INTANGIBLE CULTURAL HERITAGE AND SUSTAINABLE DEVELOPMENT

Drawing on debates about intangible cultural heritage (ICH) safeguarding at the local and international levels, *Intangible Cultural Heritage and Sustainable Development: Inside a UNESCO Convention*, explores the theoretical and practical implications of the intertwinement between these policy fields.

Considering how sustainable development (SD) priorities are influencing representations of ICH, the volume questions how they are expanding the frontiers of the heritage realm and unsettling accepted understandings of the social uses of heritage. The contributing authors, who hail from a variety of different contexts and disciplinary backgrounds, explore these issues from a unique vantage point as both scholars and actors of the processes they analyze. Playing different roles in the implementation of the Convention, their positioning as insiders allows for a unique analytical perspective that is based on first-hand engagement with the practices of the Convention.

Intangible Cultural Heritage and Sustainable Development: Inside a UNESCO Convention sheds light on the complexity, potential, and consequences of combining ICH and SD at the policy-making level and in heritage practices on the ground. It will be of interest to academics and students working in heritage studies, development studies, anthropology, archaeology, international law, political science, international relations, and sociology.

Chiara Bortolotto holds UNESCO Chair in Intangible Cultural Heritage and Sustainable Development at CY Cergy Paris University.

Ahmed Skounti is Professor of anthropology and heritage at the National Institute of Archaeology and Heritage Sciences (INSAP), Morocco.

Key Issues in Cultural Heritage

Series Editors: William Logan and Laurajane Smith

The following list includes only the most-recent titles to publish within the series. A list of the full catalogue of titles is available at: www.routledge.com/Key-Issues-in-Cultural-Heritage/book-series/KICH

Urban Heritage in Divided Cities
Contested Pasts
Edited by Mirjana Ristic and Sybille Frank

Migrant, Multicultural and Diasporic Heritage
Beyond and Between Borders
Edited by Alexandra Dellios and Eureka Henrich

Design and Heritage
The Construction of Identity and Belonging
Edited by Grace Lees-Maffei and Rebecca Houze

Toxic Heritage
Legacies, Futures, and Environmental Injustice
Edited by Elizabeth Kryder-Reid and Sarah May

Intangible Cultural Heritage and Sustainable Development
Inside a UNESCO Convention
Edited by Chiara Bortolotto and Ahmed Skounti

For more information about this series, please www.routledge.com/Key-Issuesin-Cultural-Heritage/book-series/KICH

INTANGIBLE CULTURAL HERITAGE AND SUSTAINABLE DEVELOPMENT

Inside a UNESCO Convention

Edited by Chiara Bortolotto and Ahmed Skounti

Routledge
Taylor & Francis Group
LONDON AND NEW YORK

Designed cover image: © Maria Toutoudaki / Getty Images

First published 2024
by Routledge
4 Park Square, Milton Park, Abingdon, Oxon OX14 4RN

and by Routledge
605 Third Avenue, New York, NY 10158

Routledge is an imprint of the Taylor & Francis Group, an informa business

British Library Cataloguing-in-Publication Data
A catalogue record for this book is available from the British Library

ISBN: 978-1-032-15434-3 (hbk)
ISBN: 978-1-032-15433-6 (pbk)
ISBN: 978-1-003-24415-8 (ebk)

DOI: 10.4324/9781003244158

Typeset in Times New Roman
by Apex CoVantage, LLC

CONTENTS

SERIES GENERAL CO-EDITORS' FOREWORD

This series of edited books was conceived as a platform for disseminating innovative research in heritage studies around specific research themes. The series aims to help identify and set agendas in new research areas in heritage studies. It showcases areas and issues often overlooked in more mainstream research that has tended to narrowly focus on technical heritage management and preservation issues. While challenging the traditional research focus, the series, nonetheless, is concerned with critical and reflective engagements with the practical and policy applications of research. With the development of the critical heritage studies movement, the ability to question and interrogate the nature of heritage and the social and political consequences it has on policy and practice and on people's lived experiences has become increasingly important. Interest in heritage preservation is never apolitical and simply technical, and the developing field continues to explore "heritage" as a social and political construct encompassing all those places, artifacts, and cultural expressions inherited from the past, which, because they are seen to reflect and validate our identity as nations, communities, families, and even individuals, are worthy of some form of respect and protection.

What is named as "heritage" results from a selection process, a process that intersects with the practices of remembering and forgetting, commemoration, leisure and tourism, and the development and expression of historical consciousness. This selection can often be "top down" and regulated by experts, policy, and legislation, but it is equally a process "from below" that can challenge or ignore established forms of heritage making and selection and thus foster new ways of thinking about heritage and its relationship to the past and the present.

Heritage has a complex relationship with both the past and the present and can be used in both positive and negative ways. For example, it may be used to foster respect for cultural and social diversity, provide community and individual self-esteem, and challenge prejudice and misrecognition. Equally, it may be used to foster exclusion, and the maintenance of misrecognition and prejudice, or it can be used to promote undemocratic political agendas and rally people against their neighbors in civil and international wars, ethnic cleansing, and genocide. Heritage is highly political and entwined with contemporary struggles over social justice and equity and is, as a consequence, integral to the setting and reimagining of aspirations for the future.

Gönül Bozoğlu and Laurajane Smith

CONTRIBUTORS

Janet Blake is Associate Professor of law at the University of Shahid Beheshti (Tehran), where she is a member of the Centre of Excellence for Education for Sustainable Development. She was involved in developing, drafting, and implementing the 2003 Intangible Cultural Heritage Convention and is a Global Facilitator for UNESCO. Her publications include *International Cultural Heritage Law* (2015) and (co-edited with Lucas Lixinski) *UNESCO's 2003 Intangible Heritage Convention – A Commentary* (2020).

Chiara Bortolotto holds the UNESCO Chair in Intangible Cultural Heritage and Sustainable Development at CY Cergy Paris University. Her research explores the social life of the Convention for the safeguarding of the intangible cultural heritage and the performative power of administrative apparatuses through an ethnography of the UNESCO policy world. She is a member of the French Committee for Ethnologic and Intangible Heritage and of the UNESCO global network of facilitators for the 2003 Convention.

Philipp Demgenski is Junior Professor at the Institute of Anthropology, Department of Sociology, at Zhejiang University. He is also Senior Researcher in the project "Constructing Urban Futures in Asia" at the Max Planck Institute for Social Anthropology. His research focuses on intangible cultural heritage policy and practice and socio-spatial transformation in contemporary China.

Ellen Hertz is Professor of Anthropology at the University of Neuchâtel, Switzerland. From 2009 to 2014, she directed a large interdisciplinary research program on the implementation in Switzerland of the 2003 Convention for the safeguarding of intangible cultural heritage. With Hervé Munz, Florence Graezer Bideau, and

Walter Leimgruber, she published the results of this research in *Politiques de la tradition: le patrimoine cultural immatériel* (2018).

Marc Jacobs, PhD, is a professor of heritage studies at the University of Antwerp (ARCHES, Faculty of Design Sciences), and he also holds the UNESCO chair on critical heritage studies and the safeguarding of intangible cultural heritage at the Vrije Universiteit Brussel. He participated as a reflexive expert in and since the meetings of the drafting group of the 2003 UNESCO convention. Jacobs has been an active member of the Belgian delegation in the General Assembly and the Intergovernmental Committee of the 2003 Convention since 2006. Belgium formed part of the Committee from 2012 to 2016, when Chapter VI of the Operational Directives for the Convention was negotiated and adopted.

Kristin Kuutma is Professor of Cultural Studies, holding the UNESCO Chair on the Applied Studies of Intangible Cultural Heritage at the University of Tartu, Estonia. She is a leading expert at the UNESCO National Commission and represents Estonia on the Intergovernmental Committee for the safeguarding of intangible cultural heritage. Her research in cultural anthropology focuses on ethnographic practice and disciplinary knowledge production, critical analyses of heritage policy-making, and issues of intersectional representation.

Aba Sadki, PhD, in Human Geography from Université de Montréal, is Postdoctoral Fellow at la Chaire de recherche sur l'immigration et les communautés franco-ontariennes, University of Ottawa. He is also a PhD student in Anthropology at the Institut National des Sciences de l'Archéologie et du Patrimoine (Rabat, Morocco). His research focuses on North–South mobilities, global tourism, gentrification, and space appropriation conflicts, with a focus on Moroccan World heritage sites.

Carlos Sandroni teaches ethnomusicology at the Federal University of Recife, Brazil. He is the author of *A Respectable spell: transformations of samba in Rio de Janeiro*. He was a visiting professor at the University of Texas at Austin (2007) and the Indiana University at Bloomington (2015). His main research interests are the history of Brazilian popular music and the labeling of some of its genres as ICH.

Hanna Schreiber is an adjunct professor at the Faculty of Political Science and International Studies at the University of Warsaw, Poland. She situates her academic work on the crossroads of international law, international relations, ethnography, and history. Her current research is aimed at the application of Elinor Ostrom's concepts and methodology to the field of UNESCO global heritage regimes. She is the President of the Intangible Cultural Heritage Board of the City of Warsaw and UNESCO Global Facilitator for the 2003 Convention.

Ahmed Skounti is Professor of anthropology and heritage at the National Institute of Archaeology and Heritage Sciences (INSAP), Morocco. His research area revolves about local and global heritage-making processes. He has been working with the UNESCO World Heritage Convention for more than two decades. He contributed to the drafting of the UNESCO Intangible Cultural Heritage Convention and was chair of its Evaluation Body in 2015 and 2017. He is a member of the 2003 Convention facilitators' global network.

Rieks Smeets was head of UNESCO's Intangible Heritage Section from the spring of 2003 on, and from the summer of 2006 Secretary of the Convention. Before, he worked as a descriptive linguist at Leiden University, specializing in languages of the Caucasus and linguistic policies. After retiring from UNESCO, he has been active in the Convention's capacity-building program, as an author and trainer; he also has assisted groups and organizations in diverse countries in dealing with the Convention and has published on the Convention's history and implementation.

Benedetta Ubertazzi is a partner at the law firm Studio Ubertazzi in Milan and Associate Professor of European Union Law at Milano – Bicocca University, Italy. She is a UNESCO Facilitator for the global capacity-building program for the effective implementation of the 2003 Convention on safeguarding intangible cultural heritage. She situates her academic and practical work at the crossroads of international law and intellectual property law. In 2022, she published her book on Intangible Cultural Heritage, Sustainable Development, and Intellectual Property with Springer. She is a member of the doctoral board on intangible cultural heritage of the University of Milan Bicocca.

Julien Vuilleumier is a trained anthropologist and scientific collaborator at the Swiss Federal Office of Culture (FOC), where he is in charge of the 2003 Convention. As of 2017, he has acted as coordinator of the Swiss nominations for the lists of the 2003 Convention; he is also a scientific advisor to the Swiss Delegation within the intergovernmental committee.

THE RISE OF SUSTAINABLE DEVELOPMENT IN THE CONVENTION FOR THE SAFEGUARDING OF THE INTANGIBLE CULTURAL HERITAGE

The Convention for the Safeguarding of the intangible cultural heritage (hereafter, the ICH Convention) turns 20 at a time when humanity is facing formidable challenges such as climate change, persistent inequalities, and armed conflicts. It is in this context that the sustainable development goals (SDGs) were developed and accepted. Today, sustainable development (SD) has become a pervasive concept, affecting every aspect of our lives (Sachs, 2015). With the mainstreaming of the 2030 Agenda for sustainable development across all UN agencies, SD has also become a key priority for the United Nations Educational, Scientific, and Culture Organization (UNESCO). Framed within this organization, intangible cultural heritage (ICH) is therefore increasingly being rethought and mobilized in relation to the SD.

In its focus on the rapidly growing interconnections between ICH and its safeguarding on the one hand, and SD on the other, this volume offers critical reflections on this development, which has marked the ICH policy field over the last decade and will shape its future. The contributing authors show how the ICH Convention is currently at a crucial crossroads, where new and unconventional directions for heritage policies are taking form. In fact, over the last ten years, a number of issues related to SD, particularly its economic uses, have emerged in debates within the international heritage community. This led to the adoption in 2016 of a new chapter on SD and ICH safeguarding at the national level in the *Operational Directives for the Implementation of the Convention for the Safeguarding of the Intangible Cultural Heritage* (hereafter, the Operational Directives or ODs), which guide the implementation of the Convention. SD is also a major concern for heritage practitioners who continue to invest in ICH as a means of sustaining or improving their livelihoods. In considering how social and cultural practices, *reprocessed* under the Convention as intangible cultural heritage elements, are mobilized by the SD discourse on both the local and international levels, this volume examines the complexity and unintended

DOI:10.4324/9781003244158-1

consequences of combining ICH and SD for both policy-making and actual heritage practices. Grounded on the authors' unique dual positions as researchers interested in the ICH policy field and as actors within the legal, institutional, and political apparatus created by or under the Convention, this volume responds to the call to undo dichotomies between epistemological and policy objectives that are increasingly regarded as "unproductive" (Larsen et al., 2022: 6).

In what follows, we first briefly describe attempts made to place culture and ICH within global SD policies, as well as present the ICH Convention as a normative framework. We then discuss the complex positionality of the authors. Finally, we introduce the main topics tackled in the chapters of this volume.

UNESCO and sustainable development

In September 2022, the World Conference on Cultural Policies and Sustainable Development – MONDIACULT was held in Mexico City, 40 years after the first MONDIACULT organized by UNESCO in 1982. In the discourse of the Organization, this latter event is presented as the first call to take culture into account as a dimension of development strategies (Arizpe, 2004). Indeed, in their 2022 final declaration the conference leaders again advocated for a stronger role of culture in development policies and development plans and sought to secure full-fledged cultural objectives in the development agenda beyond 2030 (UNESCO, 2022: 4).

In point of fact, UNESCO has engaged in a debate over the economic function and legal protection of folklore since the 1970s, with member States from the Global South voicing the need to better integrate culture[1] and development (Labadi, 2022). Wiktor-Mach (2019) notes that the process of convergence between culture and development began to emerge in the 1980s, and underlines the will of countries from the Global South to play an active role in the global heritage regime. This led not only to the broadening of the notion of heritage but more significantly to the design of new policies globally. At the request of the United Nations, UNESCO launched the World Decade for Cultural Development (1988–1997), based on the idea that "culture should be regarded as a direct source of inspiration for development, and in return, development should assign to culture a central role as a social regulator" (Mayor, 1988: 5). During this period, the World Commission on Culture and Development, established by UNESCO, published its report *Our Creative Diversity* (1996), calling for a rethinking of conventional development strategies. This was followed by the Intergovernmental Conference on Cultural Policies for Development, organized by UNESCO in Stockholm in 1998. Inspired by *Our Creative Diversity*, participants emphasized that "SD and the flourishing of culture are interdependent" (UNESCO, 1998: 13) and urged UNESCO Member States to "make cultural policy one of the key components of development strategy" (ibid.: 14). Interestingly, in an effort to highlight the economic potential of culture, the conference also hosted the first UNESCO Business Forum on Enterprise, Human Development, and Culture in the Global Age.

Yet, the role of culture, or more specifically that of cultural heritage, in SD was neither recognized nor integrated into the development strategies agreed upon at the UN level and reflected first in the Millennium Declaration (2000–2015) and subsequently in the 2030 Agenda for SD (2015–2030). In fact, the Millennium Development Goals adopted in 2000 leave out culture altogether. Meanwhile, while it might be assumed that culture permeates all of the 17 SDGs established by the 2030 Agenda, the latter do not explicitly embrace culture as a crucial factor in SD. In fact, despite UNESCO's increasing efforts to have the role of culture recognized in SD policies, culminating in the organization of the international congress "Culture: Key to sustainable development" convened by UNESCO in 2013 in Hangzhou, the 2030 Agenda mentions culture just six times, in general terms, with only Goal 4.7 referring explicitly to "culture's contribution to sustainable development" (UN, 2015). Heritage is mentioned only once, in Goal 11.4, which calls to "strengthen efforts to protect and safeguard the world's cultural and natural heritage" (UN, 2015). Thus, no evident link has been instituted between heritage protection and safeguarding on the one hand and SD on the other.

The ICH convention and sustainable development

Since its entry into force in 2006, the Convention has become an influential normative instrument. As of June 2023, 181 States have ratified, approved, or accepted the Convention, 76 elements have been inscribed on its List of Intangible Cultural Heritage in Need of Urgent Safeguarding, and 567 on its Representative List of the Intangible Cultural Heritage of Humanity, while 33 programs, activities, and projects have been inscribed in the Register of Good Safeguarding Practices. A multitude of diverse actors at the local, national, and international levels engage on a daily basis with the concept of ICH and implement their, sometimes very different, understandings of the Convention. A global intangible cultural heritage apparatus has thus emerged, with increasingly defined contours.

An already substantial body of literature outlines the origins and development of the 2003 Convention over its first decade, showing how its elaboration has offered an opportunity to challenge both the hegemony of the "Authorized Heritage Discourse" (Smith, 2006) and State-driven heritage making. This normative instrument has sought to create a new heritage protection paradigm (Blake, 2017; Bortolotto, 2011; Hafstein, 2007; Lixinski, 2013) based on a dynamic process of "safeguarding" as opposed to conservation, the term of the art for heritage protection in the World Heritage regime. The new paradigm is also devoid of any references to "authenticity" (Deacon and Smeets, 2013; Su, 2018; Bortolotto, 2020), a concept that remains at the core of the World Heritage apparatus (Brumann, 2017; Gfeller, 2017). Despite its difficult articulation with States' interests and sovereignty, and despite the language of the Convention diluting the potential agency of the communities, groups, and individuals (CGIs), this effort has reflected a push for heritage self-determination (Bortolotto, 2015). The latter emerged as a key policy principle in the heritage field in the late 1990s (Seitel, 2001) and has, since the beginning, been present in the debates of the Committee (Aikawa-Faure, 2004, 2009).

The Convention is a complex policy apparatus comprising a legal text with its Operational Directives, governing and advisory bodies, a secretariat and state players, and satellite and non-state actors such as accredited non-governmental organizations (NGOs) (Skounti, 2017). As a treaty, it is binding for its States Parties. Following its preamble, the Convention states its purposes (Art. 1) and defines intangible cultural heritage as practices, representations, expressions, knowledge, and skills transmitted and recreated from generation to generation and that communities, groups and, in some cases, individuals, recognize as their cultural heritage (Art. 2). The article also states that ICH that is inconsistent with the requirements of SD will not be considered under the Convention. Obligations of the States signing the Convention include taking the necessary measures to ensure the safeguarding of the ICH present on their territories (Art. 11), establishing and updating ICH inventories (Art. 12), contributing to the ICH Fund (Art. 25–28), and submitting periodic reports on the implementation of the Convention, including the state of safeguarding of elements inscribed on the lists of the Convention (Art. 29–30). Other actions expected of the States Parties include the adoption of a general policy including legal, institutional, and educational measures as well as awareness-raising and capacity-building (Art. 13–14). The States Parties are also expected to ensure, within the framework of their safeguarding activities, the widest possible participation of communities, groups, and individuals (CGIs) in the management of their ICH (Art. 15).

The organs governing the Convention are the General Assembly of the States Parties (Art. 4) and the Intergovernmental Committee composed of 24 elected States Parties (Art. 5–9). These bodies are supported by the UNESCO Secretariat, which organizes and informs their sessions and oversees the implementation of the Convention at the international level. This includes the organization of expert meetings and the preparation of Operational Directives, as well as capacity-building activities for the implementation of the Convention at the national level. Other actors contributing to the implementation of the Convention are ad hoc consultative bodies (Art. 8.3) and NGOs accredited by the General Assembly (Art. 9). The so-called Evaluation Body assists the Committee by recommending decisions concerning the inscription of elements on the Lists of the Convention, the inclusion of good safeguarding practices in the Convention's Register, and the award of some forms of international assistance. The lists established by the Convention are the Representative List of the Intangible Cultural Heritage (Art. 16) and the List of Intangible Cultural Heritage in Need of Urgent Safeguarding (Art. 17), while the Register of Good Safeguarding Practices is based on Art. 18. All three mechanisms are expected to contribute, each in its own way, to the safeguarding of ICH. Finally, the General Assembly, on the recommendation of the Intergovernmental Committee, adopts and amends, as needed, the ODs. In 2015, the Committee adopted the

"Ethical Principles for Safeguarding Intangible Cultural Heritage" in order to emphasize the central role of communities, groups, and individuals in the implementation of the Convention.

Although SD was occasionally discussed during the meetings leading up to the first draft of the Convention (see Blake, this volume), before its rise as a key objective of the Convention, SD was only remarked on "in passing" in the Preamble and Article 2 of the Convention. The former considers ICH a "mainspring of cultural diversity and a guarantee of sustainable development" and the latter refers to respect of SD as a requirement for international recognition of any ICH element submitted for inscription on the Lists established by the Convention. In the first versions of the ODs, SD is mentioned twice in a rather marginal way, highlighting the fact that it was initially not an issue in UNESCO ICH discourse. The first refers to the conditions for financial contributions to the ICH Fund, which should be "compatible with the aims and principles of the Convention, with existing international human rights instruments, with the requirements of SD or with the requirements of mutual respect among communities, groups and individuals" (Paragraph 73). The second encourages the media "to contribute to raising awareness about the importance of the intangible cultural heritage as a means to foster social cohesion, SD and prevention of conflict, in preference to focusing only on its aesthetic or entertainment aspects" (Paragraph 111).

Other, less explicit, references to SD can also be found in the ODs. Paragraphs 116 and 117, adopted in 2010, amend the ODs to address commercial activities related to intangible heritage, one of the key issues that have occupied the governing bodies of the Convention since the latter's entry into force. Specifically, paragraph 116 acknowledges the existence and even the importance of commercial activities that may emerge from certain forms of intangible cultural heritage and contribute to the local economy and social cohesion. Paragraph 117 meanwhile invites States Parties to avoid any misappropriation and alteration of the significance of elements of the intangible cultural heritage through commercial use.

With the ubiquitous interest in SD reconfirmed in the UN's 2030 Agenda, mainstreaming SD became an even stronger priority for UNESCO, and SD was integrated into its various programs and sectors, including the ICH Convention. As early as the occasion of the tenth anniversary of the Convention in 2013, the Chengdu International Conference on Intangible Cultural Heritage called on the international community to continue its efforts "to renew its commitment to the fundamental principle of the Convention that ICH is a guarantee of sustainable development" (UNESCO, 2013). That same year, the Intergovernmental Committee decided that "a new chapter of the Operational Directives on the safeguarding of intangible cultural heritage and SD *at the national level* be drafted" (Decision 8.COM 13.a) (our emphasis).

Thus, in 2016, a new chapter on the linkages between intangible cultural heritage and SD was added to the ODs to frame the articulation between the two and guide States Parties to the Convention in promoting SD through ICH. Its structure mirrors that of the 2030 Agenda, organized around three dimensions (social, economic, and environmental), with the addition of a fourth dimension on peace. As thoroughly described by M. Jacobs (this volume), 28 new paragraphs were discussed by the Intergovernmental Committee and black-boxed to become this sixth chapter before being adopted – and discussed again – by the General Assembly. This process, regarded by R. Smeets clearly as a "reorientation" (this volume), was crucial in reshaping the policy priorities of the Convention.

Writing about and engaging with: the complex positionality of "two-hat" authors

Academics, civil servants, representatives of civil society organizations, former members of the UNESCO secretariat, UNESCO consultants – the authors of this book have all actively, and often passionately, engaged with the Convention. Most have worn several of the aforementioned "hats." Some were key actors in the drafting of the Convention and have played an active role in shaping its subsequent implementation at the international level, for instance by contributing to the work of its governing bodies as members of national delegations. Others have been trained by the UNESCO Secretariat to work as facilitators within its capacity-building program and collaborate with national or local institutional and social actors in drawing up ICH inventories, assisting with the preparation of nominations to the international Lists of the Convention, and helping to design legislation, policies, and programs for safeguarding ICH. As academics with expertise in the field of ICH, or active NGO members, some have also been involved in ICH mechanisms and programs at the national level.

Hailing from different disciplinary fields (anthropology, ethnomusicology, international law, linguistics), all of the authors are also actors in the policy field analyzed in this volume, playing the role of cultural brokers on the ground (Kurin, 1997; Jacobs, 2014; Baron, 2021) and of norm entrepreneurs in the international arena (Finnemore and Sikkink, 1998). As R.F. Bendix, K. Bizer, and D. Noyes highlight, researchers in some disciplines (e.g., economics or law) often engage with policy-making and implementation in order to formulate recommendations or problem-solve (Bendix, Bizer and Noyes, 2017). The analytical effort here aims to optimize the policy apparatus. However, for anthropology and assimilated disciplines whose hermeneutic perspective questions and endeavors to understand this apparatus as a social world, the role of "participant decision-makers" (Arizpe, 2013: 147) comes with the much-dreaded risk of "going native" (Bierschenk and Olivier de Sardan, 2019) and its relevant ethical challenges (Escobar, 1991), inevitably spurring "collaborative dilemmas" (Bortolotto, 2017).

In some cases, this commitment to ICH, be it the establishment of policy and legal frameworks or safeguarding ICH on the ground, entangles a normative and moral outlook with analytical and descriptive perspectives. The authors of this volume do not separate their engagement with the Convention from their analytical view and speak as actors of the object they are analyzing, as increasingly observed in the study of international organizations (Sapignoli, 2017). In most instances, as "heritage believers" (Brumann, 2014) they are explicit advocates of ICH safeguarding who are "speaking within the patrimonial regime" and for whom therefore "the moral imperative to conserve is self-evident" (Hafstein, 2018: 9). This proximity to "UNESCO speak," as, for instance, explicitly acknowledged by J. Blake, together with having an agenda in the ICH field may entail being "embedded" or, put differently, "being pulled in and to critique on its terms instead of critiquing its terms" (Hafstein, ibid.).

If adopting the technocratic language of heritage policies makes it more difficult to unpack the latter (Riles, 2004), the choice of not only "studying up" (Nader, 1968) but also "engaging up" (Ceribašić, 2019) arguably has its own epistemological potential and affords a unique analytical perspective when coupled with reflexivity. The cultural intimacy (Herzfeld, 2005) of seasoned insiders embedded (Bonhomme, 2007; Spencer, 2010) in their own object of analysis means they can read UNESCO documents and grasp their meaning beyond their actual content. This is all the more important since, as M. Halme-Tuomisaari points out in her work on UN human rights bureaucracies,

> the real insights or mechanisms of impact are rarely available for discovery through textual sources, through focusing on the issues that they address, and are, conversely, embedded in broader dynamics and logics and even in desires to make certain things opaque or invisible.
>
> *(Halme-Tuomisaari, 2018: 466)*

This is, in fact, how R. Smeets uniquely contributes to this volume, taking stock of his experience as head of the ICH unit since 2003 and as Secretary of the Convention from its entry into force in 2006 until 2008. His long-term and firsthand experience with the management of the Convention, coupled with rigorous analysis of available data, allows him to see in the rise of SD a radical shift for the Convention, as opposed to its natural or constitutive essence as the UNESCO narrative has subsequently framed it.

The choice to leave the safe zone of distancing and actively participate in the controversies that are the object of the analysis not only triggers methodological and epistemological conundrums but also comes with ethical dilemmas. As asked by an ethnomusicologist who engaged with the implementation of the Convention as a member of the Evaluation Body established in 2015: "What about the wrongs we commit? Even more, what about wrongs we do not even recognize?" (Ceribašić, 2019: 252). At the same time, adding analytical depth to policy debate is regarded by many engaged scholars precisely as a moral duty. As De Cesari argues,

> There are great advantages in being close to policy-making because this makes our critical task more effective. Analyses and critiques of UNESCOization and

heritage as regime are helpful precisely because we can put them to use by feeding the fruits of our necessarily critical work back into policy-making.

(2013: 411)

Several authors in this volume reflexively consider their perspective as academics exploring policy-making in their own field of expertise. In doing so, they cautiously consider the very conditions that shaped and made the research process possible in the first place, thereby contributing to producing knowledge on the very process of knowledge production (Bourdieu, 2001). M. Jacobs's reflexive stance is particularly striking. In describing his own passionate efforts to establish SD as a key priority of the Convention, he insists on "the tensions, the drama, and the momentum" that he experienced while "in the cockpit" as the most active spokesperson of the Belgian delegation to UNESCO ICH meetings. In shedding light on how the human factor shapes international policy-making, M. Jacobs furthermore provides evidence that active and sometimes ardent engagement with the Convention spurs hope and enthusiasm as much as frustration. He demonstrates the added value of reflecting on affects and emotions as crucial components of international decision-making.

Reflexivity also exposes how the emotions that drive heritage bureaucracy are triggers revealing the values underpinning particular professional cultures (Bortolotto, forthcoming). For example, in considering how decontextualized ICH performances spur embarrassment among some ICH experts and safeguarding advocates, Chiara Bortolotto and P. Demgensky highlight how distress provoked by the violation of assimilated cultural codes reveals the cultural intimacy that binds the international heritage expert community. Passion and zeal are evident in several texts. H. Schreiber, as a legally trained heritage scholar and practitioner, consciously advocates for the integration of commons governance in the ICH field, based on her five-year tenure on the Polish Intangible Heritage Council (2013–2018), where she experienced the dilemmas of intervening in the governance of ICH on the local, national, and international levels. She also reflects on how the language of heritage making differs from that developed in critical heritage studies.

Ahmed Skounti and A. Sadki objectivate their work as experts involved in the heritage project around the Jemaa el-Fnaa Square in the Medina of Marrakech and their moral commitment to community participation. They also point out the difficulty of managing the potential impact of their dual position as researchers and heritage professionals on their interactions with ICH bearers during fieldwork. A comparable concern is discussed by C. Sandroni, namely his awareness of his own role in shaping representations of *forro* as "traditional" music in the process of its heritagization. Similarly, in facing the contradictions and dilemmas of working with technocratic mechanisms and the "utopia of rules" (Graeber, 2015), a reflexive approach to their own role in this process allows E. Hertz and J. Vuilleumier to consider the double edge of bureaucracy, in particular "periodic reporting," one of the mechanisms through which UNESCO tries to enforce the integration of SD into ICH. This perspective allows the authors to interrogate from within the material, political, economic, and administrative conditions that make the ICH and SD linkage possible.

In questioning the role of the researcher and offering examples of different ways of integrating knowledge production and engagement with policy agendas and societal issues, this volume contributes to current debate over the need to "defy sharp divides between the 'pure' or 'academic' and its implicit 'other', whether labeled as 'applied' or simply 'non-academic'" (Larsen et al., 2022: 5). Wearing two hats or more, whether voicing critical perspectives or not, the contributors navigate labyrinthine paths, passing from involvement to distancing, from engagement to a more neutral stance, and vice versa. In doing so, they contribute to a "continuous reconsideration of the researcher's inquisitive and exploratory and critical stance in relation to heritage related policies, strategies and institutional patterns, or the act of knowledge production in general" (Kuutma and Vaivade, 2021: 467).

The chapters

The volume addresses the international legal and policy frameworks governing the relationship between ICH safeguarding and SD, different modes of conceiving the ownership of ICH and its use as a resource, ongoing negotiations that shape local understandings of the linkage of ICH and SD within particular social contexts, and finally, economic uses of ICH and their relationship to broader political economic issues.

J. Blake observes that both human rights and SD are introduced in the Preamble of the Convention and frame the definition of ICH. Here, they embody the universalizing aim of the Convention, where ICH is characterized as the "heritage of humankind," in a constant tension with the specific values and norms of particular communities, reflected in the promotion of cultural diversity. While human rights standards and sustainability differ in form and approach, they are both articulated as universal values structured around a set of policy goals to be adopted globally, and share many objectives. Blake argues that they go hand in hand and one is unlikely to be achieved without the other. At the same time, she highlights the fact that they are based on very different approaches, respectively qualitative and quantitative. Articulating SD with human rights therefore allows us to take into account the quality of SD and its impact on individuals (ultimately its human dimension), rather than focusing primarily on quantitative indicators.

Based on a study of UNESCO documents and his own experience as Head of the UNESCO ICH Section and as Secretary of the Convention, Smeets traces the progressive emergence of SD in the history of the Convention, which has led to a crucial shift – a "reset" – in the understanding of the Convention's objectives. He shows how and why no attention was paid to economic issues and very little to "sustainability" during the drafting and early years of the Convention and how, under the impetus of the UNESCO Secretariat, SD became a core concern in the implementation of the Convention after 2012. The increasingly manifest pursuit of SD, promoted by the UN worldwide, and by UNESCO in the ICH arena, gained prominence in the discussions and decisions of the Convention's governing bodies and ultimately led to the decision to add a new chapter to the ODs, rather than simply amending the existing ODs on commercial uses of ICH. Smeets shows how Western European positions on the new chapter differed substantially from those of the Global South. In this process, and as a consequence of UNESCO's attempt to position itself within the broader UN debate by lobbying for culture to be recognized as a fourth pillar of SD, Smeets highlights a strategic reorientation in the representation of ICH, from "fragile" to a driver for and enabler of SD.

M. Jacobs retraces the drafting of Chapter VI of the Operational Directives, entitled "Safeguarding intangible cultural heritage and SD at the national level," and sheds light on the different positions taken by individual States in this process. Drawing on actor–network theory and translation sociology, Jacobs documents how, during the drafting of the Convention, SD issues were conceptualized mainly in terms of the economic uses of ICH and related Intellectual Property Rights (IPRs) matters. However, because of their controversial nature, these were, as he notes, "put in a fridge" to allow for the smooth adoption of the Convention. In observing the way these issues were then eventually put back on the table, Jacobs shows that although UNESCO was not able to strongly influence the ways SD was defined at the UN level, the framework established by Agenda 2030 black-boxed the implementation of the Convention. Furthermore, by reflexively assessing his own role in this process, he illustrates the impact of a particular delegation on global policy-making.

In her chapter, K. Kuutma shows how "community" is the result of the heritagization process, not its premise (the people gathered in an NGO, for instance). Such a group structures itself in order to pursue particular objectives. Kuutma contends that the ICH format generates a new policy of cultural management that brings about conceptual and social change or a "process of cultural change that depends on interaction, knowledge transfer, and shifts in agency." The author draws on multi-sited ethnographic observations as well as on her long-standing work with the 2003 Convention. Drawing on examples from Estonia, Scandinavia, Greece, and Ethiopia, she illustrates how, while building national heritage frameworks, multi-layered heritage making ultimately implies a reorganization of power interactions and hampers access to resources for local actors. Kuutma also discusses issues of self-determination, State distrust, and confusion over ICH's deictic reference, all of which are brought about by State mediation within the ICH Convention. She concludes by stressing how heritage can serve as a vehicle for finding strength through embracing change.

B. Ubertazzi observes that the progressive implementation of the ICH Convention raised concerns over the relationship between the market and ICH. In the debates of the Committee, it was argued that certain ICH elements should avoid the market in order to be better safeguarded. However, according to the Convention and its current Operational Directives, ICH is expected to be compatible with sustainable development, a paradigm with economic, social, and environmental dimensions. In an effort to achieve "economic sustainability," the Convention's ODs favor commercial activity that is consistent with safeguarding ICH. Such activities can pose, however, certain perils for ICH, often termed "misappropriation." The author examines the issue of misappropriation from a legal perspective, at both the UNESCO ICH international scale and the level of communities on the ground. In so doing, she tackles the uses of intellectual property rights and other safeguarding measures, including benefit-sharing agreements and codes of ethics (all of which must align with the UNESCO 2015 Ethical Principles), as potential answers to such misappropriation.

H. Schreiber claims that since the adoption of the Convention, ICH discourse has involved issues concerning its nature and management. Central themes include the listing mechanisms and the modes of community participation at all levels of ICH governance. She analyses these two key areas through the lens of "the commons," "common-pool resources (CPRs)," and "polycentric governance," concepts coined by Nobel laureate Elinor Ostrom. In particular, the author asks: How might institutional analysis methodology and Ostrom's key concepts shed greater light on the nature of ICH, ICH lists, and the difficulties experienced in governing ICH? Institutional and legal analysis and ethnographic methods are mobilized to provide insights on challenges related to the *glocal* governance of ICH, as observed in the process of global reflection on the reform of the Convention's listing mechanisms, organized by the Secretariat in 2021–2022. Schreiber shows that Ostrom's principles on governing CPRs and polycentric governance can indeed illuminate and guide ongoing glocal ICH policy initiatives. She furthermore highlights crucial aspects that should be taken into account when designing new institutions and regulations.

A. Vaivade explores the connection between ICH safeguarding and SD through issues of social inclusiveness, with a particular focus on the rights of Indigenous peoples. Although the Preamble of the ICH Convention includes Indigenous groups among the communities that contribute to enriching cultural diversity and human creativity, it refers to these actors only in vague and implicit terms and not as specific legal subjects. This is also reflected in the practical intergovernmental implementation of the Convention, where Indigenous peoples remain absent, as distant objects rather than as active actors. Vaivade observes a "striking" geographical and relational distance separating them from the governmental representatives who discuss their heritage and make decisions on its safeguarding at the international level. Interestingly, Vaivade shows how explicit reference to Indigenous peoples and attention to the safeguarding of their heritage was introduced in parallel with the rise of SD as a priority pursuit of the Convention and increased concern for social inclusiveness and cohesion. Though it remains a "discursive strength," the revision of the ODs in 2016, the adoption of the Ethical Principles in 2015 and of the Overall Results Framework for the 2003 Convention in 2018, influenced by the 2030 Agenda and its concern over social inclusiveness, have seen a first reference to "Indigenous peoples," otherwise only evoked in the Preamble of the Convention.

J. Vuilleumier and E. Hertz explore the ways ICH is associated with environmental sustainability in the design and implementation of Swiss heritage policies, and how this transforms the understanding of ICH. Focusing on water management systems and wild plant horticulture, both officially recognized as ICH, they argue that material conditions grounded in political and economic infrastructures determine the actual sustainability of development projects associated with "living traditions." At the same time, institutional and policy interventions aimed at promoting environmental sustainability necessarily embed cultural practices in economic, social, and political projects. Both examples therefore illustrate what UNESCO calls an "intersectoral" approach, crucial for the viability of these practices and their contribution to SD. This can be particularly challenging for public institutions that fragment their interventions, addressing specific aspects of the same phenomenon. For instance, the success and effectiveness in terms of SD of the "invented tradition" around Swiss medicinal herbs depend on a synergy between scientific research, tourism, politics, and cultural actors, as well as an interest in medicinal herbs that goes well beyond the mountain population represented as the "tradition bearers." In this sense, the articulation of ICH and SD reflects a modernizing project rather than a nostalgic look at the past.

Chiara Bortolotto and P. Demgenski consider the association between ICH and economic development. Building on an ethnography of the policy chain linking the Convention's governing bodies where this relationship is normatively defined, with its implementation in China, they nuance and complexify the idea of "decontextualization." While presented in UNESCO discourse as the essence of "bad" commercialization, they argue that decontextualization is actually already part and parcel of the implementation of the Convention at the international level. In China, where the commercialization of ICH is an integral part of a poverty alleviation strategy and is explicitly encouraged by national laws and regulations, ICH transmitters perform their practice or sell their products in the many so-called "ICH exposition parks" or on online platforms specializing in the sale of ICH products. Rather than seeing themselves as heritage victims, they embrace this form of decontextualization as empowered entrepreneurs. Against the backdrop of the Convention's participatory principle and its troublesome relation to neoliberal ideology, these examples paint a more complex picture of decontextualization and its different perceptions by the actors involved in heritage making.

In examining the impact of the inclusion of the Cultural Space of Jemaa el-Fnaa Square in Marrakech on the Representative List, Ahmed Skounti and A. Sadki, like Blake, suggest that sustainability, particularly from an economic standpoint, is conditioned by community participation. In its integration of cultural and economic activities, the square provides an example of the complex impact of a heritage listing, as well as the disappointment of heritage bearers when their expectations of deriving a sustainable livelihood from it are not met. As an example of the absence of acknowledgment of these practitioners, Ahmed Skounti and Sadki highlight their non-involvement in the requalification project implemented on the Square. The resulting frustration unsurprisingly accelerated the decline of some of the ICH practices. The COVID-19 pandemic further underscored the lack of recognition of these actors, whose informal activities excluded them from any official state support that might have compensated for their loss of income due to the interruption of tourism. Intriguingly, while the pandemic exacerbated existing inequalities, it also saw new means and opportunities for transforming storytelling emerge through new technologies.

In the last chapter, C. Sandroni, drawing on experiences in Brazil with *samba* and *forro*, discusses different ways of valuing musical expressions as heritage or as commercial products. In exploring the controversial issue of ICH commercialization, Sandroni describes the strategies adopted by different players to avoid the embarrassment caused by the acknowledgment of what is, in fact, often an intrinsic aspect of the social life of ICH, especially in the music and dance sectors. He shows how a narrative of authenticity is used to distinguish between heritage and commercial dimensions. In the case of both samba and forro, specific versions emphasizing the origins of the practice are endowed with heritage status in order to clearly separate their identity from related pieces in the pop music industry. In light of the national recognition of these two music genres, Sandroni reflects on whether (and how) mass media diffusion might be integrated into the fabric of ICH. He argues that, contrary to received wisdom, mass diffusion could play a positive role in the sustainability of traditional music.

Note

1 UNESCO defines culture as "the set of distinctive spiritual, material, intellectual and emotional features of society or a social group, that encompasses, not only art and literature but lifestyles, ways of living together, value systems, traditions, and beliefs" (UNESCO, 2001).

Bibliography

Aikawa-Faure, N. (2004) 'An historical overview of the preparation of the UNESCO international convention for the safeguarding of the intangible cultural heritage', *Museum International*, 56(1–2), pp. 137–149. doi: 10.1111/j.1350-0775.2004.00468.x.

Aikawa-Faure, N. (2009) 'From the proclamation of masterpieces to the convention for the safeguarding of intangible cultural heritage', in Smith, L. and Akagawa, N. (eds.) *Intangible Heritage*. London: Routledge, pp. 13–44.

Arizpe, L. (2004) 'The intellectual history of culture and development institutions', in Rao, V. and Walton, M. (eds.) *Culture and Public Action*. Stanford: Stanford University Press, pp. 163–184.

Arizpe, L. (2013) 'Comment parvenir à un consensus. De la Commission sur la culture et le développement à la Convention de 2003', *Gradhiva*, 18, pp. 146–165. doi: 10.4000/gradhiva.2738.

Baron, R. (2021) 'Cultural brokerage revisited', *Journal of Folklore Research*, 58(2), pp. 63–104. doi: 10.2979/jfolkrese.58.2.03.
Bendix, R. F., Bizer, K. and Noyes, D. (2017) *Sustaining Interdisciplinary Collaboration: A Guide for the Academy*. Urbana: University of Illinois Press.
Bierschenk, T. and Olivier de Sardan, J. P. (2019) 'How to study bureaucracies ethnographically?', *Critique of Anthropology*, 39(2), pp. 243–257. doi: 10.1177/0308275X19842918.
Blake, J. (2017) 'Anthropology in international law: The case of safeguarding intangible cultural heritage', in Nafziger, J. A. R. (ed.) *Comparative Law and Anthropology*. Cheltenham: Edward Elgar, pp. 135–152.
Bonhomme, J. (2007) 'Anthropologues embarqués', *La Vie des idées*. Available at: www.laviedesidees.fr/Anthropologues-embarques.html.
Bortolotto, C. (2011) 'Le trouble du patrimoine culturel immatériel', in Bortolotto, C. (ed.) *Le patrimoine culturel immatériel: enjeux d'une nouvelle catégorie*. Paris: Éditions de la Maison des sciences de l'homme, pp. 21–43. Available at: http://terrain.revues.org/14447.
Bortolotto, C. (2015) 'UNESCO and heritage self-determination: Negotiating meaning in the intergovernmental committee for the safeguarding of the ICH', in Adell, N. et al. (eds.) *Between Imagined Communities and Communities of Practice: Participation, territory and the Making of Heritage*. Göttingen: Göttingen University Press, pp. 249–272.
Bortolotto, C. (2017) 'Collaborative dilemmas in the age of uncertainty.' Available at: https://allegralaboratory.net/collaborative-dilemmas-in-the-age-of-uncertainty/.
Bortolotto, C. (2020) 'Le patrimoine immatériel et le tabou de l'authenticité : de la pérennisation à la durabilité', in Csergo, J., Hottin, C., and Schmit, P. (eds.) *Le patrimoine culturel immatériel au seuil des sciences sociales*. Paris: Éditions de la Maison des sciences de l'homme, p. [online]. doi: 10.4000/books.editionsmsh.16377.
Bortolotto, C. (forthcoming) 'The embarrassment of heritage alienability: affective choices and cultural intimacy in the UNESCO lifeworld', *Current Anthropology*.
Bourdieu, P. (2001) *Science de la science et réflexivité*. Paris: Éditions Raisons d'agir.
Brumann, C. (2014) 'Heritage agnosticism: A third path for the study of cultural heritage', *Social Anthropology*, 22(2), pp. 173–188. doi: 10.1111/1469-8676.12068.
Brumann, C. (2017) 'How to be authentic in the UNESCO World Heritage system: Copies, replicas, reconstructions, and renovations in a global conservation arena', in Forberg, C. and Stockhammer, P. (eds.) *Copies, Replicas, Reconstructions, and Renovations in a Global Conservation Arena*. Heidelberg: Heidelberg Publishing, pp. 269–287.
Ceribašić, N. (2019) 'On engaging up and expertise in ethnomusicology: The example of expert services in the programme for safeguarding intangible cultural heritage', in Hemetek, U., Kölbl, M., and Sağlam, H. (eds.) *Ethnomusicology Matters: Influencing Social and Political Realities*. Wien: Bohlau Verlag, pp. 233–256. doi: 10.7767/9783205232872.233.
Deacon, H. and Smeets, R. (2013) 'Authenticity, value and community involvement in heritage management under the world heritage and intangible heritage conventions', *Heritage and Society*, 6(2), pp. 1–15.
De Cesari, C. (2013) 'Thinking through heritage regimes', in Bendix, R., Eggert, A., and Peselmann, A. (eds.) *Heritage Regimes and the State*. Göttingen: Göttingen University Press, pp. 399–413.
Escobar, A. (1991) 'Anthropology and the development encounter: The making and marketing of development anthropology', *American Ethnologist*, 18(4), pp. 658–682.
Finnemore, M. and Sikkink, K. (1998) 'International norm dynamics and political change', *International Organization*, 52(4), pp. 887–917. doi: 10.1017/S0020818300028460.

Gfeller, A. E. (2017) 'The authenticity of heritage : Global norm-making at the crossroads of cultures', *American Historical Review*, 122(3), pp. 758–791.
Graeber, D. (2015) *The Utopia of Rules: On Technology, Stupidity, and the Secret Joys of Bureaucracy*. Brooklyn: Melville House.
Hafstein, V. T. (2007) 'Claiming culture: Intangible heritage Inc., Folklore ©, traditional knowledge™', in Hemme, D., Tauschek, M., and Bendix, R. F. (eds.). Münster: Lit Verlag, pp. 75–100.
Hafstein, V. T. (2018) *Making Intangible Heritage. El Condor Pasa and Other Stories from UNESCO*. Bloomington: Indiana University Press.
Halme-Tuomisaari, M. (2018) 'Methodologically blonde at the UN in a tactical quest for inclusion', *Social Anthropology*, 26(4), pp. 456–470. doi: 10.1111/1469-8676.12583.
Herzfeld, M. (2005) *Cultural Intimacy: Social Poetics in the Nation-State*. 2nd edn. London: Routledge.
Jacobs, M. (2014) 'Development brokerage, anthropology and public action', *Volkskunde*, 115(3), pp. 299–318.
Kurin, R. (1997) *Reflections of a Culture Broker: A View From the Smithsonian*. Washington, DC: Smithsonian Institution Press.
Kuutma, K. and Vaivade, A. (2021) 'Academic and research engagements alongside professional or public entanglements in the field of intangible cultural heritage', *Slovensky Narodopis-Slovak Ethnology*, 69(4), pp. 466–472.
Labadi, S. (2022) *Rethinking Heritage for Sustainable Development*. London: UCL Press. Available at: www.researchgate.net/publication/269107473_What_is_governance/link/548173090cf22525dcb61443/download%0Awww.econ.upf.edu/~reynal/Civil wars_12December2010.pdf%0Ahttps://think-asia.org/handle/11540/8282%0Awww.jstor.org/stable/41857625.
Larsen, P. et al. (2022) 'Anthropological engagement in the international sphere', *TSANTSA–Journal of the Swiss Anthropological Association*, 27, pp. 108–129. doi: 10.36950/tsantsa.2022.27.7801.
Lixinski, L. (2013) *Intangible Cultural Heritage in International Law*. Oxford: Oxford University Press. doi: 10.1093/acprof:oso/9780199679508.001.0001.
Mayor, F. (1988) 'The world decade for cultural development', *The UNESCO Courier: A Window Open on the World*, 41(11), pp. 4–6.
Nader, L. (1968) 'Up the anthropologist : Perspectives gained from studying up', in Hymes, D. (ed.) *Reinventing Anthropology*. New York: Vintage Books, pp. 284–311.
Riles, A. (2004) 'Real time: Unwinding technocratic and anthropological knowledge', *American Ethnologist*, 31(3), pp. 392–405. Available at: http://scholarship.law.cornell.edu/facpubhttp://scholarship.law.cornell.edu/facpub/996.
Sachs, J. D. (2015) *The Age of Sustainable Development*. New York: Columbia University Press. doi: 10.1007/s00382.
Sapignoli, M. (2017) 'A kaleidoscopic institutional form: Expertise and transformation in the UN permanent forum on indigenous issues', in Sapignoli, M. and Niezen, R. (eds.) *Palaces of Hope: The Anthropology of Global Organizations*. Cambridge: Cambridge University Press, pp. 78–105.
Seitel, P. (ed.) (2001) *Safeguarding Traditional Cultures: A Global Assessment*. Washington, DC: Smithsonian Institution, Center for Folklife and Cultural Heritage.
Skounti, A. (2017) 'The Intangible cultural heritage system: Many challenges, few proposals', *Santander Art and Culture Law Review*, 2017(2), pp. 61–76. doi: 10.4467/2450050XSNR.17.017.8423.
Smith, L. (2006) *Uses of Heritage*. London and New York: Routledge.

Spencer, J. (2010) 'The perils of engagement a space for anthropology in the age of security?', *Current Anthropology*, 51(October), pp. 289–299. doi: 10.1086/653421.

Su, J. (2018) 'Conceptualising the subjective authenticity of intangible cultural heritage', *International Journal of Heritage Studies*. Routledge, 7258, pp. 1–19. doi: 10.1080/13527258.2018.1428662.

UNESCO (1998) *Intergovernmental Conference on Cultural Policies for Development, Stockholm. Final Report* [Online]. Available at: https://unesdoc.unesco.org/ark:/48223/pf0000113935 (Accessed 5 March 2023).

UNESCO (2001) Universal Declaration on Cultural Diversity. Available at: https://en.unesco.org/about-us/legal-affairs/unesco-universal-declaration-cultural-diversity

UNESCO (2013) *Chengdu International Conference on Intangible Cultural Heritage in Celebration of the Tenth Anniversary of UNESCO's Convention for the Safeguarding of the Intangible Cultural Heritage. Chengdu Recommendations* (Chengdu, China, 14–16 June 2013). Available at: https://ich.unesco.org/doc/src/20548-EN.pdf (Accessed 5 March 2023).

UNESCO (2022) *UNESCO World Conference on Cultural Policies and Sustainable Development – MONDIACULT 2022* (28–30 September 2022, Mexico City). Final Declaration. Available at: www.unesco.org/sites/default/files/medias/fichiers/2022/10/6.MONDIACULT_EN_DRAFT%20FINAL%20DECLARATION_FINAL_1.pdf (Accessed 5 March 2023).

United Nations (2015) *Transforming Our World: The 2030 Agenda for Sustainable Development*. Available at: https://wedocs.unep.org/20.500.11822/9814.

Wiktor-Mach, D. (2019) 'Cultural heritage and development: UNESCO's new paradigm in a changing geopolitical context', *Third World Quarterly*, 40(9), pp. 1593–1612. doi: 10.1080/01436597.2019.1604131.

PART I

The international legal and policy framework

Sustainability as a political and moral imperative

1

SUSTAINABLE DEVELOPMENT AND HUMAN RIGHTS IN SAFEGUARDING ICH

Positive goals or an internal contradiction?

Janet Blake

1.1. Introduction

I write this chapter from the perspective of an international law specialist (albeit with a background in Classics) and within that particular "universe of discourse." I have been engaged since 1999 up until now with the intergovernmental system of UNESCO as an independent expert and, more recently, as a representative of a non-governmental organization accredited to the Convention. My first direct engagement with UNESCO over the 2003 Convention was as the author of the preliminary study exploring the possibility of setting new standards for safeguarding this heritage (referred to at that time as "traditional cultural and folklore"). Although this was a "technical and legal" study, cultural and anthropological considerations were prominent in the background research. Subsequently, I acted as Rapporteur of the (non-governmental) Restricted Drafting Group that produced the first preliminary draft of what became the 2003 Convention on safeguarding intangible cultural heritage. From this perspective, I cannot distance myself wholly from what is often dismissed as "UNESCO speak" but which is, in fact, the technical language of international law[1] or ignore such international law principles as the sovereignty and equality of States (Crawford, 2019) whereby a treaty is only as good as the intentions of the States that drafted it. It is a political reality that an international treaty involves a series of compromises in order to reconcile the various priorities and interests of the negotiating States: It would be naïve to imagine that negotiating States to any treaty (with the possible exception of treaties in the rather special field of human rights) would prioritize the interests of a group of non-state actors over their own.

It is true that the States Parties to the 2003 Convention are also Parties to the main human rights treaties, in particular the International Covenant on Economic,

DOI:10.4324/9781003244158-3

Social, and Cultural Rights ("ICESCR," 1966) (United Nations, 1966b). The right to participate in cultural life (enshrined in Article 15(1)) encompasses the rights of access to and enjoyment of cultural heritage, which, according to more recent thinking, includes the importance of civil society participation in heritage protection (from identification through designing and managing policies and plans) and assigns a priority of interest to heritage bearers and the local inhabitants of areas where the heritage is based (Human Rights Council, 2011). This is present in the subtle accommodation between the requirement for the full participation of communities (groups and, in some cases, individuals) ("CGIs") in safeguarding intangible cultural heritage ("ICH") and an almost exclusive reservation of sovereignty otherwise expressed in the 2003 Convention. The challenge is how we can reconcile these two apparently contradictory approaches, and this is the space in which critical heritage studies can play a particularly important role, as can international human rights law: Within the international law discipline, human rights provides the "critical" viewpoint since it is the sole area in which States are held accountable to their citizens for their behavior (Dixon, 2013). This is why I emphasize the human rights aspects of this treaty here when speaking of sustainable development.

1.2. Human rights and sustainable development: primary contexts of the 2003 convention

1.2.1. The sustainable development context

The route by which sustainable development entered the Convention text is instructive, initially included in two of the key documents from expert meetings convened during 2001 and 2002. At an expert meeting held in Turin in 2001, it was noted that "international efforts to safeguard intangible cultural heritage must be founded on universally accepted human rights, equity and sustainability" and that the definition of ICH for the Convention should include reference to "the resources, spaces and other aspects of social and natural context necessary to their sustainability" (UNESCO, 2001a: Preamble at 12(a) and Recommendations at 7). It also called for a proclamation of best practices that "(iv) involve women to the fullest extent of their potential participation; (v) enhance the social and ecological sustainability of the group and region" (Ibid.: Recommendations at 14). This connects the ICH–sustainable development nexus with both its gender aspects and also the idea of social and ecological sustainability whereby (a) societies (and people's livelihoods) need to be sustainable and (b) safeguarding ICH also aims at and/or ensures ecological sustainability.

These additions are suggestive of an expert view that goes beyond a simple recitation of international policy agendas to a more contextual understanding of the relationship being described. A follow-up expert meeting held in Rio de Janeiro in 2002, taking a somewhat more utilitarian approach, typified ICH "as a potential resource for sustainable development" and noted that "actions concerned with the safeguarding of intangible cultural heritage, should encourage innovation and creation" (UNESCO, 2002a: paragraphs 10 (i) and 10 (ii) €, respectively). This latter reference points to an important characteristic of ICH for supporting sustainable development, namely the capacity of its bearers to innovate in response to changing conditions. From this, we can see that non-governmental experts play a rather specific and nuanced role in the development of the text, even though they may also serve as members of official delegations in intergovernmental meetings; moreover, they may also be paid by UNESCO as consultants to produce documentation for the statutory bodies, capacity-building materials, information brochures, etc.

Following this, the reference to sustainable development in the 2003 Convention was incorporated into the intergovernmental processes through the outcome document of a ministerial meeting held in Istanbul in the lead-up to drafting the preliminary draft treaty. This noted that:

> Laying the foundations of true sustainable development requires the emergence of an integrated vision of development based on the enhancement of values and practices involved in the intangible cultural heritage. Alike (sic) cultural diversity, which stems from it, intangible cultural heritage is a guarantee for sustainable development and peace.
>
> *(UNESCO, 2002b: Paragraph 6)*

The first part of the second recital of the treaty's Preamble grew out of this: "Considering the importance of the intangible cultural heritage as a mainspring of cultural diversity and a guarantee of sustainable development." It is also clear that some valuable ideas (related to social and ecological sustainability, the gender dimensions of development, innovation) introduced by non-governmental experts have been lost in this process. Even the intergovernmental ministerial meeting proposed the vision of "an integrated vision of development" which would have been much more far-reaching than the rather bland formulation that eventually made it into the Convention text. This would have reflected the central idea that sustainable development can operate as an integrating principle which can help to resolve some of the paradox mentioned in the title of this chapter. Sadly, and rather predictably, the final treaty text as negotiated incorporates the idea of sustainable development in a form that feels closer to a box-ticking exercise to acknowledge its place in international policy-making at the time. The other reference to sustainable development in the Convention is in a negative formulation in the definition of ICH which requires it to be "compatible with . . . sustainable development" (Article 2(1)).

What is also of interest here is to consider how the rather flexible model of the 2003 Convention[2] has allowed room for it to evolve and develop over time. This evolution is not isolated in the Convention's framework but reflects shifts in the understanding of sustainable development within international (and national) policy-making. There is still a long way to go in having the full international acceptance of the centrality of the role that culture – and particularly cultural heritage – can play in achieving sustainable development, especially the sustainability of communities as called for by sustainable development goal ("SDG") 11.4. This is despite several attempts by UNESCO to articulate this, from the report of the World Commission on Culture and Development (World Commission on Culture and Development, 1996), through the Stockholm Declaration and Action Plan (1998) to more recent efforts made in the lead-up to the adoption of the SDGs in 2015. The reference in Target 4 of SDG 11 to "sustainable communities" is very much in tune with an understanding that the survival of ICH depends on the survival of ways of life – without viable bearer communities, ICH cannot be sustainable.

This, in turn, leads us to the concept of viability that lies at the heart of safeguarding ICH, as defined in Article 2(3) of the Convention. Safeguarding policies and measures, including international actions, should be undertaken with the aim of ensuring the future viability of this heritage, an approach that is wholly consonant with the philosophy of sustainable development as "development that meets the needs of the future without compromising the ability of future generations to meet their own needs" (World Commission on Environment and Development, 1987). Crucially, the viability of ICH cannot be ensured without ensuring the future sustainability of its CGIs; this, in turn, cannot be ensured without securing their capacities and livelihoods which rely, in large part, on protecting their economic, social, cultural, and other rights. This may well represent another area in which a critical examination is required to investigate whether safeguarding practices do respect the rights of CGIs sufficiently and whether associated endeavors to ensure sustainability are really favorable to these rights. This presents a conundrum since there will be cases where safeguarding ICH elements (and the cultural rights of the bearer community) will threaten the rights of individual community members or groups within communities, while supporting the economic rights of CGIs through commercialization might risk the future "viability" of an element from the viewpoint of the Convention.

1.2.2. The human rights context

The other main context to the Convention emphasized in the Preamble, and given prominence by its placement in the first recital, was that of international human rights standards. This was a strong signal that (a) human rights represented an essential context within which the 2003 Convention would operate and (b) the treaty, including the scope of the definition of ICH, should be interpreted and applied with reference to international human rights standards. Of course, this referencing of human rights can be viewed somewhat cynically in view of the weak enforcement of human rights standards and the continuing violation of these standards by Governments worldwide. At the same time, its inclusion in the Preamble is important since it situates all of the treaty's provisions within that legal framework and adds a degree of "bite" to a series of somewhat general obligations.

Both the Universal Declaration on Human Rights (at Article 27) (United Nations, 1948) and the International Covenant on Economic, Social, and Cultural Rights ("ICESCR" at Article 15(1)) (United Nations, 1966a) cited in the Preamble articulate the right to participate in cultural life. This is the primary human right relating to access to and enjoyment of cultural heritage and includes the rights to create heritage and to enjoy access to one's own and other's cultural heritage and of a community to develop its cultural heritage (Blake, 2015: Chapter 8). In addition, the International Covenant on Civil and Political Rights ("ICCPR" at Article 27) (United Nations, 1966b) protects the rights of ethnic, religious, and linguistic minorities who constitute a large number of the "communities, groups and . . . individuals" (CGIs) accorded a central position in the 2003 Convention. Moreover, the freedoms of expression and association contained in the ICCPR (Articles 19 and 22) are often essential for heritage practice while the economic rights and the right to education of the ICESCR (Article 13) are also necessary for the continued viability of bearer communities and their heritage. The definition of ICH in the 2003 Convention (Article 2(1)) underlines the significance of this heritage for the identity of its associated CGIs and their ability to respond to the environment around them.

Human rights also place a limit on the elements that can be treated as "intangible cultural heritage" for the purposes of the Convention (Francioni, 2020) by excluding those that are clearly harmful to human rights and contain serious discriminatory aspects. A recent example of the removal of an element from the Representative List of Intangible Cultural Heritage of Humanity (RL) on human rights grounds related to the Aalst Carnival element (Belgium). The violations in question concerned stereotypical depictions of Jews and caricatures of Second World War deportations being shown during the carnival on three separate occasions (UNESCO, 2019).[3] This human rights limitation is an important safeguard but can create very challenging situations where elements that are supported by their bearer community are judged according to externally set universal standards and values to contravene human rights standards and denied the official status of "ICH." This could obviously give rise to a contradictory outcome in which the well-being of the community as a whole is set against the rights and well-being of subaltern groups and individual members who do not wish the element to be recognized.[4] These cases also clearly demonstrate that a lack of mutual respect and dialogue within and between bearer communities and other social groups has the potential to give rise to serious issues, drawing attention to the importance of the value of mutual respect called for in the Convention's definition of ICH.

Significantly, this is the first UNESCO heritage treaty to make such explicit reference to human rights in its Preamble, a signal of the increased attention accorded to cultural rights since the late 1990s (Symonides, 1998) which coincided with greater recognition of Indigenous peoples' rights and the heritage of countries of the global "South." One outcome of this was a shift from protecting "national heritage" toward protecting the rights of CGIs, as both individuals and members of communities and groups; this, in turn, implies acknowledgment of some form of community-based right to cultural heritage (Jakubowski, 2017) and a related shift in the heritage safeguarding paradigm from a top-down, state-led model to one in which CGIs play a much more active and even proactive role (Blake, 2016). Notably, the 2003 Convention requires the participation of CGI at all stages of safeguarding ICH, from its identification through to designing and managing safeguarding plans. This is a further expression of its human rights orientation which is a logical approach toward safeguarding a form of heritage that primarily exists in the human person. However, the theoretical ideal of deep CGI involvement underpinning this treaty and the reality of its implementation by States Parties are frequently far removed from each other, and it is challenging to see how CGI participation in the 2003 Convention's operation can be better realized (Waterton and Watson, 2011; Lixinski, 2013; Jacobs, Neyrink and Van der Zeijden, 2014; Adell, Bendix, Bortolotto and Tauschek, 2015).

1.3. Shared objectives but different approaches

In many ways, human rights and (sustainable) development share similar objectives since both are concerned with improving the quality of life and opportunities for different sections of a given population, as well as society as a whole. At the same time, they have important differences which we should take into account here, an idea well-expressed by Alston when he wrote of human rights and development as being like "ships passing in the night" (Alston, 2005). Although they may be heading toward a similar destination, they are not following the same course and they use quite different means to reach it. An example of how the two approaches are very closely related but equally far-removed might be the case of a country where 98.2% of primary school-aged girls attend school. This is a high achievement from a development perspective while, although it would still regard this positively, a human rights approach would also ask why 1.8% of girls do not go to school; importantly, it seeks to identify who is responsible, culpable, and accountable for this among various governmental and social actors and institutions (UNDP, 2000). This desire to delve into the quality of the process as well as the quantitative data is one that is shared in the 2003 Convention as is now apparent from the Overall Results Framework (ORF) adopted in 2018 (UNESCO, 2020), which combines both qualitative and quantitative indicators.

The second recital of the Preamble twins the idea of cultural diversity with sustainable development, where the former is presented as a guarantee for the latter. Since cultural diversity is understood as a human rights value, we see here that it is also the linking concept between human rights and sustainable development approaches and objectives. As one of the main foundations for developing the 2003 Convention,[5] the Universal Declaration on Cultural Diversity (UNESCO, 2001b) recognizes that cultural diversity is a "source of exchange, innovation and creativity" as well as a "common heritage of humanity" (Ibid., Article 1). Preserving and promoting cultural diversity by safeguarding ICH run as a common theme and purpose through the 2003 Convention, from its definition to international inscriptions on the RL.[6] Defending cultural diversity is "inseparable from respect for human dignity" that therefore "implies a commitment to human rights . . . in particular the rights of persons belonging to minorities and those of indigenous peoples" (Ibid., Article 4). The aforementioned human rights limitation on what we count as "ICH" in the Convention is mirrored in the rider that cultural diversity cannot be invoked "to infringe upon human rights guaranteed by international law, nor to limit their scope" (Idem). It also makes the linkage with development, seeing cultural diversity as a phenomenon that "widens the range of options open to everyone; it is one of the roots of development" (Ibid., Article 3), making it clear that this is a form of development that allows people and societies to "achieve a more satisfactory intellectual, emotional, moral and spiritual existence". Here, then, we see how the defense of cultural diversity (with in-built safeguards) is both a human rights imperative and an important basis for achieving human and sustainable development. Of course, these are fine-sounding and rather rhetorical assertions, and it is important to examine them more closely in order to identify any potential contradictions they may encompass when actually applied on the ground.

1.4. Human rights and sustainability: a mutual or a contradictory relationship?

Human rights standards and sustainability, although quite different in form and approach, have many shared objectives and one is unlikely to be achievable without the other. This mutuality is one of the complexities built into the 2003 Convention that we need to understand in order to judge how far its implementation has really contributed toward achieving these goals. At the time of its drafting and even today, there remain many unanswered questions as to how these twin objectives can be achieved in a way that answers the requirements of each.

1.4.1. Human rights and development

In considering the relationship between human rights and (sustainable) development, a key idea was expressed in the UDHR (1948) in Article 28 which, sadly, has not yet been fully articulated as a norm in international human rights law.[7] This article stated: "Everyone is entitled to a social and international order in which the rights and freedoms set forth in this Declaration can be fully realized". The significance of this statement was underlined by Mohammed Bedjaoui,[8] who described it as the "alpha and omega" of human rights law and who argued cogently that this right, including an equitable international economic order and the associated right of all States to (sustainable) development, is as fundamental as self-determination[9] for the achievement of human rights (Bedjaoui, 1991). The *Proclamation of Tehran* (1968) drew out the relationship between human rights and development in its Preamble in the following terms: The achievement of lasting progress in the implementation of human rights is dependent upon sound and effective national and international policies of economic and social development.

Today, we would include cultural rights in the list of rights mentioned here and, in so doing, make the connection directly between the objectives of the 2003 Convention and this viewpoint. If we bring this discussion forward to the early 1990s, we see that the 1992 Rio Declaration (UNCED, 1992) that formally articulated the concept of sustainable development for the international community was adopted one year before the 1993 Vienna Declaration on Human Rights (United Nations, 1993), which was an authoritative expression of the state of human rights law at that time. In addition to containing a section dedicated to the rights of Indigenous people (paragraphs 28–32), the Declaration also recognizes

> the inherent dignity and the unique contribution of indigenous people to the development and plurality of society and strongly reaffirms the commitment of the international community to their economic, social and cultural well-being and their enjoyment of the fruits of sustainable development.
>
> *(Article 20)*

The rights of women and children to participate in and enjoy the fruits of development are also noted elsewhere in this instrument. There are numerous references to development and the "interrelationship between development, democracy and human rights" (Article 74) in the Declaration, which notes also that to achieve lasting progress toward fulfillment of the right to development requires not only national-level policies and measures but also "equitable economic relations and a favourable economic environment at the international level" (Article 11). The Vienna Declaration (1993) is the closest that the international community has yet come to really putting Article 28 of the UDHR (1948) into action. However, this was swiftly followed by the Uruguay round of GATT in 1994 at which the World Trade Organization was established and the new GATT Agreement (WTO, 1994) was adopted: which can be seen as a direct response to the Rio and Vienna Declarations by the dominant capitalist trading blocs (Shiva, 1999).

What remains to be seen is whether the push-back from countries of the South in UNESCO[10] and other international fora can be successful in reversing the pernicious impacts of the WTO agreements (GAT, GATS, and TRIPS) on international economic equity and associated social and cultural rights. On a positive note, a UN Special Rapporteur on the right to development was appointed in 2016 by a UN General Assembly Resolution (UNGA, 2016) that notes (in its Preamble) that "the 2030 Agenda is informed by the Declaration on the Right to Development and that the right to development provides a vital enabling environment for the full realization of the sustainable development goals" and called for "the elaboration of a comprehensive and coherent set of standards for the implementation of the right to development." This work is now in progress and raises the possibility of a standard-setting instrument in this area in the future, which would help considerably to integrate development with human rights in international law (Ibid., paras. 13 (C) and 14, respectively).

The relationship between human rights and development is a complicated one since, on the one hand, more economic development may make it easier for governments to protect their citizens' rights. On the other hand, however, if the model of development followed is narrowly focused on economic growth, then human rights may actually suffer for the benefit of short-term economic gains. This does not mean that we need to sacrifice human rights for development, but rather that our concept of development must be one that integrates them and takes a holistic view of development as having socio-cultural as well as economic dimensions. Both the notions of human development[11] and sustainable development respond to this requirement for a more holistic view of development. There is, in fact, an important complementary character to the relationship between human development and human rights, with human development's focus on people's capabilities and the freedoms they enjoy complemented by the emphasis in human rights on individuals' claims against the State and individuals to facilitate these capabilities (Donnelly, 2003).[12] However, it is important to recognize also that the aims and objectives of human rights and development are not the same, as was pointed out by Alston writing about the millennium development goals (MDGs, 2000–2015), which preceded the sustainable development goals. He noted that "although the SDGs have a great deal in common with human rights commitments . . . the two agendas resemble ships passing in the night, even though they are headed for very similar destinations" (Alston, 2005, p. 755).

An important difference is that a human rights approach emphasizes the distribution of these outcomes across a population and highlights inequities in delivery in a way that simply considering aggregate figures does not.[13] In this way, taking a human rights approach to development issues shifts the focus to *the quality of the process*, rather than simply measuring outcomes as the development approach does (Gauri, 2003). This challenge of finding ways of capturing the quality of the process bedeviled measurement of the MDGs and will no doubt also be a challenge in measuring the sustainability of policies through the sustainable development goals (SDGs, 2015–2030) also. This is because they are a set of quantitative indicators that describe the progress of a country toward achieving certain development outcomes but do not show *how* these are achieved. An example that illustrates this problem well concerns the quantitative indicator of how many girls of primary school age go to school. The indicator may show that 98% attend school, a very positive picture of that country's success in achieving this indicator. However, a human rights focus would ask why 2% of these girls do not go to school (and who is responsible), which adds a wholly new dimension to our understanding.

A similar quantitative versus qualitative challenge has been faced in developing the ORF for the 2003 Convention (UNESCO, 2020) and the detailed assessment factors for each of the core indicators that measure progress in achieving the objectives of the Convention attempt to capture the quality of the process. Hence, if we take core indicator 1, this measures the "[e]xtent to which competent bodies and institutions and consultative mechanisms support the continued practice and transmission of ICH," which is primarily quantitative in character while assessment factor 1.3 tries to capture a more qualitative picture. This asks whether "[b]road and inclusive involvement in ICH safeguarding and management, particularly by the communities, groups and individuals concerned, is fostered through consultative bodies or other coordination mechanisms." Time will tell how successfully the ORF (and the new periodic reporting tool that is aligned with it) can capture this qualitative aspect.

1.5. Local specificities and global goals

This prominence accorded to human rights and sustainable development presents a further potential contradiction in this treaty's underlying conceptual framework, namely the constant tension between its universalizing mission – as expressed through universal standards and global goals, as well as the notion of ICH as a "heritage of humankind" – and the emphasis it places on cultural diversity and the significance of this heritage to local communities, groups, and even individuals. For example, UNESCO's 1970 Convention (UNESCO, 1970) mixes global with national priorities, attempting to balance the right of all people to enjoy the world's cultural property with the right of the State of origin to retain its cultural property or have it restored. The idea of "global cultural heritage" is constructed from the concept of a "universal heritage of mankind" and further supported by applying universal human rights standards to evaluating and even selecting it. When we seek to satisfy both the global and the local in our international heritage safeguarding paradigm, we inevitably set a number of competing interests against each other. Should we characterize heritage as a 'cultural heritage of (hu)mankind', or should it be viewed primarily as a source of value and identity to local and Indigenous communities?

This tension has become particularly apparent in the 2003 Convention in view of the emphasis it places on CGI involvement in safeguarding their ICH including, crucially, the identification of elements of ICH for safeguarding. In the Preamble to this treaty, there is an interesting attempt to strike a balance between these two requirements. The fifth recital refers to "the universal will and the common concern" to safeguard this heritage, which expresses a notion that this is of universal importance to the international community while avoiding the direct assertion that it is a common heritage per se. The sixth recital expresses recognition of the important role played by "communities, in particular indigenous communities, groups and, in some cases, individuals . . . in the production, safeguarding, maintenance and re-creation" of ICH, thus "helping to enrich cultural diversity and human creativity." Here, then, the specificity of ICH for its concerned CGIs is acknowledged, while placing its safeguarding within the broader framework of the globalist ambition of (global) cultural diversity and the creativity of human cultures worldwide. This is a delicate balancing act and one that papers over some of the internal contradictions it sets up.

The idea of the "Representative List of the Intangible Cultural Heritage of Humanity" reiterates this approach since it is "representative" by dint of representing as wide a range as possible of the different types of ICH while this also, somehow, represents a global value as a "heritage of humanity." In theory, this duality can be finessed with the variety of "representative" elements contributing to the diversity of the heritage of humankind it presents. In practice, this is more challenging since the elements can only be nominated by States Parties, many of which retain a more elitist World Heritage-based view of the inscription process. According to this theory, it should be possible and even common for quite mundane elements that hold important significance for their related CGIs to be inscribed (and some have been).[14] However, the vast majority of elements nominated for international inscription have been proposed on the basis that their inscription would showcase and even glorify the country's heritage. This is in direct contradiction to the spirit of the 2003 Convention and the underlying philosophy of the RL but is hardly surprising since the States Parties that have become used to the "hit parade" thinking of world heritage nominations. This distinction between CGI-specific significance and global value was always going to be a rather esoteric fudge to allow the inclusion of a listing mechanism that would attract new States Parties while tacitly expecting them to respect the philosophy of representativeness.

Economic, social, and cultural globalization can also create contradictory outcomes, with the potential for both positive and negative impacts on ICH. This is noted in the Preamble (fourth recital):

> Recognizing that the processes of globalization and social transformation, alongside the conditions they create for renewed dialogue among communities, also give rise, as does the phenomenon of intolerance, to grave threats of deterioration, disappearance and destruction of the intangible cultural heritage.

With regard to commercial activities in general, as stated in the Operational Directives to the Convention (at OD 116) (UNESCO, 2020), these can present both benefits and dangers. On the plus side, they can contribute to improving the living standards of CGIs, enhance local economies, and contribute to social cohesion. On the deficit side, they "might affect the nature and viability" of the ICH elements concerned, thus leading to an unsustainable outcome for the heritage in question.

In the second recital of the Preamble, the reference to ICH as a "guarantee" of "truly" sustainable development is worth examining. First, ICH is seen as making a fundamental contribution toward achieving sustainable forms of development, which is quite different from the attitude of earlier decades where traditional cultural practices were viewed as a break in economic development (Douglas, 2004). Second, the kind of development that is being envisaged here is one that encompasses various aspects of sustainability, including socio-cultural ones, as well as the idea that it should continue to be sustainable for both communities and their heritage into the future. A tool that has recently been developed for evaluating the performance of Parties in implementing the Convention, the Overall Results Framework (ORF), may well prove useful in critically examining how successful States Parties have been in working toward sustainable development through their safeguarding policies and measures. The ORF addresses a number of specific measures that can be relevant to fulfilling the requirement to guarantee sustainability. Four of its core indicators (out of 26) cover (i) the extent to which policies as well as legal and administrative measures in the fields of culture and education and other fields reflect the diversity of ICH and the importance of its safeguarding and are implemented (Indicators 11, 12, and 13, respectively) and (ii) how far they respect customary rights, practices, and expressions, particularly as regards the practice and transmission of ICH (Indicator 14). Questions related to these indicators are now found in the periodic reporting tool for the Convention.

Interestingly, the ORF also includes some clearly human rights-related notions, such as "inclusive" and "inclusively" as applied to CGI involvement in safeguarding generally which is understood to mean "inclusive of all sectors and strata of society, including indigenous peoples, migrants, immigrants and refugees, people of different ages and genders, persons with disabilities and members of vulnerable groups" (UNESCO, 2018, footnote 5). It also encourages States Parties to provide "disaggregated data or to explain how such inclusiveness is ensured" which should help greatly in evaluation. Addressing policy-making in fields outside culture, the ORF refers to "inclusive social development" (Ibid., Assessment Factor 13.2) and "inclusive economic development" (Ibid., Assessment Factor 13.4). The former includes reference to food security, health care, and gender equality which are all relevant to sustainable development goals but also have important human rights aspects as well since they respond to the rights to food and health and the principles of non-discrimination and equality. The latter is less straightforward since it touches on the sustainable development objectives of sustainable livelihoods, productive employment, and decent work, all of which echo qualitative human rights measurements; however, these could set up a conflict with the idea of the viability of ICH elements if, when seeking to monetize ICH elements, the original significance for its CGIs is lost or severely diluted. This adds a level of complexity to the requirements placed on States Parties with regard to how they implement the 2003 Convention and it opens up important questions concerning the role States should play in the cultural arena and their relationships with non-state actors, including private individuals and the private sector (Lankarani and Fines, 2013).

1.6. In conclusion – sustainable development as a principle of integration

This chapter has taken the two main international policy and legal frameworks within which the 2003 Intangible Heritage Convention of UNESCO was developed, international human rights standards and sustainable development, and sought to expose potential contradictions thrown up by this in the treaty's implementation. Participation is a fundamental principle of human rights and, in the Convention's framework, this implies the deep and direct participation of CGIs in the process of safeguarding ICH, from its identification to its management. Sustainable development is understood as encompassing the sustainability of the heritage and its related communities, while ICH safeguarding can contribute toward more sustainable forms of development.

Although quite different in their form and approaches, human rights and sustainable development have many shared objectives and each of them is unlikely to be easily achieved without the other. This mutual dependency, then, is one of the complexities built into the 2003 Convention that needs to be unpicked if we are to understand how far its implementation has really contributed toward achieving these aims; it also gives rise to a not-inconsiderable potential for these two to become contradictory. An example of such potential paradoxical outcomes of the treaty's architecture includes the case of ICH elements that are seen by their cultural community as socially and/or economically beneficial but that are considered – by external evaluators – as in contravention of international human rights standards. Indeed, we have seen that there is a continuous tension between its universalizing mission as expressed, for example, in the characterization of ICH as a "heritage of humankind" contrasted with the emphasis it places on participation and cultural diversity, which represents a strongly localized viewpoint.

The goal of sustainable development encompasses some of these tensions while also providing a possible route out of them. Sustainable development has primarily been articulated as a global policy goal (albeit one achieved through national-level measures) and has been articulated as a universal goal and value. This is particularly true of the sustainable development goals (2015–2030) and their associated Agenda 2030 which have become part of how the performance of States Parties to the 2003 Convention is measured.[15] However, in its stated aim of balancing economic, environmental, and socio-cultural objectives, sustainable development potentially offers a means of reconciling some of the conflicts and contradictions identified in this chapter. This view is supported by two cases with an environmental subject matter heard before the International Court of Justice (ICJ). In the earlier of the two cases, the *Gabcikovo Nagyamoros* case (1997) between Hungary and Slovakia which concerned a shared watercourse, the Court noted the "need to reconcile economic development with protection of the environment [which] is aptly expressed in the concept of sustainable development" (International Court of Justice, 1997, paragraph 140). In the more recent *Pulp Mills* case (2010), concerning pollution of a shared river between Uruguay and Argentina, the ICJ referred in its majority judgment to the "balance between economic development and environmental protection that is the essence of sustainable development" (International Court of Justice, 2010, paragraph 177). Here, the Court acknowledged sustainable development as an integrating notion that has an important role to play in the legal balancing of potentially conflicting interests.

Since sustainable development comprises economic, environmental, and socio-cultural "pillars," this balancing could just as well be seen as a principle that can serve to provide a balance between economic and cultural interests as economic and environmental ones. This balancing of interests involves the reconciliation of differing interests between various stakeholders in any given situation and so has the potential also to support much greater real integration and involvement of CGIs (and other actors) in the operation of the 2003 Convention. Since it is becoming increasingly recognized that sustainable development is an approach that must be respected by governments when putting into place policies and legislation, as well as when implementing existing legislation, this may well be seen over time to provide a resolution to some of the apparent internal contradictions in the 2003 Convention.

Notes

1 It is sometimes forgotten in more critical literature that actions related to implementing the 2003 Convention are taken within the framework of an international treaty and are thus governed by the principles and methods of international law, including the use of specific terms of art with particular meanings.
2 This model usually involves a somewhat general main text with detailed (and relatively easy to revise) Operational Directives, Guidelines, or similar for the implementation of the broad obligations it sets out.
3 The Intergovernmental Committee for the Safeguarding of the Intangible Cultural Heritage removed the Aalst Carnival from the RL in 2019 (Decision 14.COM 12).
4 Such situations could result from individuals seeking to diverge from traditions, such as intra-community marriage, where the bearer community as a whole regards that as essential for preserving their social cohesion and collective identity.
5 The development of the 2003 Convention responds very directly to no. 13 of the Main Lines of Implementation of the 2001 Declaration, which enjoins: "13. Formulating policies and strategies for the preservation and enhancement of the cultural and natural heritage, *notably the oral and intangible cultural heritage*, and combating illicit traffic in cultural goods and services" (emphasis added).
6 The best way to understand the concept of "representative" here is that the inscribed elements, taken together, represent the global diversity of ICH elements and their related CGIs.
7 UNGA Res. 41/128 of 4 December 1986. However, this was adopted by the international community in that universal forum has never gained status as a binding norm of international law and remains in the somewhat uncertain territory of the "solidarity" human rights.
8 A previous President of the International Court of Justice who was the Chairperson of the Restricted Drafting Group of the 2003 Convention and President of the three intergovernmental sessions that negotiated the final treaty text.
9 Enshrined in joint Art. 1 of the two 1966 International Covenants.
10 The adoption of the 2005 Convention on the Protection and Promotion of the Diversity of Cultural Expressions adopted by UNESCO on 20 October *2005* at the 33rd session of the General Conference can be seen, alongside the 2003 Convention, as part of this pushback.
11 As conceived by Amartya Sen in the late 1980s and applied in the Human Development Reports of UNDP.
12 Donnelly (2003, p. 111) explains this as follows: "A developmental perspective is aggregate and focuses on production. Economic and social rights, by contrast, are concerned

with distributions of goods, services, and opportunities, which must be guaranteed to every person even when pursuing the most noble social goals."

13 UNDP, *Human Rights and Human Development*, Human Development Report, 2000.

14 The "Hawker culture in Singapore: community dining and culinary practices in a multicultural urban context" element inscribed on the RL in the name of Singapore in 2020 can be seen as an example where people from diverse backgrounds gather for breakfast, lunch, and dinner in hawker centers, which serve as "community dining rooms." They are both a part of the ordinary lives of many people in Singapore while also holding a special significance for the CGIs who use them. More information can be found at < https://ich.unesco.org/en/RL/hawker-culture-in-singapore-community-dining-and-culinary-practices-in-a-multicultural-urban-context-01568> accessed on 9 June 2021.

15 The relationship between each of the 26 core indicators and the ORF is made clear in the Guidance Notes that accompany them. These are available online at <https://ich.unesco.org/en/overall-results-framework-00984#guidance-notes-by-indicators> (accessed September 22, 2021).

References

Adell, N., R. F. Bendix, C. Bortolotto and M. Tauschek (eds.) (2015) *Between Imagined Communities and Communities of Practice*, Göttingen: Universitätsverlag Göttingen.

Alston, P. (2005) 'Ships passing in the night: The current state of the human rights and development debate seen through the lens of the Millennium Development Goals', *Human Rights Quarterly*, 27(3), pp. 755–829.

Bedjaoui, M. (1991) 'The right to development', in Mohammed Bedjaoui (ed.) *International Law: Achievements and Prospects*, Leiden: Martinus Nijhoff/UNESCO.

Blake, J. (2015) *International Cultural Heritage Law*, Oxford: Oxford University Press.

Blake, J. (2016) 'Development of UNESCO's 2003 convention: Creating a new heritage protection paradigm?', in Peter Davis and Michelle L. Stefano (eds.) *Intangible Cultural Heritage*, London and New York: Routledge.

Crawford, J. (2019) *Brownlie's Principles of International Law*, 9th edn., Oxford: Oxford University Press.

Dixon, M. (2013) *Textbook on International Law*, 7th edn., Oxford: Oxford University Press.

Donnelly, J. (2003) *Universal Human Rights in Theory and Practice*, 2nd edn., New York: Cornell University Press.

Douglas, M. (2004) 'Traditional culture – let's hear no more about it,' in Vijayendra Rao and Michael Walton (eds.) *Culture and Public Action*, Stanford: Stanford University Press, pp. 85–119.

Francioni, F. (2020) 'Article 2(1): Defining intangible cultural heritage', in Janet Blake and Lucas Lixinski (eds.) *A Commentary on UNESCO's 2003 Convention on Safeguarding Intangible Cultural Heritage*, Oxford: Oxford University Press, pp. 48–57.

Gauri, V. (2003) *Social Rights and Economics: Claims to Health Care and Education in Developing Countries*, Policy Research Working Paper No. 3006. Washington, DC: World Bank.

Human Rights Council (2011) *Report of the Independent Expert in the Field of Cultural Rights, Farida Shaheed*, adopted by the Human Rights Council seventeenth session, agenda item 3, 21 March 2011. Geneva: United Nations.

International Court of Justice (1997) *Case Concerning the Gabcikovo-Nagymoros Project* (Hungary/Slovakia), Judgment, I.C.J. Reports 1997, p. 7.

International Court of Justice (2010) *Pulp Mills on the River Uruguay* (Argentina v. Uruguay), Judgment, I.C.J. Reports 2010, p. 14.

Jacobs, M., Neyrink, J. and Van der Zeijden A. (2014) 'UNESCO, brokers, facilitators and mediation: Critical success (f)actors for the safeguarding of intangible cultural heritage', *Volkskund*, 115(3), pp. 249–256.

Jakubowski, A. (ed.) (2017) *Cultural Rights as Collective Rights – An International Law Perspective*, Leiden: Brill Nijhoff.

Lankarani, L. and Fines, F. (eds.) (2013) *Le Patrimoine Culturel Immatériel et les Collectivités Infraétatiques*, Paris: Éditions A. Pedone.

Lixinski, L. (2013) *Intangible Cultural Heritage in International Law*, Oxford: Oxford University Press.

Shiva, V. (1999) 'Ecological balance in an era of globalization', in Nicholas Low (ed.) *Global Ethics and Environment*, London and New York: Routledge, pp. 47–69.

Symonides, J. (1998) 'Cultural rights: A neglected category of human rights', *International Social Science Journal*, 50, pp. 559–71.

UN Conference on Environment and Development (UNCED) (1992) *Final Declaration*, Rio de Janeiro, New York: United Nations.

UNDP (2000) *Human Development Report – Human Rights and Human Development*, New York: UNDP.

UNESCO (1970) *Convention on the Means of Prohibiting and Preventing the Illicit Import, Export and Transfer of Ownership of Cultural Property*, United Nations, Treaty Series, vol. 823, 231.

UNESCO (2001a) *Final Report of the "International Round Table on 'Intangible Cultural Heritage – Working Definitions'"*, 14–17 March, Turin, Italy, available online at: https://ich.unesco.org/doc/src/00077-EN.pdf (accessed 28 September 2021).

UNESCO (2001b) *Universal Declaration on Cultural Diversity Adopted by UNESCO General Conference*, 2 November 2001.

UNESCO (2002a) *International Expert Meeting on Intangible Cultural Heritage: Priority Domains for an International Convention*, Rio de Janeiro, Brazil, 22–24 January 2002, Doc. RIO/ITH/2002/WD/1O.

UNESCO (2002b) *Final Communiqué of the Third Round Table of Ministers of Culture "Intangible Cultural Heritage, mirror of cultural diversity"*, Istanbul, Turkey 16–17 September 2002.

UNESCO (2019) *Decision of the Intergovernmental Committee: 14.COM 12*, Doc. LHE/19/14.COM/12.

UNESCO (2018) *Agenda Item 10 of the 7th General Assembly Meeting in Paris*, 4–6 June 2018, Doc. ITH/18/7.GA/10 Rev.

UNESCO (2020) *Basic Texts of the 2003 Convention for Safeguarding the Intangible Cultural Heritage*, available online at https://ich.unesco.org/doc/src/2003_Convention_Basic_Texts-_2020_version-EN.pdf (accessed 26 August 2021).

United Nations (1948) *Universal Declaration on Human Rights*, United Nations General Assembly Resolution 217 A(III).

United Nations (1966a) *International Covenant on Economic, Social and Cultural Rights*, United Nations, Treaty Series, vol. 993, p. 3.

United Nations (1966b) *International Covenant on Civil and Political Rights*, United Nations, Treaty Series, vol. 999, p. 171.

United Nations (1993) *Vienna Declaration on Human Rights and Programme of Action*, United Nations General Assembly, Doc. A/CONF.157/23.

United Nations (2016) *United Nations General Assembly Resolution of 5 October 2016*, Doc. A/HRC/RES/33/14.

Waterton, E. and S. Watson (2011) *Heritage and Community Engagement. Collaboration or Contestation?* New York and London: Routledge.
World Commission on Culture and Development (WCED) (1996) *Our Creative Diversity*, Paris: UNESCO Publishing.
World Commission on Environment and Development (1987) *Our Common Future*, United Nations, New York, Doc. A/42/427.
World Trade Organization (WTO) (1994) *General Agreement on Tariffs and Trade*, International Legal Materials, vol. 33, p. 1153.

2

THE REORIENTATION OF A CONVENTION

UNESCO, intangible heritage, and sustainable development

Rieks Smeets

2.1. Introduction[1]

When it was adopted, UNESCO's 2003 *Convention for the Safeguarding of the Intangible Cultural Heritage* (the Convention) was meant to contribute to the safeguarding, identification, and visibility of that heritage, the recognition of its values and functions, and to appreciation of and respect for it. In the process, cultural identities would be reinforced, and cultural diversity and human creativity promoted.[2] The Convention reserves important roles in the recognition and safeguarding of ICH for communities, groups, and "where appropriate" individuals who "create, maintain and transmit" that heritage.

With the more tangible heritage of the North being well served by the 1972 *World Heritage Convention*, the 2003 Convention was meant to make up for a widely felt neglect within UNESCO of the more intangible, fragile heritage of the Global South. As such, it was promoted by UNESCO and welcomed by many states.

The 2003 Convention does not mention the economic functions of ICH and leaves legal protection to other instruments. The Convention mentions that ICH is constantly recreated by communities and groups "in response to their environment," but it does not, as opposed to the 1992 *Biodiversity Convention*, refer to actual or possible contributions of traditional practices and knowledge to a sustainable natural environment.[3] Article 1 of the Convention (*Objectives*) does not mention "development" or "sustainable development" (SD), and in the early implementation of the Convention, SD did not play a role of any importance.

That situation changed from 2009 onward, when UNESCO started envisaging an SD-focused reorientation of the Convention. In 2014, the Secretariat of the Convention already claimed that SD was "at the heart of the Convention,"

DOI:10.4324/9781003244158-4

and in 2016, the envisaged reset culminated in the adoption of a new chapter of the Convention's *Operational Directives* (OD). In it, ICH is presented as a "driver and guarantee of SD," a "strategic resource to enable SD," and a "powerful force for inclusive and equitable economic development," while "safeguarding and sustainable development" are mentioned as twin goals of the Convention.[4]

Section 2.2 is about the attention paid by UNESCO until roughly 1985 to economic aspects of folklore and its legal protection and about the lesser interest in such issues in the 1990s. Section 2.3 shows how, during the initial preparation of the Convention, no attention was paid to economic issues and very little to "sustainability." Section 2.4 is about the introduction of two references to SD in the draft Convention. Section 2.5 shows how the uneasy hesitance to discuss economic issues started disappearing under the Young Convention, while SD remained unexplored. Section 2.6 covers the mobilization of the Convention by UNESCO for its ambitions concerning culture and SD – and for itself – at the UN level. Section 2.7 presents the making of OD Chapter VI, called *Safeguarding intangible cultural heritage and sustainable development at the national level.* Section 2.8 discusses positions from states/regions toward *Chapter VI.* Section 2.9 indicates how the new chapter influences certain mechanisms of the Convention and how it takes into consideration "communities, groups and individuals" (CGIs).

The Governing Bodies of the Convention are its General Assembly (GA) and Intergovernmental Committee. The Committee, which functions under the control of the GA, meets once a year, the GA every second year.[5] The Director-General (DG) of UNESCO prepares the agendas of the Committee and instructs – usually through the Assistant Director-General for Culture – the Secretariat of the Convention *sensu stricto*. The Committee elects the Evaluation Body (EB), by which it is advised on various issues, including listing of ICH elements and the interpretation of the Convention. Like the Committee and the GA, the EB, assisted by the Secretariat *sensu stricto*. The Convention has two Lists and a *Register of Good Safeguarding Practices*.[6]

During the final phase of the preparation of the Convention and the first two years of its implementation (till mid-2008), the author of this paper worked at UNESCO, first as head of the ITH Section and later also as Secretary of the Convention.[7] He observed earlier phases of that preparation as a member of Dutch delegations to UNESCO.

2.2. Economic aspects of folklore till 2000[8]

In the 1970s and 1980s, many states – many of them engaged in post-colonial state-building – were interested in promoting and protecting folklore.[9] Until 1985, UNESCO intensively engaged itself with the protection of folklore, often in cooperation with WIPO, the *World Intellectual Property Organization*. Both organizations assisted in the preparation of, for instance, the 1976 *Tunis Model Law on Copyright for Developing States*, which seeks *inter alia*

> *to prevent any improper exploitation and to permit adequate protection of the cultural heritage known as folklore, which constitutes not only a potential for economic expansion, but also a cultural legacy intimately bound up with the individual character of each people.*[10]

The 1982 UNESCO-WIPO *Model Provisions for national laws on the protection of expressions of folklore against illicit exploitation and other prejudicial actions* contained similar language.

UNESCO in 1985 decided to work toward an international legal instrument on the protection of folklore, without WIPO. Although the resulting 1989 *Recommendation on the Safeguarding of Traditional Culture and Folklore* recognized the "social, economic, cultural and political importance" of folklore, and in spite of its product-oriented definition of folklore, it primarily promoted the interests of researchers.[11] Few countries started implementing the *1989 Recommendation*, the preparation of which had been guided by UNESCO's Copyright Division.

The *1989 Recommendation* largely ignored the outcomes of *Mondiacult*, a trailblazing world conference on cultural policies UNESCO had organized in 1982. *Mondiacult* had reached an agreement on a – wide – definition of culture that included tangible and intangible heritage, and also "modes of life," "value systems, traditions and beliefs," and "the fundamental rights of the human being." The resulting *Mexico City Declaration* claimed *inter alia* that education and culture needed to be drawn in to achieve "genuine development," the aim of which was "the continuing well-being and fulfilment of each and every individual."[12] This, to my knowledge, was the first time culture and development – whatever their definitions – were linked in a high-level UNESCO document.

When in 1992 the Culture Sector of UNESCO was summoned by Director-General Major to take up ICH, it was inspired more by *Mondiacult* than by the *Recommendation*: Focus was to be placed on the function and values of ICH, the involvement of practitioners, and on pilot projects in safeguarding. A 1993 expert meeting, invited to discuss an *Outline for a new ICH Sub-programme* that the Culture Sector had prepared, approved the proposed program.[13] It ignored economic aspects of ICH, while warning against phenomena such as "folklorization," "excessive tourism," "unbridled commercialization," and "decontextualization." "Sustainability," SD, and pragmatic views on ICH were still far away.[14] The meeting suggested the creation of two programs that UNESCO indeed would develop in the 1990s.

These two new programs focused on excellency and "outstanding value," echoing *World Heritage* approaches. In 1993, UNESCO's Executive Board endorsed the *Living Human Treasures* program.[15] LHT systems recognized excellent practitioners and supported them, also financially, in transmitting their skills and knowledge. UNESCO stopped supporting this program, which found implementation in about 25 states, when the Convention became operational.[16]

A program called *Proclamation of Masterpieces of the Oral Heritage of Humanity* was created in 1997/8; it represented a large-scale exercise in listing ICH internationally.[17] The program's nomination form asked about the "contemporary cultural and social role in the community concerned" of nominated elements and cultural spaces; economic aspects were not asked for, but problematized. For instance, when asking for information about "durability and possible risks of disappearance," the form suggested among the possible risks "economic and technological development" and "development of tourism."[18] Three proclamations (2001, 2003, 2005) yielded 90 *Masterpieces* in 70 countries.

A large-scale conference, organized by UNESCO and the Smithsonian Institution (Washington DC, 1999), put the *Recommendation* in its grave, criticizing its definition and focus, and suggesting that a more appropriate legal instrument be created.[19] The conference's *Action Plan*, which insisted on legal protection for ICH, referred nowhere to economic functions.[20] Its Preamble, however, linked ICH and development by stating that practitioners should

> *contribute expertise that is crucial to local, national, and international policy-making in such areas as health, environment, education, youth, gender, conflict resolution, the peaceful coexistence of ethnic groups, sustainable, human development, and inclusive civic participation as well as fighting chauvinism and intolerance.*
>
> (Seitel, 2001, p. 303)

Later in 1999, UNESCO's General Conference authorized the Organization to study "the feasibility of adopting a new normative instrument on the safeguarding of traditional culture and folklore."

2.3. Preparations for developing a convention (2001–2002) – sustainability enters

In an exploratory study ordered by UNESCO, the Organization was advised "to address the question of safeguarding intangible heritage primarily from the cultural perspective" (Blake, 2001, p. 3) and to leave the "protection of the economic rights of tradition-holders to other, specialist Agencies" (ibid., 84). These positions were consistently advocated by UNESCO during the further preparation of the Convention. Blake recommended nevertheless states "to support tradition-holders in exploiting the commercial potential of their traditional culture" (ibid., 86), which "can contribute significantly to the economies of developing countries" (ibid., 79).

Then followed five expert meetings (March 2001–June 2003) that resulted in a working draft for the Convention and an unofficial glossary of ICH-related terms. The first meeting (Turin, March 2001) introduced the term "sustainability" in a new definition for ICH, which started as follows[21]:

> *Peoples' learned processes along with the knowledge, skills and creativity that inform and are developed by them, the products they create, and the resources,*

spaces and other aspects of social and natural context necessary to their sustainability[22]*;*

The Turin participants also emphasized that "international efforts to safeguard ICH must be founded on universally accepted human rights, equity and sustainability and on respect for all cultures that also have respect for other cultures." They further drew UNESCO's attention to safeguarding practices that "enhance the social and ecological sustainability of the group and region."[23]

In October 2001 UNESCO adopted the *Universal Declaration on Cultural Diversity*, which included a *Mondiacult*-based definition of culture.[24] Para. 14 of its *Action Plan* asks for "protecting traditional knowledge, in particular that of indigenous peoples," and for "recognizing the contribution of traditional knowledge, particularly with regard to environmental protection and the management of natural resources."

The second meeting was held in Rio de Janeiro (January 2002).[25] The Turin and Rio meeting reports do not mention debates about the economic aspects of ICH or about the relationship between ICH and SD. When addressing these meetings, UNESCO DG Matsuura did not refer to such subjects either. Still, when discussing a case study "a key concern to participants [of the Rio meeting, RS] was the crucial connection between intangible cultural heritage, environmental harmony, and economic sustainability."[26]

Next came two meetings of a "Select Drafting Group" (SEL). In his address to SEL-1 (March 2002), which started from a zero draft for the Convention, prepared on the basis of the *World Heritage Convention*, DG Matsuura insisted that approaches under the future Convention should be of a cultural nature.[27] UNESCO also suggested "to base the Convention on principles contained in the *Universal Declaration of Human Rights* and the *2001 Declaration*."[28]

Just before SEL-2 (June 2002), a *Glossary meeting* prepared definitions for ICH-related concepts.[29] Its definition for ICH was centered around "practices and representations" that, *inter alia*, should be "consistent with universally accepted principles of human rights, equity, sustainability, and mutual respect between cultural communities." These same four elements had already been mentioned in Turin. SEL-2 accepted with minor changes the *Glossary Meeting*'s definition of ICH, which was included in a new draft *(the First Preliminary Draft)* of the Convention.[30]

UNESCO then organized a *Round table of Ministers of Culture* (September 2002, Istanbul), to mobilize outside UNESCO support for the Convention to-be and the recognition of culture as a pillar for SD.[31] The *Istanbul Declaration* called ICH a fundamental source of cultural identity and an "essential factor in the preservation of cultural diversity" (para.1). Para. 4 mentioned "the extreme vulnerability" of the ICH, which is threatened, among other things, by "excessive merchandising." Para. 6 stated that "alike cultural diversity" ICH is "a guarantee for sustainable development and peace." Para. 6 further stated that "laying the foundations of true sustainable development requires the emergence of an integrated vision of development based on the enhancement of values and practices involved in the intangible cultural heritage."[32] The "fragile" ICH, the neglect of economic aspects of ICH, and "ICH as a guarantee for SD" would reappear in the Convention, whose effective preparation started the following week.

2.4. The intergovernmental process (2002–2003) – SD mentioned twice in the draft convention

UNESCO then organized an *Intergovernmental Meeting of Experts on the Preliminary Draft Convention for the Safeguarding of the Intangible Cultural Heritage* (IME), which would consist of three sessions: IME-1 (September 2002), IME-2 (February/March 2003), IME-3 (June 2003), with an *Intersessional Working Group* to speed up the process (April 2003). The IME process started from the post-SEL-2 draft of the Convention, which contained "sustainability" in its definition of ICH.

Addressing IME-1 DG Matsuura said, with the *Istanbul Declaration* fresh in mind, that ICH "plays an essential role in the construction of identities, cultures and visions of the world, and consequently, on the road towards genuine sustainable development."[33] In the ICH arena, he would not come back on SD until late 2009. The records of none of the IME sessions mention discussion about the economic aspects of ICH.

Since IME-1 achieved few results, UNESCO called for comments on the draft it had distributed. The comments, received from 58 states and 3 NGOs, were presented in two useful documents: *Compilation of amendments* (CA: 1352 amendments) and *Compilation of general comments* (CGC).[34] Two states used "economic" in their comments: Colombia proposed to mention "the right of communities, nations and indigenous peoples to reap economic benefit" from their ICH. Benin (and "Africa Group") stated that ICH, in view of its socio-economic importance for communities, constitutes "an important factor of development." Italy, Ethiopia, and Portugal, too, linked ICH and SD in their comments, with Portugal specifying that "safeguarding of cultural diversity and creativity" would contribute to "the survival and sustainable development of human society on a universal scale."[35]

After IME-2, UNESCO published another *Compilation of amendments* that 12 states spontaneously had submitted "during IME-2."[36] Some concerned SD, with Brazil, proposing to mention (p. 8) the importance of ICH "as a resource for sustainable development and improving the quality of life of communities." Honduras stated (p. 10) that "an integrated vision of development based on the enhancement of values and practices involved in the intangible cultural heritage was needed."

2.4.1. SD in the preamble of the convention

UNESCO produced during IME-2 a new draft Preamble, revised "in the light of the discussions, and at the request of various delegations," in which the following new consideration was found: "*Considering* the importance of the ICH as the crucible of cultural diversity and the key to sustainable development."[37]

The new draft Preamble was first discussed by IME-3, which replaced "crucible" by "mainspring," and "the key to" by "a guarantee of," thus returning to the *Istanbul Declaration* language. Three references were added:

> *Considering the importance of the intangible cultural heritage as a mainspring of cultural diversity and a guarantee of sustainable development, as underscored in the UNESCO Recommendation on the Safeguarding of Traditional Culture and Folklore of 1989, in the UNESCO Universal Declaration on Cultural Diversity of 2001, and in the Istanbul Declaration of 2002,*[38]

2.4.2. SD in the definition

The post-SEL-2 definition of ICH had stated that ICH is: "consistent with universally accepted principles of human rights, equity, sustainability, and mutual respect between cultural communities".

IME-2 transformed that phrase into a separate *caveat* sentence, following the definition, in line with proposals made by Uganda and Germany.[39] The new sentence read:

> *For the purposes of this Convention, only relevant is the intangible cultural heritage that is consistent with universally recognized human rights international instruments, as well as with the principles of justice, equity, sustainability, and mutual respect between communities, groups and individuals.*[40]

IME-3 changed the definition again, a process not covered in the records.[41] The "principles of justice and equity" were eliminated from the *caveat* sentence and "sustainability" was replaced by "SD." This resulted in:

> *For the purposes of this Convention, consideration will be given solely to such intangible cultural heritage as is compatible with existing international human rights instruments as well as with the requirements of mutual respect among communities, groups and individuals, and of sustainable development.*

According to the reports, during the SEL and IME meetings the relationship between ICH and SD never was a substantial topic of debate among the drafters of the Convention, who did not even bother to refer to the *Biodiversity Convention*, whose trail-blazing article 8.j was well known to them, if only thanks to Blake (2001, pp. 67–69).[42]

I can confirm this for IME, and other witnesses testify to the same. Noriko Aikawa, director of UNESCO's ITH section till April 2003, wrote several articles about the history of the Convention. In Aikawa (2007), which covers in particular "conceptual developments," no reference is made to sustainability or SD. Aikawa (2009, p. 35) mentions SD once, when speaking about the *2001 Declaration*. Janet Blake, who assisted UNESCO as a consultant at IME-1 and IME-2, in her 2006 *Commentary on the Convention*, when discussing the *caveat* sentence, explained that at the time compatibility with "human rights" was considered more important than the "requirements," whereby the wording chosen "further weakens the strength of this since "requirements" is a rather vague term, open to various readings."[43]

2.5. The Young Convention – economy enters

The instructions I received from DG Matsuura as Secretary of the brand-new Convention were to promote its ratification and to prepare ODs that would allow the Convention to become operational quickly.[44] SD was not an issue in his briefings.

The term "SD" occurring just a handful of times in the records of the first nine sessions (2006–2010) of the Organs of the Convention, and the absence of SD-related items from their agendas, confirms that the relationship between ICH and SD was not really discussed by the Governing Bodies in that period.[45] UNESCO apparently wanted the Convention to gain weight before mobilizing it for a new orientation.

After the entry into force of the Convention (June 2006), three chapters of ODs were prepared by Secretariat and Committee and adopted by 2.GA in 2008. These ODs provisionally regulated key mechanisms of the Convention, such as listing (including the integration of the 90 *Masterpieces* in the Representative List), awarding financial assistance, accreditation of NGOs, and periodic reporting.[46] In these ODs, neither economic or commercial issues, nor SD were mentioned.

The Committee and its advisory bodies were confronted early on with economic aspects of ICH proposed for listing. A fourth OD chapter, approved in 2010, consequently included a section (OD/116–117) on *Commercial activities related to intangible cultural heritage*. In that section, which recalls discussions at UNESCO from the early 1980s, it is claimed that commercial activities can improve the living standards of communities and "enhance the local economy, and contribute to social cohesion." The section also asks for sustainable tourism and for "finding a proper balance between the interests of the commercial party, the public administration and the cultural practitioners."

Two early mentions of SD appeared in 2010 elsewhere in the ODs: Modified OD/73 stated, Echoing the *caveat* sentence, that the Fund of the Convention should not accept contributions "from entities whose activities are not compatible with . . . the requirements of sustainable development or with the requirements of mutual respect among communities, groups and individuals."[47] New OD/111 encouraged the media to raise awareness "about the importance of ICH as a means to foster social cohesion, sustainable development and prevention of conflict, in preference to focusing only on aesthetic or entertainment aspects." Both ODs were proposed by the Secretariat and – according to the records – approved by the Organs of the Convention without debate.

2.6. UNESCO mainstreaming SD in the ICH arena

The Rio 1992 *Earth Summit* gave a major impetus to UN reflections and ambitions in the field of SD. It adopted the *Rio Declaration*, which distinguished an economic, a social, and an environmental pillar for SD, and *Agenda 21*.[48] It also launched the *Biodiversity Convention. Agenda 21* and many more high-level meetings led to the *2000 Millennium Development Goals*, the *2015 Sustainable Development Goals* and, eventually, *Agenda 2030*.[49] In these Goals and Agendas, culture plays a modest role, in spite of UNESCO's long-standing efforts to have culture acknowledged as a fourth pillar (or dimension) of SD.[50] In September 2022, another UNESCO-organized *Mondiacult* Conference again called for the inclusion of culture ("a global public good") "as a specific goal in its own right" in future UN SD goals.[51]

Around 2010, UNESCO started mobilizing its heritage conventions for its attempt to secure a significant place for culture in the *2015 SD Goals*.[52] With ICH covering large areas of "culture," as defined in the *Declaration on Cultural Diversity*, the 2003 Convention became a favorite battleground.

In October 2009, at 4.COM, DG Matsuura in his farewell speech in the ICH arena, kicked off:

> *safeguarding intangible heritage is not only essential to preserving the world's cultural diversity, but also to building more effective and sustainable development strategies.*[53]

His successor, DG Bokova (2009–2017), developed this idea further at 3.GA (June 2010), where she said:

> *I also plan to launch several major initiatives to demonstrate culture's contribution to development in a concrete way. The Convention states clearly in its preamble: "intangible heritage is a guarantee of sustainable development". It is time for us to transform these words into a commitment on the part of the international community – into a commitment that will be acted upon.*[54]

DG Bokova repeated her message at 5.COM (2010).[55] At the opening of 4.GA (June 2012), she

> *spoke of the work by the United Nations that would lead to a new development agenda beyond 2015, adding that the recognition of cultural diversity in this agenda was an essential prerequisite, which she described as a personal priority. She stated that the safeguarding of the intangible cultural heritage was a key component of this advocacy.*[56]

By 2011, the Secretariat and Committee had started following the DG. In decision 6.COM 7.10, for instance, the Committee encouraged States Parties

> *to integrate considerations of SD into safeguarding measures proposed in nominations to the Urgent Safeguarding List and requests for International Assistance, and to propose for possible selection for the Register . . . programmes, projects or activities that place SD at their core.*[57]

Occurrences of "SD" in meeting records of the Governing Bodies started increasing in 2011, with UNESCO officials and the *Consultative Body* leading the way, and states following in 2012.[58] Compatibility with SD became a consideration in inscription decisions.

In 2012, the *Consultative Body* reported to 5.COM "that the question of over-commercialization arose in several of the files presented to it" and that guidance was needed. It suggested the Committee amend OD/116–117 on *Commercial activities*. The Committee duly invited "the Secretariat to propose draft directives about the topic."[59]

In between, in 2012, UNESCO requested an evaluation report about the implementation of the Convention from its *Internal Oversight Office* (IOS).[60] The Committee received the report in 2013, with two elaborate decisions based on it, prepared by DG UNESCO.[61] It adopted these far-reaching decisions, without much discussion. Four of the 26 IOS recommendations referred to SD.[62]

Also at 6.COM (2013), the Secretariat, considering that the issue of commercialization exceeded the subject of OD Chapter IV, recommended developing a new OD chapter. It stated that such a chapter

> *could respond to the lacunae noted in the recent evaluation by the Internal Oversight Service, which noted that at present the ODs 'do not explain how ICH is expected to foster sustainable development and whether particular ICH domains foster SD more than others.*[63]

The Secretariat suggested that an expert meeting might prepare a draft for the new chapter which, after discussion in the Committee, could be adopted by the General Assembly in 2016. The Committee, encouraged by, in particular, Türkiye, Morocco, and Belgium, accepted the Secretariat's proposal.[64] Türkiye proposed to host the meeting.

2.7. Developing *Chapter VI*

At that meeting (Istanbul, September 2014), 12 experts and UNESCO staff discussed a draft chapter prepared by UNESCO.[65] It presented four sets of ODs under headings borrowed from the 2012 UN Report *Realizing the Future We Want For All*, namely (i) Inclusive social development; (ii) Environmental sustainability; (iii)

Inclusive economic development; and (iv) Peace and security.[66] Follow-up drafts were discussed by the Committee and the General Assembly.[67]

2.7.1. In the Committee

During the debate at 9.COM (2014), Belgium asked for relevant recommendations from the *IOS-13 Report* to be taken into account. There was discussion whether IP rights could be mentioned (they could); Mongolia was happy that the development of communities was given attention. There were critical comments, too: Saint Lucia noted that the Convention is not about development as such and that it was not the Committee's role to promote tourism or commercialization. Afghanistan found that "there was a general tendency at UNESCO to reduce everything to sustainable development."[68]

Based on the 9.COM discussions, and on "previous work undertaken by the Secretariat on the subject" and "recent developments in intergovernmental negotiations for the 2030 development agenda," the Secretariat presented a new draft at 10.COM.[69] In its presentation, one reads (para. 4) that "in close connection to the spirit of the Convention the document positioned culture at the heart of development goals."[70]

At 10.COM (2015) numerous amendments were made.[71] Brazil insisted on deleting references to the 2012 UN "information document" *Realizing the Future We Want for All*, and replacing these by references to the formally approved *2030 Agenda*. The Republic of Korea proposed – unsuccessfully – to make the text under discussion an annex to the ODs as it was more "policy-oriented" than "technical."[72]

2.7.2. In the General Assembly

The General Assembly (6.GA) spoke at length about the scope and the tone of the chapter. The draft still featured the four headings copied from *Realizing the Future We Want for All*, including *Peace and Security*, which is not found in *Agenda 2030*. Brazil did not want the ODs to go beyond what was agreed in New York; "peace" was fine, but "security" was beyond the mandate of the Convention. That position was shared by, for instance, Zimbabwe and Saint Vincent and the Grenadines. Venezuela considered that "it was not a good idea to risk politicization of the Convention with issues that were inconsistent with its mandate, and which in fact detracted from the original text of the Convention."[73]

Brazil also, seconded by Venezuela and other states, objected to the ambitions of the chapter: By means of safeguarding ICH, one should not try to solve "all the problems of the world." Kuwait agreed, and so did China, while otherwise welcoming the chapter. Brazil further stated that "no single country in the world was able to 'fully include and recognize the intangible cultural heritage of indigenous peoples, migrants, immigrants and refugees, people of different ages and genders, persons with disabilities, and members of vulnerable groups.' " That "was so politically correct that it was impossible to implement." Ecuador stated that "the objective of the Convention" should not be confused with "the objectives of UNESCO, even if they had a bearing on each other." The Philippines wished to know how paragraphs "of a recommendatory nature" would be operationalized. "Would States Parties be expected to take all of these into account when submitting nominations to any of the Lists? Would they be expected to take them into account when producing periodic reports?"[74] Bangladesh warned that "the Assembly should exercise caution in that it should not in any way impose unnecessary limitations on developing countries or on their ability to submit nominations to the Lists."[75]

Most intervening European countries (outspokenly so Belgium, Latvia, and Türkiye), Morocco, and the Secretariat were opposed to significantly changing the text as reformulated after 10.COM.[76] Austria "was happy with the text since it reflected the importance of traditional knowledge and skills in the context of sustainable development." Greece reminded that ICH "concerned the livelihoods of people with the issues of sustainable development at its core." Some delegations (Belgium, Greece, Türkiye), and the Secretary of the Convention, considered that the text had been spoken about long enough in the Committee, which led to discussion about the sovereign status of the GA. Italy and Portugal worked hard to reconcile positions.[77]

Eventually, GA.6 left most of the chapter untouched; most changes were made to its last section, the name of which was changed from *Peace and Security* into *Intangible Cultural Heritage and Peace*.[78]

After the adoption of *Chapter VI*, the debate resumed, when India suggested to transform the adopted text into a policy document,[79,80] The Philippines, Serbia, Palestine, and Brazil supported India, stating that the adopted text was not really operational, that it was far-reaching, that much was not yet clear, and that the World Heritage approach could be followed. OD-chapter status of the already adopted text was defended by Belgium (referring to the *IOS-13 Report*), Cyprus, France, Germany, Greece (recalling that SD is not mentioned in the *World Heritage Convention*), Italy, Latvia, Morocco, Netherlands, Norway, Peru, and Türkiye. The text remained an OD chapter.[81]

2.8. Positions of states, European states, and UNESCO

While there was strong support for *Chapter VI* from in particular West-European states, East-European states (but Latvia), Asian and Sub-Saharan states showed themselves less interested, or not interested at all. At 9.COM and 10.COM only eight committee members, out of 24, participated in the debates, with Belgium, Latvia, and Saint Lucia intervening at both sessions. Not a single Sub-Saharan Committee member took the floor. At 6.GA, most interventions concerning *Chapter VI* came from European and Latin American states. Brazil (28), Belgium (15), and Morocco (13) together made over one-third of all interventions. Sub-Saharan States made only 6 and East-European States 5.[82] Critical comments came mainly from Asian and Latin American states, that is from regions that have vast experience in mobilizing ICH for local development. Remarkably, Japan, the main sponsor of the Convention, did not take the floor, on this issue.[83]

Many states from the Global South had welcomed the Convention and its lists. They had understood that the Convention was meant to be a flexible instrument, accommodating visions and ambitions from different regions. They may have experienced a rude awakening when informed by IOS – read UNESCO – that many states misunderstood the Representative List.

States from the South have relatively many inscriptions on the Urgent Safeguarding List against few inscribed safeguarding practices and accredited NGOs, and fewer elements on the Representative List than aspired for. They sometimes receive earmarked financial assistance from other States Parties.

West-European states, many of which had been opposed to, consecutively, the *Masterpieces Programme*, and/or Convention for ICH, and or listing viable ICH, in general, were late in ratifying the Convention.[84] Northern states nevertheless quickly assumed dominant positions: They "have" 11 of 29 inscribed good safeguarding practices, only a few elements on the Urgent Safeguarding List and over half of accredited NGOs (in violation of OD/93). This might give the impression that Western countries are relatively rich in expertise and better in safeguarding. When Western countries understood that the Convention might become a tool for pursuing SD, they generally were happy to jump on that bandwagon. The way *Chapter VI-* was forced through, and the high-handed way West-European delegates sometimes expressed themselves, contributed to fueling North–South dichotomies in sessions of the Governing Bodies.

2.9. Preliminary effects of the reset

2.9.1. On mechanisms

As UNESCO had envisaged, the implementation of the Convention is becoming more SD-oriented. After 2016 first followed the preparation, and adoption in 2018, of an intricate *Overall Results Framework* – as recommended by the *IOS-13 Report*. It contains 26 *core indicators* and 86 *assessment factors* and aims as its highest impact that ICH:

> *is safeguarded by communities, groups and individuals who exercise active and ongoing stewardship over it, thereby contributing to sustainable development for human well-being, dignity and creativity in peaceful and inclusive societies.*[85]

Relations between ICH safeguarding and social and economic development, and environmental sustainability, are explicitly mentioned in assessment factors for *core indicators 13* and *15*. It draws, however, the attention that in the quote above safeguarding and contribution to SD are not presented as twin objectives, as they had been in *Chapter VI*. Contribution to SD is rather presented – in the spirit of consideration 2 of the Preamble – as a positive by-effect of safeguarding. This adjustment resulted from an expert meeting UNESCO organized in September 2016 in Beijing that prepared a high-level results map as a first step on the road to the adoption of the *Framework* by 7.GA.[86]

The *Framework* served as the basis for a revision of Form ICH-10 that States Parties have to use when reporting about the implementation of the Convention (see Article 29). The cumbersome form imposes reporting against 25 core indicators.

The Convention's reset has started affecting the listing mechanisms as well. In January 2023, various Forms were revised. While criterion 2 for the *Representative List* was not changed, the instruction in the revised Form ICH-02 on how to meet that criterion was reduced to ticking SD goals to which the nominated element is considered to contribute, and explaining the selection made. Similarly, requests for the transfer of an element from the *Urgent Safeguarding List* to the *Representative List* have to demonstrate *inter alia* – see new OD/39.2.b – how the element contributes to SD. The first objective of the *Representative List*, "to ensure better visibility" of ICH, is getting out of sight (see Article 16).

2.9.2. For communities, groups, and individuals

Chapter VI also affects the relations between States Parties, CGIs, and their ICH. The Convention and the *Ethical Principles* that the Committee adopted in 2015, assign the primary role in the recognition and safeguarding of ICH to CGIs concerned. The *Ethical Principles* and various Forms that states parties have to use in their contacts with the Committee require free, prior, and informed consent from CGIs for actions of third parties – including authorities – concerning their ICH.[87]

The terms "consent" and *Ethical Principles* do not occur at all in *Chapter VI*, but its OD/171.c wishes development programs that affect ICH to respect "ethical *considerations*." In a text prepared over two years this choice for shadowy "considerations" (rather than the well-established "*principles*" that were adopted one year before the adoption of *Chapter VI*) must be deliberate. Fortunately, "free, prior and informed consent" and the *Ethical Principles* reappear in both the *Framework* and questions States Parties are confronted with in Form ICH-10.

Chapter VI seems to encourage states to judge by themselves the value of ICH for development goals and to use ICH in programs, inside and outside communities and groups concerned, without having to obtain their consent. This would not be in conformity with *Ethical Principle* 6, which states that "each community, group or individual should assess the value of its own ICH and this ICH **should not be subject to external judgements of value or worth**" (bold as in original). A strengthened position for the state vis-à-vis communities and groups seems to suit policies that promote culture – and hence ICH – as a "common public good." That expression does not befit ICH as it used to be understood under the Convention.

ICH practices also run the risk of decontextualization if it would become standard practice to request that safeguarding plans should involve considerable numbers of persons who are not bearers of expressions concerned. OD/174, for instance, promotes safeguarding plans that are "fully inclusive of all sectors and strata of society, including: Indigenous Peoples, migrants, immigrants and refugees; people of different ages and genders; persons with disabilities and members of vulnerable groups, in conformity with Article 11."[88] The Periodic Reporting Form's assessment factor 16.1 adds to this list "groups with different ethnic identities." Including "all strata and sectors of society" may be feasible in broad development plans, for ICH safeguarding plans conditions are different,[89] and *Ethical Principle* 12 orders that CGIs "should never be alienated" from their ICH. The way *Chapter VI* speaks about CGIs leads to erosion of the prerogatives of GCIs as rather generally understood before 2016.

The 2015 World Heritage SD *Policy Document* refers to the 2007 UN *Declaration on the Rights of Indigenous Peoples* and also otherwise takes Indigenous Peoples seriously.[90] What is more, in 2017 the WH Committee – of all Committees – launched an *International Indigenous Peoples Forum for World Heritage*.[91] A source of inspiration – one might think – for the 2003 Convention.

While the Convention mentions CG(I)s six times (against SD twice), there is no special OD chapter about their role in the implementation of the Convention; in spite of insisting Latin American states, the Committee did not wish to investigate options for structural representation of community representatives in its sessions. Few of the accredited NGOs can be considered community organizations. UNESCO, which has – as we saw – solid means to influence the implementation of the Convention, apparently is not interested in a reasonable involvement of CGIs, including Indigenous Peoples, in the implementation of the Convention at the national and international levels.[92]

One would have liked to hear practitioners and community representatives speak – invited and at their own initiative, in Committee sessions and high-level expert meetings – about past, actual, and possible contributions of their practices, knowledge, and skills to the development of their ICH, their communities, their environment, and – possibly – society at large. The reorientation of the Convention apparently was not meant to serve their interests. One hopes states parties will continue supporting CGIs in safeguarding activities that have other primary goals than the pursuit of SD and that they will not make use of ICH in development activities without the free, prior, and informed consent of Indigenous Peoples and other communities and groups, and individuals concerned.

Notes

1 Thanks are due to Harriet Deacon for her valuable comments on earlier versions of this contribution.
2 See Articles 1 (*Objectives*), 11, 12, 15 to 18. "Article(s)" with capital "A" refers to Articles of the Convention. All quoted URLs as checked in early February 2023.
3 For the *Biodiversity Convention*, see www.cbd.int/convention/text/

4 See, respectively, OD/170, 173, 184, and 176; for the ODs, see https://ich.unesco.org/en/directives
5 Under the 2003 Convention, the GA is the sovereign body (Article 4.1) as opposed to the *World Heritage Convention*'s GA (which has mainly administrative tasks).
6 For the *Representative List*, the *Urgent Safeguarding List*, and the *Register*, see Article 16–18 and ODs 39.3 and 44.
7 I left between 2.GA, the second session of the GA, and 3.COM, the third session of the Committee.
8 For UNESCO's action in the field up to 1989, see Sherkin (2001); for UNESCO's action in the 1980 and 1990s, and the preparation of the Convention, see Blake (2001) and Aikawa (2007) and (2009). See also under events on the website of the Convention.
9 See Martinet (2019, pp. 32–38).
10 See section 6 of www.wipo.int/edocs/pubdocs/en/wipo_pub_812.pdf
11 For the *Recommendation*, see https://unesdoc.unesco.org/ark:/48223/pf0000092693
12 See para. 10 of https://culturalrights.net/descargas/drets_culturals401.pdf
13 For the meeting report, see CLT/ACL/93/IH/01; its Annex VII presents the *Outline*.
14 The *Brundtland Commission* published its definition of SD in 1987
15 See annex 2 of https://unesdoc.unesco.org/ark:/48223/pf0000111165/PDF/111165eng.pdf.multi
16 See https://ich.unesco.org/en/living-human-treasures
17 See https://ich.unesco.org/en/proclamation-of-masterpieces-00103. In May 1998, UNESCO's Executive Board inserted "and Intangible" between "Oral" and "Heritage" in the program's name.
18 See the program's *Implementation Guide* at https://unesdoc.unesco.org/ark:/48223/pf0000124628/PDF/124628engo.pdf.multi
19 See Can et. al (2001).
20 For the Proceedings of the Conference, papers read, and its *Action Plan*, see Seitel (2001).
21 For the meeting's *Final Report*, see https://ich.unesco.org/doc/src/00077-EN.pdf, for its *Action Plan*: https://ich.unesco.org/doc/src/05220-EN.pdf
22 Here "sustainability" boils down to the long-term viability of ICH.
23 See *Action Plan*, Consideration 12.a and Recommendation 14.
24 For the *Declaration*, see https://unesdoc.unesco.org/ark:/48223/pf0000127160/PDF/127160qaa.pdf.multi
25 *Final Report* available at https://ich.unesco.org/doc/src/00074-EN.pdf
26 Ibid., page 11.
27 For the SEL-1 report: https://ich.unesco.org/doc/src/00070-EN.pdf.
28 See p. 7 of https://ich.unesco.org/doc/src/05352-EN.pdf
29 For the resulting *Glossary Intangible Cultural Heritage*, see https://ich.unesco.org/doc/src/00265.pdf
30 For the SEL-2 report: https://ich.unesco.org/doc/src/05152-EN.doc
31 For DG's address, see https://unesdoc.unesco.org/ark:/48223/pf0000127500_eng/PDF/127500eng.pdf.multi
32 For the *Istanbul Declaration*, see https://ich.unesco.org/doc/src/00072-EN.pdf
33 My translation, from French. See https://unesdoc.unesco.org/ark:/48223/pf0000127502/PDF/127502fre.pdf.multi. For the IME/1 records, see https://unesdoc.unesco.org/ark:/48223/pf0000129000
34 See, for CA CLT-2002/CONF.203/3 Rev, for CGC: CLT-2003/CONF.205/5
35 See for Colombia CA/137, for Benin CA/72, for Italy CA/36, for Ethiopia CA/787, and for Portugal CGC/47.
36 See CLT-2003/CONF.206/2.
37 See page 7 of the "Semi-consolidated Draft," dated April 2003, CLT-2003/CONF-206/1. The IME-1 and IME-2 records do not mention discussions about the Preamble. Blake (2007, p. 26) mentions Portugal as a source for the new consideration.
38 The *1998 Recommendation* does not mention SD at all.

39 Uganda (CA/367) proposed to separate the consistency requirement from the definition, as "a guide to qualification for safeguarding"; for Germany see CA/768, 1344.
40 The IME-2 records, see https://unesdoc.unesco.org/ark:/48223/pf0000130016, do not cover this transformation of the definition (see para. 13). An Annex presents, however, the four Articles IME-2 agreed about, one of which contains the definition.
41 For the draft prepared for IME-3, see CLT-2003/CONF.206/2. For the IME-3 report: https://unesdoc.unesco.org/ark:/48223/pf0000131274_eng
42 Blake (2001) was made available at all SEL and IME meetings.
43 Cf. Blake (2006: 36). See also Janet Blake's chapter in this volume.
44 Just before my retirement, the Section ITH had a drink celebrating the 100th ratification; Mr Matsuura joined us.
45 At the first Extraordinary Committee Session (May 2007), India (records para. 238) advocated "to have NGOs as well as practitioners for advisory assistance" with a background in "sustainable development, human rights and so on." At 3.GA (2010) (records para. 398) Colombia unsuccessfully proposed to include "SD" in new OD/117.
46 For the 2008 ODs, see https://ich.unesco.org/doc/src/ICH-Operational_Directives-2.GA-EN.pdf
47 See ITH/09/4.COM/CONF.209/8. Apparently, OD/73 was never applied, though it might have been on a few occasions.
48 For the *Rio Declaration*: https://culturalrights.net/descargas/drets_culturals401.pdf; for *Agenda 21,* see www.un.org/esa/dsd/agenda21/
49 See, for instance, https://research.un.org/en/docs/dev/2000-2015, https://research.un.org/en/docs/dev/2016-2030, www.sdgfund.org/mdgs-sdgs
50 For *Agenda 2030*, see https://sdgs.un.org/2030agenda. Its para. 36 acknowledges uncommittedly "that all cultures and civilizations can contribute to, and are crucial enablers of, sustainable development."
51 See www.unesco.org/sites/default/files/medias/fichiers/2022/10/6.MONDIACULT_EN_DRAFT%20FINAL%20DE CLARATION_FINAL_1.pdf
52 See https://en.unesco.org/sustainabledevelopmentgoals
53 https://unesdoc.unesco.org/ark:/48223/pf0000184518
54 https://unesdoc.unesco.org/ark:/48223/pf0000188355/PDF/188355eng.pdf.multi
55 https://unesdoc.unesco.org/ark:/48223/pf0000189974/PDF/189974eng.pdf.multi
56 See para. 2 of ITH/14/5.GA/INF.1.
57 See https://ich.unesco.org/en/6com
58 *Report of the Consultative Body on its work in 2012*, ITH/12/7.COM/7, par 53. The *Consultative Body* preceded the *Evaluation Body*.
59 See Committee Decision 7.COM 7.6. ITH-13–8.COM-13.a-EN
60 See *IOS-13 Report References*
61 See Decisions 8.COM.5.c.1 and 8.COM.5.c.2
62 IOS entered on Committee ground when explaining (para. 211) that not all States Parties rightly understood the purposes of the *Representative List.* A follow-up 2021 IOS-evaluation stated that it was the purpose of the *Urgent Safeguarding List* that was not understood – see LHE/21/16.COM/INF.10 Rev (Key Finding 7).
63 See ITH/13/8.COM/13.a, para. 7
64 See Decision 8.COM 13.a
65 See ITH/14/EXP/3-EN
66 See www.un.org/millenniumgoals/pdf/Post_2015_UNTTreport.pdf
67 For the post-Istanbul draft, see ITH/14/9.COM/13.b-EN; for the post-9.COM draft, see ITH/15/10.COM/14.a_EN; for the post-10.COM draft, see ITH/16/6.GA/7-EN, page. 14–22. For the final version, see https://ich.unesco.org/en/directives.
68 See the 9.COM records (ITH/15/10.COM/4), in particular paragraphs 381, 382, 383, 385 and 386.

69 See https://ich.unesco.org/en/Decisions/10.COM/14.a
70 See para. 4 of ITHH/15/10.COM/14.a.
71 See para. 1139–1240 of the 10.COM records: ITH/16/11.COM/4
72 See the records of 10.COM (ITH/16/11.COM/4) for Brazil's (para. 1146, 1152) and Korea's (para. 1150) comments.
73 See for the interventions referred to here para. 223–236 of the 6.GA records: ITH/18//7/. GA/INF.1
74 For answers, see OD/176, and section 9 below.
75 For the interventions referred to in this paragraph, see the 6.GA records: Brazil (para. 150, 178, 223, 143), Venezuela (228), Kuwait (203), China (197), Brazil (337), Ecuador (168), Philippines (212), Bangladesh (265).
76 Türkiye's keen support of the chapter seems to fit in a tradition, which says that countries that host UNESCO expert meetings, consider these meetings a success, and support their outcomes.
77 For interventions referred to in this paragraph, see the 6.GA records: Austria (para. 132), Belgium (250, 311, 381), Latvia (145), Greece (226), Türkiye (380), Secretary (214, 273), Morocco (295), Greece (194).
78 See 6.GA records, par. 192–197.
79 Ibid. par. 373–470.
80 The World Heritage Committee in 2015 approved a *Policy Document for the Integration of a Sustainable Development Perspective into the Processes of the World Heritage Convention; see* WHC-15/20.GA/INF.13
81 Over-reaching (see for instance OD/177!) *Chapter VI* did not bring the called-for clarity on economic functions and commercial aspects of ICH.
82 The GA meets in Paris, where all member states have representations. The Committee would make an important contribution to the environment if it would also hold its sessions in Paris.
83 The GA did not vote about the chapter. UNESCO's ruling bodies in principle avoid voting, preferring to reach an agreement through chair- and UNESCO-steered consensus.
84 Aikawa (2009, pp. 19–20 and 33–34). For the first 103 ratifications, see *The Intangible Heritage Messenger 10*, at https://ich.unesco.org/doc/src/00447-EN.pdf
85 See https://ich.unesco.org/en/overall-results-framework-00984
86 See https://ich.unesco.org/en/news/a-first-look-at-the-future-of-the-convention-00192
87 For the *Ethical Principles for Safeguarding Intangible Cultural Heritage*, see https://ich.unesco.org/en/ethics-and-ich-00866; see Forms ICH-01, ICH-02, and ICH-03 at https://ich.unesco.org/en/forms
88 Article 11 offers no justification for this enumeration, which was adapted from UN documents.
89 As noted in the 6.GA debates by – for instance – Brazil, Kuwait, and China.
90 See http://whc.unesco.org/en/documents/138856, WHC-15/20.GA/INF.13. The 2003 Convention's webpage *ICH and Indigenous peoples* lacks ambition, see https://ich.unesco.org/en/indigenous-peoples (last accessed on 3-3-2023).
91 See https://iipfwh.org/
92 As opposed to WIPO's *Intergovernmental Committee on Intellectual Property and Genetic Resources, Traditional Knowledge and Folklore* – see www.wipo.int/tk/en/igc/

References

Aikawa, N. (2007) 'The conceptual development of UNESCO's programme on intangible cultural heritage' in Blake, J. (ed.) *Intangible cultural heritage: Challenges and approaches*. Buillth Wells: Institute of Art and Law, pp. 43–72.

Aikawa, N. (2009) 'From the proclamation of masterpieces to the convention for the safeguarding of intangible cultural heritage' in Smith, L. and Akagawa, N. (eds.) *Intangible Heritage*. London – New York: Routledge, pp. 13–44.

Blake, J. (2001) *Developing a new standard-setting instrument for the safeguarding of the intangible cultural heritage – Elements for consideration.* Paris: UNESCO. Available at: https://unesdoc.unesco.org/ark:/48223/pf0000123744

Blake, J. (2006) *Commentary on the 2003 UNESCO convention on the safeguarding of the intangible cultural heritage*. Buillth Wells: Institute of Art and Law.

Can, A. et al. (2001) 'The 1989 *Recommendation* ten years on: Towards a critical analysis' in Seitel, P. (ed.).

IOS-13 Report (2013) *Evaluation of UNESCO's standard-setting work of the culture sector, Part I.* P Prepared by Barbara Torggler, Ekaterina Sediakina-Rivière and Janet Blake (consultant). Paris: UNESCO. Available at: https://ich.unesco.org/doc/src/IOS-EVS-PI-129_REV.-EN.pdf

Martinet, Lily (2019) *Les expressions culturelles traditionnelles en droit international.* Paris: IRJS Editions.

Seitel, Peter (ed.) (2001) *Safeguarding traditional cultures: A global perspective*. Washington, DC: Smithsonian Centre for Folklife and cultural heritage. Available at: https://ich.unesco.org/doc/src/00111-EN.pdf.

Sherkin, S. (2001) 'A historical study on the preparation of the 1989 Recommendation on the safeguarding of traditional culture and folklore: Preliminary results' in Seitel, P. (ed.).

3

HOW AND WHY THE SDGs ENTERED THE PARADIGM OF SAFEGUARDING INTANGIBLE HERITAGE: THE "SIXTH CHAPTER"

Marc Jacobs

Paris, UNESCO Headquarters, July 1, 2016, 10 a.m., Agenda Item 7. Twenty-eight paragraphs were ripe to be black-boxed as the Sixth Chapter of the Operational Directives (henceforth: ODs) of the 2003 UNESCO *Convention for the Safeguarding of the Intangible Cultural Heritage*. After years of simmering, they came just in time, made compatible and hooking up with another black box, closed in 2015 by the General Assembly of the United Nations: *Transforming our world: the 2030 Agenda for Sustainable Development*. As foreseen in article 7e of the 2003 Convention, its Intergovernmental Committee (COM, if preceded by a number it refers to a specific meeting) had submitted a coherent set of draft ODs to the General Assembly of that Convention for approval. It could have taken just 5 minutes. But it did not. Why all the delay and anxiety? Primarily because one of the 24 member states of the COM submitted a whole series of amendments, in the big arena of the General Assembly. A diplomat from Brazil, Marcelo Dantas, was now assertively questioning the section on "peace and security" and was trying to curtail what he saw as sustainable development experiments. It took many hours (and two off-screen negotiations between Belgium and Brazil), to adopt the original set of ODs 170–197, now with weakened security ambitions and the deletion of references to low-carbon and other burning energy issues.

But there was another strategy unfolding.[1] During the 7 hours of discussions, one can detect concerted maneuvers by diplomats of Permanent Delegations to UNESCO, introduced by India, supported by Brazil, but above all performed by a dynamic duo (foreshadowing the dynamics in the COM in the following years): Palestine/Mounir Anastas and the Philippines/Jesus Enrique Garcia. At the moment the (pre)scripted reality of the adoption of the Sixth Chapter was about to be realized, the diplomat of Palestine elegantly hijacked the meeting by asking for the floor, by-passing the chairperson, and the Secretariat-prompter-steering-function,

DOI: 10.4324/9781003244158-5

and immediately passing it on to his colleague from the Philippines to speak first, so Jesus could give an assist. As seasoned diplomats like Photini Panayi (Cyprus) tend to be awake, points of order followed, red-flagging this bold last-minute attempt at a diplomatic *coup de théâtre*. So, plan B had to be activated to save the face of the diplomats involved.

Plan B for diplomats is often bashing or giving extra tasks to the Secretariat: in this case, leading to an extra decision under item 7, inviting the UNESCO personnel responsible for the 1972, 2003, and 2005 Conventions to collaborate more. The failed plan A was to demote the adopted ODs to a policy note: not including a new Chapter in the Operational Directives after all, and hence not throwing a towing line to the departing UN steamship called 2030 Agenda with a cargo full of sustainable development goals (SDGs), in a format intended to be implemented in the States Parties. And also, not to install a system that could be combined with follow-up mechanisms like periodic reporting and a Theory of Change in the format of an Overall Results Framework.

Imagine you were there, on July 1, 2016. Not in the safe observer's backbenches or armchairs watching the streaming online, or today, consulting the audiovisual recordings. No, in the cockpit itself, with access to the microphone, to feel the tensions, the drama, and the momentum. Aborting or pushing the baby back in full delivery or settling for just the head (ODs 170–176) was not acceptable for some delegations like that of Belgium. The Sixth Chapter could have been deleted, debunked, or emasculated as a "policy document," by using the diplomatic power play tricks as in the COMs of the 1972 World Heritage Convention to force inscriptions on the Lists (Brumann, 2021). But on July 1, 2016, this was not the case: Five minutes after the lunch break, the vast majority of the members of the General Assembly of the Convention performed the decision as prescripted by the other organs of the Convention: the UNESCO Secretariat and the Intergovernmental Committee. *Chapter VI: Safeguarding intangible cultural heritage and sustainable development at the national level* was adopted.

3.1. Apostrophes and black boxes matter

Twenty-eight new paragraphs were added to something Bruno Latour (1987) called a "black box" in his book *Science in action*: a set of powerful articles, directives, and principles that frame, legitimate, and influence heritage policies and practices all over the world (Jacobs, 2020a). As part of the *Basic Texts*, the (paragraphs of) Chapter VI now could function as a (set of) "boundary object"(s): "both plastic enough to adapt to local needs and the constraints of the several parties employing them, yet robust enough to maintain a common identity across sites" (Star & Griesemer, 1989, p. 393; Bowker, 2015). The 17 SDGs themselves are a strong example of how powerful (a black box that functions as) a boundary object can be for influencing and coordinating policy, initiatives, and practices across levels, scales, and sectors. As the Actor-network Theory glossary of Mike Michael spells out:

"Anything that operates as black-boxed is thus resistant to problematization and can therefore be used for making associations and building networks" (Michael, 2017, p. 154). Since September 2015, the black-boxed frame of the SDGs has largely colonized and canalized the relationship between safeguarding intangible cultural heritage and the broad spectrum of what "sustainable development" might mean. Despite its advocacy for promoting culture as the fourth pillar (next to ecology, economy, and social development) for the post-2015 Agenda, UNESCO saw the aspirations overruled in 2015 and sidetracked for at least the next 15 years. This makes focusing on the months before and after the launch of the SDGs and how different entities within UNESCO reacted to this evolution interesting, for instance by comparing what the organs of the 1972 and the 2003 heritage Conventions did and how their instruments were adapted.

Heritage is only mentioned explicitly under the umbrella of SDG11: "Make cities inclusive, safe, resilient and sustainable." One of the targets, numbered 11.4, reads "Strengthen efforts to protect and safeguard the world's cultural and natural heritage." At first sight, it just refers to the 1972 Convention Concerning the Protection of the World Cultural and Natural Heritage. But do notice the Saxon genitive, the apostrophe, and an s between "world" and "cultural," leaving some room for maneuvering for the alternative intangible cultural heritage paradigm. However, adding insult to injury, just one clumsy indicator associated with this target is given, a cost-oriented look at an old-fashioned heritage interpretation.[2] The explanation about ICH in the annex of that indicator 11.4.1 is a scandal:

> It includes tangible heritage (movable, immobile and underwater), intangible heritage (ICH) embedded into cultural, and natural heritage artefacts, sites or monuments. The definition excludes ICH related to other cultural domains such as festivals, celebration, etc.[3]

Should this be interpreted as symptoms of push-back by advocates of the hardcore monuments sector, harnessing the 1972 Convention and trying, on the world stage, to put the safeguarding ICH genie back in the bottle or to appropriate it superficially (Smith and Campbell, 2017)? Time presses, climate changes, humanity re-polarizes, and there are counter scripts possible, by redistributing attention to all SDGs, by just denouncing and ignoring that indicator and calling, louder and louder as 2030 approaches, for doing a better effort next time. For the time being, however, the SDGs seem to be the strongest lever and advocacy tool available, offering chances to demonstrate what can be done with ICH safeguarding and gathering convincing arguments to make a better 2045 Agenda.

Considering that sustainability, prudence, and equity between generations are potentially the core business of heritage and as UNESCO and other actors (Rosetti et al., 2022) treated culture as an important factor (right, driver, and enabler) in sustainable development: what went so "wrong" in 2014 and 2015, before sustainable development was black-boxed into 17 goals?And how did global influencers like the different entities of UNESCO (linked to respectively the 1972 and the 2003 heritage conventions), design, respond and update their strategies?

Sophia Labadi (2022), herself former employee and consultant of UNESCO, suggests that UNESCO and in particular director-general Irina Bokova and her (failed) maneuvers in the mid-2010s to become the secretary-general of the United Nations, were to blame for the failure to grant culture, and heritage, a subtle and intelligent place in the 2030 Agenda. According to Labadi, the assertive actions of Palestine in the world heritage sites' controversies would have pushed Bokova to go for education rather than culture, to secure American support. Notwithstanding this, according to Labadi, there were two important strands in the debates concerning heritage and sustainable development in UNESCO in the pivotal years 2015–2016;

> Two texts are of particular importance for their attempt at legislating. The first is the 2015 UNESCO Policy for the Integration of a Sustainable Development Perspective into the Processes of the World Heritage Convention, which is innovative in its comprehensive attention to all four core dimensions of sustainable development. . . . The second text consists of chapters [MJ: sic] on safeguarding intangible heritage and sustainable development in the Operational Directives for the implementation of the 2003 Intangible Heritage Convention.
>
> *(Labadi, 2022, p. 76)*

Labadi focuses on the making and implementation of the *Policy Document for the Integration of a Sustainable Development Perspective into the Processes of the World Heritage Convention* (Labadi, 2019, 2021, 2022)[4] She seems critical and worried: "*Yet issues preventing the implementation of this policy are plenty, embracing its lack of inclusion in national legislations; lack of inclusion of traditional management systems; and the presence of exclusionary approaches to heritage conservation inherited from colonial times.*" As far as the Sixth Chapter of the ODs of the 2003 Convention is concerned, she remarks: "*The implementation of this text faces similar issues to those of the 2015 Policy, in addition to its non-binding nature, which means that it can simply be ignored*" (Labadi, 2022, p. 77). I argue however that the addition in 2016 of a special, sixth chapter in the Operational Directives of the 2003 Convention can make a difference, as part of the "Blue Book," the set of official Basic texts of the 2003 Convention for the safeguarding of the intangible cultural heritage.[5] Not only the factors that this arsenal is translated and mass-distributed by UNESCO, and that it functions as a "boundary object" (Jacobs, 2020b) are relevant. In particular, the inclusion, from 2018 onward, of a tool inspired by a theory of change, the Overall Results Framework, should be mentioned here. It is an instrument partly based on Chapter VI, to structure the periodic reports that States Parties must submit every six years to comply with Article 29 of the 2003 Convention. In this contribution, I reopen the black-boxing of that Sixth Chapter in the years before, intending to complement and nuance the analysis by Labadi.

3.2. Glocal ethics

A trajectory ran parallel to the creation of Chapter VI and yielded another relevant component of the "Basic Texts" since 2015: 12 Ethical Principles (Jacobs, 2017). These principles try to capture the tensions between, on the one hand, global sensitivities and agendas in the UN family and other cosmopolitan networks (as, for instance, expressed in globally promoted SDGs) and on the other hand the (g)local impact, economic realities, voices and relative autonomy of communities, groups, and individuals (CGIs). How to do good in a contemporary way, benefitting consenting CGIs, when working in the 21st century on what used to be called traditional culture and folklore in the 20th century?

In 1999, a "10 years later" assessment in Washington D.C. of the problems of the (failed) 1989 UNESCO Recommendation on the Safeguarding of Traditional Culture and Folklore, justified the need for a new Convention about traditions, feasts, and crafts. It advocated not to look away but to address issues such as tourism, marketing, sustainable development, new media, creative industries, commercialization, exploitation, appropriation, access, and benefit sharing. Both when negotiating the 2003 Convention and the first batch of ODs (launched in 2008), the debates on these topics tended to be so heated, suppressed, or in a defensive mode, that the political technique of "putting them in the fridge" (postponing further discussion and elaboration to a later, unspecified date) had to be used. The World Intellectual Property Organization in Geneva acted as an additional external fridge or *oubliette*, as issues relating to Intellectual Property were systematically delegated to this agency. It would have been very hard to reach a consensus about the 2003 Convention and the first version of the ODs in 2008 if all the challenges and opportunities that are covered by the concept of "sustainable development" would have remained on the negotiation table.

But as the tenth anniversary of the 2003 Convention approached, the nomination dossiers for the Representative list started yielding interesting problems: It seemed time to open the fridges and to start reflecting on unfreezing "sustainable development" in the definition in Article 2 of the 2003 Convention (Jacobs, 2016, 2017). An attempt to do this was made in the seventh meeting of the Intergovernmental Committee for the Safeguarding of the ICH, held at UNESCO Headquarters in Paris in 2012. The connection between ICH, the Millennium Goals, and sustainable development was spelled out by the Secretariat in (draft) decision 7.COM 6, welcoming comments on this issue in the periodic reports on the implementation of the Convention in States Parties. Belgium was the first to take the floor, picking up the assist. Yes, lessons learned from the analysis of periodic reports should influence the evolution of the ODs and also inspire much-needed guidelines on ethics. The Belgian intervention spelled out a to-do list: next to developing ethical tools (1) make a program for sustainable development, (2) introduce the notion of access and benefit-sharing inspired by the 1992 Convention on Biological Diversity, and (3) develop a more constructive view on the relationship between intangible cultural heritage and tourism. It also advocated for stronger involvement of NGO networks and the introduction of concepts (and hence roles) like specialists in participatory methods, facilitators, and heritage brokers. Overall, there were almost no other interventions, except by Latvia, Grenada, Morocco, Egypt, and the NGO Traditions pour Demain. Later in the meeting, while examining nomination files for the international Lists, issues of (over) commercialization and decontextualization were noted, accompanied by an invitation to propose new operational directives.

In 2015, the Secretariat prepared rich documents about codes of ethics and co-organized a crucial Expert Meeting in Valencia in which the idea of a single code was problematized.[6] It led to the proposal of a dual instrument: on the one hand an A4-synthetic document with a set of ethical principles and on the other hand an online platform with a toolkit based on those principles. The tenth meeting of the Intergovernmental Committee, held in Windhoek, in 2015, amended but endorsed the double proposal in decision 10.COM 15.a., with instructions for the Secretariat to develop the web application and even explicitly invited "(10) . . . accredited non-governmental organizations to participate in enriching, sharing information, following-up, and contributing to update the online platform with tools of ethics for safeguarding intangible cultural heritage."[7] The platform with a toolkit to address issues of ethics (e.g., how to manage the tensions between global agendas and SDGs and the relative autonomy of communities, groups, and individuals), was quietly stored in the fridge by the Secretariat, until today. The isolated Ethical Principles did immediately become part of the Basic Texts, but without links to interlocking texts, tools, and updating mechanisms, which are crucial to make them work (Jacobs, 2017).

3.3. 2013, Baku: 8.COM

Meanwhile, attempts were made to further develop the ODs, when the eighth meeting of the Intergovernmental Committee took place in Baku, Azerbaijan, in 2013. There, the Internal Oversight Service (IOS) of UNESCO presented a path-breaking audit document about the impact, challenges, and opportunities of ten years of working with the 2003 Convention. The authors not only discussed the connections between culture, ICH in particular, and sustainable development in UN and UNESCO documents. They sharply diagnosed that the culture sector was not yet able to make a compelling case about this link, also in relation to other sectors:

> A lot of awareness-raising and lobbying will be needed in the future to demonstrate this link. . . . This will require the culture sector to use a 'language' that speaks to these other sectors and to look at these linkages from their perspective, . . . to look at ICH through the lens of sustainable development.
>
> *(Torggler, 2013, §47–70, passim and the quote §126)*

Several proposals of the IOS to remediate this in the development of the safeguarding ICH paradigm were selectively amended and adopted (decision 8.COM 5.c.1).

In 2013, the IOS already tried to promote an innovative formula that was embraced as a twenty-first-century management technique in several international organizations, a "theory of change" with differentiated short-, mid-, and long-term outputs and impacts (see the Overall Results Framework, eventually adopted and included in the Basic Texts in 2018) as a way forward. Belgium intervened to point out that the proposed preliminary model could be much improved by the inclusion of feedback loops, by connecting the model to the periodic reporting mechanism in the 2003 Convention.[8] It was already clear that combining different Basic Texts and the periodic reports of States Parties could stimulate this updating process. What was not yet clear was how the missing element of the "lens" would look (in hindsight: Chapter VI of the ODs in combination with the black box of the SDGs).

Item 13.a of the Agenda of the 8.COM meeting was "draft amendments to the Operational Directives on safeguarding, commercialization and sustainable development." But there were no draft proposals ready yet. The Secretary of the 2003 Convention, Cécile Duvelle, evoked a series of issues to consider such as income generation, over-commercialization, tourism, the creative economy and cultural industries, crafts, new technologies, and media. She referred to the IOS evaluation and Recommendations formulated on the occasion of an International Conference on Intangible Cultural Heritage, held in Chengdu in 2013.[9] She announced that an expert meeting would be organized by her team and the Turkish National Commission for UNESCO. The delegation of Morocco reported about a meeting in Rabat in July 2013 where not only commercialization, but even alternative models about the commons' (Schreiber and Pielińsk, 2023) were on the agenda. The fridges were opened wide.

3.4. 2014, Paris: 9.COM

On November 23, 2014, the day before the start of 9.COM, held in Paris, a conference organized by the forum of the NGOs accredited to the Convention tackled the theme of cultural broker(age) and mediators and presented their involvement as critical success (f)actors for safeguarding intangible heritage and for promoting sustainable development. A special issue of a scholarly journal on this topic was presented, a publication that subsequently was distributed for free to the delegations, observers, and Secretariat of the 2003 Convention (Jacobs, 2014a, 2014b; Jacobs, Neyrinck, and Van der Zeijden, 2014). I mention this as a reminder to also consider side events of the COM meetings and to illustrate how the scholarly work of NGOs and ICH UNESCO Chairs can influence the process of making operational directives, as will become apparent further on.

Item 13.b on the agenda of 9.COM was the discussion of a draft of a new set of ODs.[10] Cécile Duvelle introduced the results of the meeting held in Istanbul a few weeks before with the participation of her team and 12 experts. These results are built on the report *Realising the Future We Want for All* (2012), based on the results of the Rio +20 Conference.[11] Hence, the recommendations resulting from this meeting were organized around social development, environmental sustainability, inclusive economic development, and peace and security as spearheads. Belgium was the first to intervene, expressing surprise. Why was an Entity of UNESCO now using that model, rather than promoting the idea of culture as the fourth pillar of sustainable development? Belgium emphasized that it was crucial to refer to *safeguarding* ICH instead of just ICH and underlined the importance of cultural brokerage. Also making bridges with the 2005 Convention on the Protection and Promotion of the Diversity of Cultural Expressions was recommended. In her intervention, the Latvian delegate underscored the importance of integrating culture in the post-2015 UN Development Agenda and regretted the missed opportunity to address intellectual property rights and to team up with WIPO. The delegation of Mongolia mentioned that similar discussions about sustainable development were also taking place at the World Heritage Committee and the ICOMOS General Assembly (cfr. Labadi, 2022). Saint Lucia pleaded for addressing issues like commercialization and tourism, human rights, and gender issues and, responding to Latvia, to consider benefit sharing. An off-beat reflection by the delegation of Afghanistan complained about the proliferation of a broad version of the notion of sustainable development and feared that this might complicate the procedures for inscriptions in the Representative List.

At that point, it seemed that the discussion was already over, as nobody else was requesting the floor. Was this all "the world" had to say, as the floor was now open also to observers, NGOs, and others? Belgium asked the floor again: "colleagues, speak up!" Should the process of safeguarding not be more central? What does fostering "scientific studies and research methodologies including those conducted by the communities themselves" mean? What about strong claims like "States Parties are encouraged to recognize that inclusive social development cannot be achieved without sustainable food security, quality health care, access to safe water and sanitation"? Is there a consensus about this? Or that States Parties will "ensure the recognition of, respect for and enhancement of those traditional farming, fishing, hunting, pastoral, food-gathering," or "traditional health practices that contribute to well-being." Or what about the Directive that

> States Parties shall endeavour to recognize and promote the contribution of intangible cultural heritage to social cohesion, overcoming all forms of discrimination . . . to transcend differences of gender, colour, ethnicity, origin, class, and locality and to those that are broadly inclusive of all sectors and strata of society including indigenous peoples, migrants, immigrants and refugees, people of different ages and genders, persons with disabilities, and members of marginalized groups.

The Belgian delegation on the one hand applauded these aspirations but on the other hand reminded the experts present that the 2003 Convention strategically adhered to a limited number of concepts, while users could then appropriate and develop them (see Jacobs, 2020b). Every novel word introduced in the ODs should therefore be considered carefully.

The Secretary of the Convention replied with a remarkable speech, a gem available at §388 in the minutes of the meeting:

> "culture was not a priori part of the agenda of sustainable development . . . One problem lay in the fact that there was no specific goal dedicated to culture, unlike education, health, and so on . . . funding associated with development, particularly the United Nations or large funding agencies, had no cultural component because most people did not understand this relationship, at least in areas that were not purely economic, for example, cultural tourism, or the marketing of cultural goods and services or crafts. It was thus a problem for UNESCO and more broadly for cultural actors in how they could demonstrate that their actions were conducive to sustainable development."

Duvelle went on to evoke the documents and reflections presented in Baku and stressed that ODs could serve other functions than to organize inscriptions on Lists. So, she suggested, why not try to impact national policies and learn from the results? She continued:

> Noting that the structure of the document was completely arbitrary, the Secretariat researched existing directives and the report *Realising the Future We Want for All* to find paragraphs from the general principles that could link up with intangible cultural heritage. Thus, the vocabulary had come from these sources, which the experts had used to try and make a connection with safeguarding intangible cultural heritage . . . the idea was to show that the safeguarding of intangible cultural heritage was not just an act of cultural preservation, but that this cultural dimension had an impact on health, environmental management, human rights, gender equality, and so on; dimensions that were part of the agenda for sustainable development. . . . The Secretary recalled that the question of scientific research 'conducted by the communities themselves' was brought forward by experts who felt that they should not create the impression that science came only from a cultureless 'scientific community' but that communities themselves were interested in studying and demonstrating how their intangible cultural heritage and safeguarding helped them in the development process. . . . The Secretary appreciated the remarks by Belgium in that every time a word was used it brought with it a history. The Secretary remarked that it was interesting to note that indigenous peoples and their established organizations were not fully integrated into the Convention and they regretted that they were absent from the Convention and the Operational Directives. The Secretary explained that the addition of words was problematic, but also omissions were equally problematic for those who wished to feel part of this family.[12]

There were only two reactions. The delegate of Morocco recalled that the meeting organized in 2013 concluded that a relationship with economics had to go far beyond a strictly commercial and statistical dimension and that the Istanbul meeting he attended, stated that going beyond was also necessary for reflections about how "intangible cultural heritage contributed to sustainable development in various ways and at various levels through health, the environment, society, culture and in other ways." Strangely enough, with such an important topic on the table, nobody else in the room reacted. The delegation of Belgium, therefore, took the floor again and added the idea that this would require the involvement of many stakeholders, and hence heritage brokers. Without further comments, the decision to finalize the work at 10.COM was taken.

It is instructive to analyze a volume on sustainability and heritage published in the spring of 2015: The manuscript was submitted to Springer Verlag in December 2014. It involved (former) personnel from UNESCO and different UNESCO Chair holders working on world heritage (the 1972 UNESCO Convention). Here, you discover that this highly informed and connected group of actors was still going for the addition of culture as the fourth dimension of sustainable development. They were still following the "culture as a fourth pillar"-strategy, advocated by the United Cities and Local Governments Committee on Culture and its Agenda 21 for Culture[13] and UNESCO, including their Hangzhou Declaration pro culture in 2013 (Yang, 2015), in particular for the 1972 Convention (Bandarin, 2015). The volume on world heritage included an extra chapter on the 2003 Convention, by Shina Erlewein. She managed to integrate information in a late phase of the editing process in 2014 and early 2015. She expressed her surprise to discover the draft amendments available online for 9.COM.13b:

> [F]urther reflection, argument and exploration are truly needed. In fact, the three-pillar approach to sustainable development as applied in the *Realizing the Future We Want For All* report is reasserted in the current draft Operational Directives to the 2003 Convention, thereby missing the opportunity to further develop a four-pillar approach stressing the contribution of culture to development as a self-standing pillar. . . . In so doing, culture, and intangible heritage as a component of culture, is reduced to a tool enabling the achievement of other goals.
>
> *(Erlewein, 2015, p. 81)*

3.5. 2015, Windhoek: 10.COM

Just two months after the UN Summit organized in New York (25–27/9/2015), where the 2030 Agenda and the 17 SDGs were black-boxed, 10.COM took place in Windhoek (30/11–4/12/2015).

Item 14 on the Agenda was the discussion of the draft ODs.[14] Duvelle explained that the document was built on the previous document and discussions in 9.COM but that it now also reflected the structure of the goals presented in the very recent report *Transforming our World: the 2030 Agenda for Sustainable Development.*[15] The paragraphs had been reshuffled, mirroring the sequence of the SDGs; the roles of NGOs and cultural brokers, and references to ethics were included. The delegation of Turkey acknowledged the importance of discussions in Chengdu (2013) and the Committee. The delegation of Brazil pleaded to remove or minimize references to the original document *Realizing the Future We Want for All* and to replace it with the 2030 Agenda. But this was refused by the Secretariat in order to preserve the reliability of their original document as a source.

Belgium intervened to express satisfaction with the swift and pragmatic hook-up with the new 2030 Agenda but appealed not to give up the fight for culture as a fourth pillar for SD or as a future goal in a post-2030 agenda. Also, the reference to Article 13 of the 2005 Convention and the insertion of brokerage were welcomed. Latvia highlighted the importance of including scientific studies and research methodologies and the significance of community involvement and reminded the issue of "intellectual property regimes." The Republic of Korea welcomed everything but raised the question whether this should be a set of operational directives or a policy document.

There were (just) three series of amendments to the proposed Chapter VI of the Operational Directives from the delegations of Belgium, Brazil, and Latvia. Brazil proposed a new paragraph 170 referring to the UN Charter, the UN Framework Convention on Climate Change and in particular the 2030 Agenda to clearly frame the notion of sustainable development and all possible interpretations in that framework, but on the proposal by Latvia and Belgium, this was transferred to the decision part of the document, so keeping specific dates and documents outside the Operational Directives. Then dozens of amendments by Belgium followed. The first was to add a sub-paragraph 171 (d) referring to 'sustainable development experts and cultural brokers for the appropriate integration of the safeguarding of intangible cultural heritage into plans, policies and programmes, including outside the cultural sector.' The delegation of the Republic of Korea asked for clarification of the wording used in Belgium's amendment, specifically the term 'cultural brokers' as the Republic of Korea was unsure whether this was commonly used in the language of intangible cultural heritage. At this point, a reference by Belgium to the publication (see Jacobs, 2014, 2014a, 2014b) that was widely distributed, proved to be convincing for the Korean colleagues and § 171 (d) as amended by Belgium was adopted. Small additions like "food preparation" in paragraph 178 opened a world for cooking and recipes. Genetic resources in paragraph 179. In the heading of VI.2.3, Belgium proposed to add "and vice-versa" after the words "the impact of tourism on safeguarding intangible cultural heritage." There were more than 40 amendments by Belgium, and they were generally accepted without much discussion. Decision 10.COM 14.a, with the new draft Chapter VI in the annex, was adopted.

Then, the delegate of Palestine, the new State Party that was at that time not yet a member of the Intergovernmental Committee, immediately took the floor and stated he preferred the way business was conducted in managing the 1972 World Heritage Convention. A working group could be set up with interested States

Parties who could work on texts, proposals, and amendments. He also warned that the draft ODs would have to pass the General Assembly. Belgium responded by referring to Article 7(e) of the 2003 Convention, spelling out the function of the Committee to prepare and submit ODs to the General Assembly for approval. Duvelle clarified that in the 1972 Convention, a Committee can amend and adopt the Operational Guidelines, necessitating procedures like working groups.[16] Following the rules, the draft Chapter VI would be presented to the General Assembly in the summer of 2016.

3.6. Conclusion

In the introduction to this article, you learned what happened that summer in Paris – an episode recorded and accessible on the ICH.UNESCO.org website. The set of ODs on sustainable development were accepted and added to the Basic Texts, but it took hours of discussions and resisting attempts to trim them down or neutralize them in the form of a mere policy document. In this chapter, I discussed structural aspects and major issues such as the implications of the adaptation of the Basic texts to the SDGs, but also the importance of contingencies and power games. I hinted at the fact that it makes a difference which delegation, and also which delegate, takes the floor and intervenes during a meeting.

This is compatible with recent research in international assemblies and arenas (Meskell, 2018; Brumann, 2021):

> Much of what happens within global organizations is like theater production. . . . As with the unfolding of a good story, there are unexpected alignments of interests that complicate the usual division of roles. Diplomats, civil servants, and activists (NGOs, the private sector, etc.) do not always stay tidily in their places, but sometimes form alliances that cross boundaries, or come into conflict in efforts that are meant to be collaborative.
>
> *(Niezen & Sapignoli, 2017, p. 3)*

In the last 15 years, several research projects have yielded a legitimate methodological space for studying meetings in UNESCO and other international organizations (e.g., Müller, 2013), operating under flags like multi-sited ethnography. A specific feature is that the researchers meet and study people "just like them," anthropologists, cosmopolitans, reflexive scholars: talking back (Islam, 2015, p. 248; Bortolotto, 2020). In most of these studies, you read about Nameplate Actors, like Switzerland or Belgium, as if there were no concrete, easily identifiable individuals behind those boundary objects like a "State Party Nameplate." These people and delegations (should) know that since the 2010s, thanks to streaming and recording and the availability of the recordings on the UNESCO.org website (also for future research), they are more than ever speaking and performing in public. They could be aware that this was partly introduced to enhance transparency, reporting, traceability, accountability, rule-following and fairness being performed, or not. Since the 2020s, the "Observers," multi-sited ethnographers for instance, are no longer just sitting in the back of the room as eyewitnesses, in the Observer Nameplate Zone (when lucky in exotic locations and luxury hotels), but now they can also do their work post-factum, at home/in their office, just like the people in the Delegations or the Secretariat can.

Following an actor, also over time, in this story "Belgium," is a tested actor–network theory method to explore controversies and get insight into the making and closing of black boxes and boundary objects (Venturini and Munk, 2022; Jacobs, 2022). Although the Belgian delegation is a larger team, sustainable development and operational directives are what I follow(ed) up (while Belgium was part of the Intergovernmental Committee in 2006–2008 and 2012–2016), so "Belgium" could have been replaced in this article by "Marc Jacobs." But is it allowed for a scholar to transgress the borders of the "observer" zone in UNESCO meetings? Can an expert "know" too much? What is the significance and added value of scholarly and other heritage specialist work grounded in a long-term (more than two decades) observation and participation, not measured in weeks but in years? I am not the only one, dozens of colleagues, including several authors in this volume, are in that case, but may hide behind the convenient nameplates of Delegations of States Parties or those of the Secretariat or Observer (or consultant).

Reflexively looking at my role, many of my interventions in and outside the Belgian delegation, shaping the Convention and then the ODs, can be explained as an actor–network theory-inspired effort in the first two decades of the twenty-first century to help craft and build an interconnected series of boundary objects (the Basic Texts) to inspire and influence heritage policy and practice. Right from the beginning, there was the option for using a limited number of words, without strictly defining them. But also tabooing other expressions, among other reasons to steer away from the overshadowing World Heritage paradigm (and strange concepts like Outstanding Universal Value) or ideologically tainted folklore constructions. The challenge then was, and is, to cultivate the "appropriate vocabulary" endeavor (Jacobs, 2020a) and occasionally try to introduce new fruitful concepts (Stefano & Wendland, 2020, p. 229*)*.

My experience feels like what Renita Thedwall (2013) called "punctuated entries" and what Helena Wulff (2002) described as "yo-yo fieldwork." In this contribution, you might have felt, from an actor going very deep in the system when yo-yo-ing, the hope in 2012 of finally going not just for saving but for transformation and the fruit in the Fridge, building expectations for tools for adequately dealing with over-commercialization, tourism, creative industries, and other challenges framed as "sustainable development issues," and sharing the "up with culture as a fourth pillar" ambitions. You learn about hopes of getting more than the 17 SDGs in 2015 and more than what was presented to the 9.COM in 2014, but also about the key intervention §388 of Duvelle in 9.COM, making the pragmatic click and going for what turned out to be 2030 Agenda-compatible. Today, the paragraphs of

Chapter VI are Basic Texts, available to be activated and combined with the Overall Results Framework (or, why not, a platform on ethical tools) and, as mentioned in OD170 and 171, ready for cultural heritage brokers and mediators to facilitate those processes. Is the 2003 UNESCO Convention primarily about inscriptions on Lists or about cultivating fruitful policies and practices?

Notes

1 Listen to 7 hours of the recorded discussion of Agenda item 7 at https://ich.unesco.org/en/7com.
2 "Indicator 11.4.1: Total per capita expenditure on the preservation, protection, and conservation of all cultural and natural heritage, by source of funding (public, private), type of heritage (cultural, natural) and level of government (national, regional, and local/municipal)."
3 https://unstats.un.org/sdgs/metadata/files/Metadata-11-04-01.pdf (Accessed: 4 January 2023, just like all other URLs mentioned in this article).
4 https://whc.unesco.org/document/139146
5 https://ich.unesco.org/en/basic-texts-00503
6 https://ich.unesco.org/en/background-of-the-ethical-principles-00867
7 https://ich.unesco.org/en/decisions/10.COM/15.A
8 https://ich.unesco.org/doc/src/ITH-14-9.COM-4_Rev.-EN.doc, p. 19
9 Chengdu International Conference on Intangible Cultural Heritage in Celebration of the Tenth Anniversary of UNESCO's Convention (14–16/6/2013).
10 https://ich.unesco.org/doc/src/ITH-14-9.COM-13.b-EN.doc; Decision9.COM 13.b; https://ich.unesco.org/doc/src/ITH-15-10.COM-4_EN.docx
11 www.undp.org/publications/realizing-future-we-want-all.
12 https://ich.unesco.org/doc/src/ITH-15-10.COM-4_EN.docx, § 388.
13 www.agenda21culture.net/sites/default/files/files/documents/multi/ag21_en.pdf
14 *ITH/15/10.COM/14.a*, leading to decision 10.COM 14.a.www.unesco.org/culture/ich/doc/src/ITH-15-10.COM-14.a_EN.docx
15 https://sustainabledevelopment.un.org/post2015/transformingourworld
16 https://ich.unesco.org/doc/src/ITH-16-11.COM-4-EN.docx, §1256–1259

References

Bandarin, F. (2015) 'Sustainability in the world heritage convention: The making of a policy framework', in Albert, M.-T. (ed.), *Perceptions of Sustainability in Heritage Studies*. Berlin: De Gruyter, pp. 35–46.

Bortolotto, C. et al. (2020) 'Proving participation: Vocational bureaucrats and bureaucratic creativity in the implementation of the UNESCO Convention for the Safeguarding of the Intangible Cultural Heritage', *Social Anthropology/Anthropologie Sociale*, 28(1), pp. 66–82.

Bowker, G. et al. (2015) *Boundary objects and beyond. Working with Leigh Star*. Cambridge, MA and London: The MIT Press.

Brumann, C. (2021) *The best we share: Nation, culture and world-making in the UNESCO World Heritage arena*. Oxford: Berghahn Books.

Erlewein, S. (2015) 'Sustainable development and intangible cultural heritage: Integrating culture into development', in Albert, M.-T. (ed.), *Perceptions of sustainability in heritage studies*. Berlin: De Gruyter, pp. 71–83.

Islam, G. (2015) 'Practitioners as theorists: Para-ethnography and the collaborative study of contemporary organizations', *Organizational Research Methods*, 18(2), pp. 231–251.

Jacobs, M. (2014a) 'Cultural brokerage, Addressing boundaries and the new paradigm of safeguarding intangible cultural heritage. Folklore studies, transdisciplinary perspectives and UNESCO', *Volkskunde*, 115(3), pp. 265–291.

Jacobs, M. (2014b) 'Development brokerage, anthropology and public action. Local empowerment, international cooperation and aid: Safeguarding of intangible cultural heritage', *Volkskunde*, 115(3), pp. 299–318.

Jacobs, M. (2016) 'The spirit of the convention: Interlocking principles and ethics for safeguarding intangible cultural heritage', *International Journal of Intangible Heritage*, 11, pp. 71–87.

Jacobs, M. (2017) 'La sauvegarde du patrimoine culturel immatériel et l'éthique', in Lempereur, F. (ed.), *Patrimoine culturel immatériel*. Liège: Presses universitaires de Liège, pp. 247–259.

Jacobs, M. (2020a) 'Article 15. Participation of communities, groups, and individuals. CGIs, not just "the community"', in Blake, J. and Lixinski, L. (eds.), *The 2003 UNESCO Intangible Heritage Convention. A commentary*. Oxford: Oxford University Press, pp. 273–289.

Jacobs, M. (2020b) 'Words matter . . . The arsenal and the repertoire: UNESCO, ICOM, and European frameworks', *Volkskunde*, 121(3), pp. 267–286.

Jacobs, M. (2022) 'Kritische nabijheid. De veldgids voor Controversy Mapping (2022) van Tommaso Venturini & Anders Kristian Munk en de erfenis van Bruno Latour', *Volkskunde*, 123(3), pp. 391–413).

Jacobs, M., Neyrinck, J. and Van der Zeijden, A. (2014) 'UNESCO, brokers and critical success (f)actors in safeguarding intangible cultural heritage', *Volkskunde*, 115(3), pp. 249–256.

Labadi, S. (2019) 'Re-examining world heritage and sustainable development', in Bharne, V. and Sandmeier, T. (eds.), *Routledge Companion to Global Heritage Conservation*. London: Routledge, pp. 15–26.

Labadi, S. (2022) *Rethinking Heritage for Sustainable Development*. London: UCL Press.

Labadi, S. et al. (2021) *Heritage and the Sustainable Development Goals. Policy Guidance for Heritage and Development Actors*. Paris: ICOMOS.

Latour, B. (1987) *Science in Action: How to Follow Scientists and Engineers through Society*. Cambridge, MA: Harvard University Press.

Meskell, L. (2018) *A Future in Ruins. UNESCO, World Heritage, and the Dream of Peace*. Oxford: Oxford University Press.

Michael, M. (2017) *Actor-Network Theory. Trials, Trails and Translations*. London: SAGE.

Müller, B. (2013) 'Introduction – lifting the veil of harmony: Anthropologists approach international organisations', in Müller, B. (ed.), *The Gloss of Harmony. The Politics of Policy-Making in Multilateral Organisations*. London: Pluto Press, pp. 1–20.

Niezen, R. and Sapignoli, M. (2017) 'Introduction', in Niezen, R. and Sapignoli, M. (eds.), *Palaces of Hope. The Anthropology of Global Organizations*. Cambridge: Cambridge University Press, pp. 1–30.

Rosetti, I. et al. (2022) 'Heritage and sustainability: Regulating participation', *Sustainability*, 14(3), pp. 1–27.

Schreiber, H. and Pielińsk, B. (2023) 'Inviting all humanity to an elite club? Understanding tensions in UNESCO's global heritage regimes through the lens of a typology of goods', *International Journal of Cultural Policy*, 29(1), pp. 113–129.

Smith, L. and Campbell, G. (2017) 'The tautology of "intangible values" and the misrecognition of intangible cultural heritage', *Heritage & Society*, 10(1), pp. 26–44.

Star, S. and Griesemer, J. (1989) 'Institutional ecology, "translations" and boundary objects: Amateurs and professionals in Berkeley's Museum of Vertebrate Zoology, 1907–39', *Social Studies of Science*, 19(3), pp. 387–430.

Stefano, M. di and Wendland, W. (2020) 'Article 13: Ethical and legal considerations in researching, documenting, and ensuring access to intangible cultural heritage', in Blake, J. and Lixinski, L. (eds.), *The 2003 UNESCO Intangible Heritage Convention: A Commentary*. Oxford: Oxford University Press, pp. 217–242.

Thedvall, R. (2013) 'Punctuated entries: Doing fieldwork in policy meetings in the European Union', in Garsten, C. and Nyqvist, A. (eds.), *Organisational Anthropology. Doing Ethnography in and among Complex Organisations*. London: Pluto Press, pp. 106–119.

Torggler, B. et al. (2013) *Evaluation of UNESCO's Standard-Setting Work of the Culture Sector Part I – 2003 Convention for the Safeguarding of the Intangible Cultural Heritage Final Report*. Paris: UNESCO Internal Oversight Service.

Venturini, T. and Munk, A. (2022) *Controversy Mapping. A Field Guide*. Cambridge: Polity Press

Wulff, H. (2002) 'Yo-yo fieldwork: Mobility and time in a multilocal study of dance in Ireland', *Anthropological Journal on European Cultures*, 11, pp. 117–136.

Yang, M. (2015) 'Culture in moving the MDGs to the post-2015 development agenda: Some reflections on the role of living heritage for sustainable development', in Albert, M.-T. (ed.), *Perceptions of Sustainability in Heritage Studies*. Berlin: De Gruyter, pp. 21–34.

PART II

Ownership, intellectual property, commons

4

OWNERSHIP AND RIGHTS

Sustainable development ideals with inequalities of recognition and resource management

Kristin Kuutma

4.1. Introduction

The UN Agenda 2030 for Sustainable Development Goals pursues ideals and guidelines that suggest linkages to broader economic, political, and social contexts. However, among the heritage system participants in the UNESCO-defined ICH domains, the tendency to align "sustainability" with preserving a practice or phenomenon for eternity can make the more inquisitive scholars doubt the coveted favorable outcome.[1] This overarching "safeguarding" is retrospective in its esteem of the historical dimension, a fixation in time, and disregard for the unavoidable dynamics and change, whereas particularly the complexity and interconnectedness of Sustainable Development Goals call for a substantial ecological shift in mindset and attitude when aspiring for a different future. My inquiry in this chapter focuses, in turn, on the entanglements of inequalities, command of agency, or subsistence in designated heritage practices: I propose to unpack the socioeconomic implications for resource management and thus inherently address the rights for self-determination and openings for alterations. Alongside the availability of resources, I will tackle inequalities in the politics of recognition.

The following connects the ICH configuration with the SDGs with a closer look at the agenda to reduce inequalities (SDG10), which links to several other goals, such as empowering communities, gender equality, endorsing livelihoods. "Intangible cultural heritage" (as well as the widely disseminated acronym "ICH") is a political signifier with modifying capacity: It conveys a meaning and identifies positions in the established heritage system. What I want to point out is the predicament with granting agency in the politics promoted by the ICH discourse. The dilemma of state control over the terms of recognition and relevant representational activities in the ICH framework sets the rules of the game in mediated

DOI: 10.4324/9781003244158-7

representation, that is, standing and speaking for someone who is not or cannot be present or speak for themselves. At the same time, representational agendas and emergent hierarchies generate possessional claims in relation to cultural heritage. Heritage legislation tends to authorize the dominant systems of ownership that reinforce power imbalances, particularly for indigenous, descendant communities and minority groups.

The ethnographic material for this chapter reflects my extensive fieldwork carried out over two decades in the context of meetings focusing on the UNESCO ICH-related policies. These discussions and debates on local, national, and international levels have given me opportunities to obtain insights in various geographic locations. Meetings as organizational devices offer fieldwork sites for relating and providing access to communicative forms of epistemic and social context (Arantes 2013; Yarrow 2017; Brown et al. 2017). By participating in miscellaneous gatherings, I have acquired instructive anthropological knowledge and data on the organizational format as well as various aspects of policy-making (see Gellner and Hirsch 2001; Shore and Wright 1997). My ethnographic observations derive from a multisite experience by following people, ideas, and policy configurations in diverse settings.[2] The fieldwork examples below introduce the Kihnu islanders, the Seto community, and the Russian Orthodox Old Believers in Estonia, a workshop in Greece, the Sámi in Scandinavia, and make reference to the Laikipiak Maasai in Kenya.

4.2. Conceptual complications

Let me start with semantics because conceptual reflections may unveil assumptions and subtle constraints that construct our understanding. All in all, the intangible cultural heritage framework brought about new concepts with contextual and contingent alterations in the field, where the proactive addition of SDGs appends further issues.[3] Sustainability as a concept poses a semantic ramification by being fluid and prone to both restrictive and generative constructs. The explosion of the term "sustainability" in the sphere of culture, the field of heritage studies included, invokes complex ethical considerations on empowerment and vulnerability. Although the compound "sustainable development" implies fleetingly the notion of change, the objectification of development or cultivating a linear progress has triggered anthropological criticism when the encounters between development policy and practice and its beneficiaries reveal unintended consequences, or in turn, affordances (see Brightman and Lewis 2017; Mosse 2005). Similarly, the more recent investigative studies of the role of culture in the age of SD propose not to look at "development" as progress but rather as a complex process played out in local contexts (Wiktor-Mach 2020; see also Meissner 2021).

What poses serious problems is the "semantic inflation" of the concepts of "culture and sustainable development," turning them into floating signifiers that cannot be genuinely used in cultural policy-making (Isar 2017, p. 148). "Culture" pervaded the mainstream development discourse rather recently, although leading to the reconceptualization of the culture–development nexus (Wiktor-Mach 2020, p. 312). The anthropological discourse, however, vehemently cautions against essentializing "culture," or perceiving it as a monolithic, clearly delineable whole, or congruent with a population group.[4] Such misconception remains still pertinent in the context of preservationist agendas and therefore abstaining from articulating it on the instrumental first page would make sense for the SDGs. Nonetheless, the analytical disciplinary standpoint underscores the aspect of diversity and pluralism that punctuates human experience on the ground in a locally meaningful way.

Living heritage is embedded in people and safeguarding is a practice that depends on the interconnectedness of knowledge systems, issues of ownership, of self-determination (cf. Logan et al. 2010; Kearney 2009). In the assemblage of intersecting concepts and practices yet another moment of affordance, or a license to change, becomes cogent – that of resilience. It relates ideationally to the management of resources, but one may draw here a contour also to the claim for agency. Resilience invokes the ability to recover from adversity or deformation, making conceptually an analogy with the ability of an ecosystem to return to its original state after being disturbed. However, in the domain of intangible cultural heritage, this designation signals already by default a change, a novel situation, a transformation.

In the discourse endorsed by the UNESCO Living Heritage Entity, the executive unit of the global organization is gradually working toward replacing the "intangible cultural heritage" with the signifier "living heritage." This noteworthy conceptual shift implies a tacit conceptual development that does not automatically transpose to the policy level. The representative infrastructure depends on an inert retrospective appraisal of cultural expressions which are transformed into highly politicized commodities signified as heritage. The national governance infrastructure works for representational celebratory inscription in designated lists and congruent static conservational purposes. Also, such state-monitored infrastructure is constantly opposing the inherent integrity and interconnectedness of SDGs that fundamentally do not subject to selective parceling, if the transformational agenda is taken seriously. The UNESCO ICH configuration and managerial regime substantiate cultural politics manifestly and functions through policy-making; therefore, we should acknowledge the existential confrontational rift identified: the inability from the perspective of cultural policy to embody the multitude of incompatible roles in relation to SD (Kangas et al. 2017, p. 131).

On the whole, the goal of this chapter is to address more specifically the issue of reducing inequalities and the issues related to economic growth, highlighting in this context the more responsible consumption and production. The following discussion highlights the issues of inclusive recognition and redistribution of agency, and affordance, defined as "entitlements to capabilities" (see Goodale 2009, p. 6, quoting philosopher Martha Nussbaum). My ideational analysis looks at the ability to engage with the social structure in question, discern veiled inequality or contested positionality, and contemplate what kind of resource is found in representation. Inequality refers to social disparity with unjust distribution of resources and opportunities. While the ICH regulatory system unavoidably propounds inequitable representation and competing claims for resource management, in indigenous as well as minority group rights framework there persist claims for acknowledgment that would lead to a substantial change in agency and recognition (see Kymlicka 2009).

4.3. Converting structural agency

The living heritage concept basically suggests a fluidity in reference and indefinite substance as that of the SD field, when we consider the scope and variety of cultural expression. Things become more concrete in the culturalized politics concerning heritage that reflects the mechanisms of governmentality and the concurrent rights-based discourses (see Coombe and Weiss 2015). Here, one should make a distinction between the spheres of lived experience and the designated UNESCO ICH domain with its re-distribution of political and socio-economic power: The consequence would be a structuring normativity of governance and policy regulations that go against the nature of cultural dynamics, mobility, and license to change. For the community, ICH is a dynamic resource, but from the state perspective, the image of ICH is stagnant by default.

Nevertheless, the prevalent actor in the UNESCO ICH configuration is the (nation)state, that is, the self-governing political entity whose administrative management also defines the heritage discourse on its territory and its epistemic and ontological parameters. Those discursive factors generate a site of contested identity and rights which reflects the domestic and global politics of recognition where cultural heritage is employed for "orchestrating differences" within the state and between states (Hafstein 2018, p. 8). The global UNESCO organization functions via governmental mediation that is substantially dependent on state-monitored activities and the prevalent political system where the quality of accountability of policy implementation as well as inclusive principles of management define it: heritage regimes are crafted within and by a particular state apparatus (see Bendix et al. 2012; Müller 2013).

A closer examination of the infrastructure at play reveals that the UNESCO governance of culture operates through structural change and strategic transformation on the ground when targeted policy-setting activities produce ultimately novel organizational configurations. What's more, the 2003 Convention Operational Directives have set it as a strategic obligation, particularly through the inventory making and community representation requirement, while this objective on the national level compels a particular organizational format as a procedural corollary on a local level. However, a UNESCO nomination does not drop into an empty space but tops an already existing format of management and representation, although on a different scale and authority.[5] The community must reinvent itself as a heritage stakeholder to comply with the UNESCO regulations and execute a certain normative turn that also shifts ownership configurations. The basically novel organizational structure is a prerequisite for the administrative logic of the Convention (and its listing) mechanism. Hence, the local situation is changed by default. This process is usually parallel to conceptual debates on what is meant by "intangible cultural heritage" as opposed to previously used terms referring to popular traditions, folk culture, or folklore, depending on regional or language contexts – I have observed such discussions time and again in various settings where the concurrent identification issue becomes germane.

Moreover, the adopted international and national ICH governance policies intertwine with modern cultural management techniques that may eventually refashion also the grassroots system of representational agency and ownership. To give an example, in Estonia the Ministry of Culture set up a Board of Intangible Cultural Heritage after the 2003 Convention was ratified and became operational. That body comprised stakeholders from researchers, cultural animators, regional, and local NGOs, to councilors from the ministerial office and the UNESCO national commission who started off by debating and redefining the conceptual sphere encompassed by the novel designator. Then, to illustrate the relevant trickle-down effect to the community level, this example extends to the Seto community inhabiting the south-eastern corner of Estonia, being particularly known for their distinct group-singing or *leelo* traditions that became inscribed on the Representative List. During the process of drafting their UNESCO nomination candidature file, the involved Seto assembled a special NGO in 2008, Leelotarko Kogo (council of master *leelo* singers) composed of representatives of *leelo*-choirs (choral groups of roughly five to ten singers), identified as the main stakeholders. Though prior networking may have occasionally occurred, such an organization of choir representatives did not previously exist. Since then, they have, among other things, regularly convened seminar meetings for debating the state of their practice.

The UNESCO-related programs initiate new organizational structures, which, from the perspective of the community, may be of service in the changing social context of a list nomination. But there may occur also competitive or even antagonistic initiatives for representational authority because communities are not homogeneous: there are different kinds of expertise and interests discernible on a community level, depending on the personal practical engagement, or position in community leadership. For instance, as it happened, in Kihnu Island – with only 700 registered inhabitants but renowned as the Representative-List-inscribed cultural space in Estonia – two competitive organizations were set up in connection with the listing while a third one emerged quite recently. Still, these new organizations may stimulate unprecedented community-based initiatives and co-operations. For example, today the Seto community is organizing joint ventures with the geographically remote Kihnu islanders, as well as actively collaborating with the Suiti in neighboring Latvia, inscribed on the Urgent Safeguarding List. Thus, such UNESCO designations enhance innovative joint ventures and communication between previously distant communities.[6]

In another context, in Greece, the national ICH-specific reconfigurations took an effective turn only when a National Scientific Committee on ICH was formed, and "the quest for the meaning of cultural expressions" took place in the last decade (Fotopoulou 2016, p. 139). Cultural specialists as well as researchers had to re-invent, reconsider, and transform terminology alongside apparent changes in the organizational formation, which incited further interpretation. Confusion about the deictic reference of ICH continued to be persistent, voiced emphatically by community representatives, as was the case during the joint discussion workshop with leaders of communities of practice at the Athens Museum of Modern Greek Culture in September 2019.[7] The observable change in functional terminology, of re-naming (i.e., "translation" in novel contexts), plays a significant role in carving out the conceptual and social – thus also economic – space for the phenomenon. Previously, like in many Southern European countries, reference was made to "cultural goods" in Greek, denoting movable items of communal and aesthetic, vernacular, or ethnological interest. Here, economic terms sneak into unpacking the conceptual field, and in the same vein, any reference to heritage suggests proprietor relations. Cultural goods mean cultural property, and property means resources with constructive significance in generating socio-cultural capital when alluding to quality of life and knowledge stock fostering cultural ecology.

The alteration in heritage authorities may shepherd into existence new political entities, albeit within a national framework. The ICH safeguarding configuration by UNESCO instigates a transformation and restructuring with an emergent organizational structure, which does not necessarily correspond to or rely on the previously functioning system.[8] Hence, some hierarchies in expertise and policy-setting institutions become altered under the aegis of the ICH conceptualization. In sum, the ICH format generates a new policy of cultural management that brings about conceptual and social change. Consequently, it can be stated that we are dealing here with the process of cultural change that depends on interaction, knowledge transfer, and shifts in agency.

4.4. Economic affordance and license to change

When addressing the realm of cultural heritage, the omnipresent social struggles around ownership and control of provenance and possession take the front stage. Although cultural governance stakeholders particularly on the national level often feel discomfort with heritage-driven economic activities where they tend to highlight the menace of "over-commercialisation,"[9] the economic sphere deserves much more nuanced approach. Its rejection may appear in conflict with local community interests.

The issues of ownership and the ability to adapt on one's own terms, that is resilience, concern crucially the option of asserting rights vis-à-vis state authorities and sustaining local livelihoods, while negotiating new economic opportunities for the community. In Estonia, the Kihnu community is facing additional existential problems in connection with the pressing renewable energy objectives. European Green Deal challenges and rising electricity costs in the early 2020s have expedited the national plans for constructing offshore wind farms where one of the targeted sites would be the seabed in the vicinity of Kihnu Island. The islanders try to make themselves heard in the debates with local municipality and government officials on how the planned turbines would affect their environment as they know it. There have emerged also initiatives to seek guidance from UNESCO-related programs, as a result of which I was interviewed in an expert capacity by the national broadcasting agency ERR on whether inscription on Representative List could endorse arguments for challenging corporate governmental and business operators.[10] The Kihnu community members seek to find consensus in assessing the imminent retributions: They have voiced their possible interest in crafting new job opportunities (for instance, as turbine guardians catering also to tourists), and not simply monetary retribution that was initially on the table.[11] On the other hand, they fear the environmental effects on the fish population, as fishing was traditionally one of the major sources of livelihood, rendered accordingly in the intangible heritage safeguarding and management plans drawn already two decades ago. What needs to be added here is the fact that the number of professional fishermen has reduced drastically in Kihnu and elsewhere in the Estonian coastal regions, due to the decline of fish stock in the Baltic Sea because of a longer and multi-factor process. But at the same time when tourism has become one of the major subsistence revenues, the islanders dread the possible consequences of novel tourist ventures, like for example the aggravatingly disturbing seabird-shooting tours in recent decades.

The realm of local economic resources is often controversial. However, economic is social by default, and thus, economic issues depend on, are embedded in, as well as reflect social relations. The representation of culture and its contextualization in history plays an instrumental role in the economic aspects of tourism, branding, and marketing. Tourism is the modern global practice that brings revenue far and wide, and ideally to the stakeholder communities. The promotion of a particular product or cultural entity entails advertising of distinctive features while marketing encompasses the whole process of researching, promoting, selling, and distributing to the potential consumers. This aggregate of functions is deemed to operate in the sphere of intangible cultural heritage today when attracting the new generation or targeting potential visitors.

With the Seto community in Estonia, the traditional singing practices – engaging mostly women – are today also substantially related to tourism. There has emerged a novel space of practice, that of organized short-term recreation camps for *leelo*-singing instruction, which appears to be concurrently a source of income for the women running such camps. This is another example of how the traditional practice may retain in a new form: intensive few days away from daily routines engages those interested in learning the artistic skills (both by locals and by outsiders) that simultaneously provide innovative means for collective practice in the modern individualistic daily life. On the other hand, when tourism becomes the most available source of income, changes occur also in the communities of practice. For example, one of the prominent Seto community activists who has been a *leelo*-singing teacher to the young for decades is today committed to running the village center that includes a restaurant with local dishes on the menu. In August 2021, she excused her absence from the discussion meetings related to *leelo*-singing by being occupied with the catering for this event and tourists: The summer period was her time to earn an income that would sustain her family through winter.

The above demonstrates how the communities singled out by the UNESCO listing mechanism in Estonia struggle to deal with their moral commitment to maintaining heritage practices and relevant livelihoods, regardless of the substantial transformations. Community members try to create new economic opportunities related to traditional practices, find ways to experience exchange, and establish partnerships through heritage-related networks, which draws added attention to license to change.

The economic potential related to intangible cultural heritage bears on the aspect of turnover, employment, and meaning with a specific role of knowledge and reputation. Even if expressive practices seemingly pertain to another category with contrasting ethos, the previous or historical means of subsistence (often related to crafts) cannot occur outside of the prevalent revenue relations. In Greece, for example, the implementation of the 2003 Convention and the relevant ICH re-branding provided another direction for a potential change and possible subsistence relief for local heritage actors during the economic crisis in the previous decade (see also Karampampas 2021). It helped them to regain control of the situation and raise their living standards. It was apparently conducted as a collaborative effort by local heritage actors with public institutions and NGOs when taking collective decisions.[12] On the ground, the branding effect of "intangible cultural heritage" has been found greatly instrumental: It helps the crafters and farmers to raise their personal and their product profiles and it elevates the status of cultural practices. Consequently, it appears that international recognition facilitates negotiations for better conditions, perhaps first and foremost in relation to governmental ordinance. The Tinian Marble craftsmanship in Greece, inscribed on the Representative List, comprises traditional celebrated crafts and know-how while the novel recognition has endorsed creative originality at the expense of the earlier practical trade of stable items (see Alivizatou 2021). However, the profile of craftsmanship has been raised, tourism is enhanced, and local actors use the nomination for public advocacy. The commercial dimension of crafts is quite explicit, and, all things considered, consumption is in essence a form of social participation. With that in mind, argumentation on whether the market is a safeguarding measure, or does it premise sustainability, may take some additional coloring when thinking about sustaining local livelihoods or creating new economic opportunities related to traditional practice.

The marked economic transformations described are at the same time occurring in parallel to the inherent change. When ICH is claimed to have made practitioners more “resilient” to market logic, one should acknowledge its concurrent evidence of imminent change. Restoration of perceived bygones or stasis is impossible because by using the signification of “intangible cultural heritage” such identification has already triggered the process of transformation that anthropologists have stated all along (e.g., Skounti 2009). Still, regardless of heritage claims and regulations being imbricated in the economic domain and politics, the expert administrators alongside many scholars regard economic processes with an inferior positioning on their ethical scales. Intangible-heritage-engaged cultural workers often appear holding a strongly felt moral principle and demonstrate discomfort toward possible commercial initiatives or practices as an unappealing ramification (see Bortolotto 2020). But from a broader and complex social perspective, an alternative liberal outlook to the affordability and upscaling of economic activities may eventually concur better with the ideals pronounced in the SDGs. Particularizations of conceptual and economic issues outline the paramount dilemma of the moral effect of the “intangible cultural heritage” designation and the instrumentality of resources. The power and the politics of representation and resources at risk due to economic (or social) transformations exposit concerns related to cultural and social rights.

4.5. Inequality, limits of representation, and change in positionality

Another aspect of representational agency comes forth when instances of contestation shed more nuanced light on the intricate issues involving rights for heritage ownership. The ICH framework instigates sentiments and policies of protectionism, nativism, and nationalism, but controversially intangible cultural heritage may be implemented as a strategy in resistance to stately regulations or centralized authoritarian policy. It is likewise significant to point out instances when the state-monitored UNESCO recognition has been modest or even failed in granting respectable community agency on an organizational level: Particularly, indigenous, but also local communities, have manifested reservations with respect to state mediations. Moments contributing to social balance can be created when local heritage actors bring their own cultural resources to bear and thus simultaneously expose the limits of governmentality as well as enlarge rights-based discourse and practice in fields of heritage politics (see Coombe and Weiss 2015). The communities and groups may appear searching for the agency in this configuration and eventually generate a change in positionality.

For example, in Estonia the inclusion of ethnic minority groups in the national imaginary of intangible heritage has been selective and overlooking the larger migratory groups from the Soviet period in the latter half of the twentieth century. As it happens, the major significance falls to groups with roots in a more distant past and with a historical status reflecting their prominence in cultural and anthropological studies. One such group foregrounded by cultural experts have been the Russian Orthodox Old Believers in Eastern Estonia, whose ancestors migrated to these lands after refusing the mid-seventeenth-century Russian church reforms, presenting today a staple Slavic minority in the national imaginary, defined by religious and agricultural practices, language, and seclusion. Significantly, their traditions uphold isolation and a historic distrust toward the government, which may have played a part in the community leaders' decision to turn down the offer for the government-sponsored UNESCO-related recognition. A position that their community gets direct access to governmental financial support through other channels was voiced unyieldingly at a consultation meeting gathered by the Estonian National Commission for UNESCO that I attended in 2005. This stance seems to continue, demonstrated by their absence on the national ICH database that evolves based on voluntary submissions.

Indigenous or descendant communities appear to be in a particularly complicated and vulnerable position in the parameters of the worldwide ICH legislation. The state-defined, monitored, and represented agency contravenes the principles of autonomous knowledge systems, self-determination and ownership rights when the degree of state control delineates and regulates issues with the politics of recognition, and possession and access to resources (see Smith and Waterton 2009; Kearney 2009). Even if experts have voiced their concern long ago, according to my observations at the intergovernmental ICH-related meetings, many administrative functionaries have remained reluctant to discuss inclusive measures for indigenous and minority groups in the UNESCO ICH policy-making framework that would call for action on the national level. More substantial moves in that direction have been taken only recently, when the UNESCO Living Heritage Entity negotiated for targeted opportunities with the United Nations Permanent Forum on Indigenous Issues (UNPFII), which demonstrates an effort to seek partnerships to further a common cause.[13] However, the participatory parity does not extend the whole way in the UNESCO-related intangible heritage discourse and representation of indigenous rights: achieving political recognition from their native countries continues to be one of the most contentious struggles for indigenous peoples (see Minde 2003). There should occur a shift toward autonomous representational agency when the interconnectedness of ICH, knowledge systems, and intellectual property become grounded as a right for cultural autonomy and self-determination (cf. Kearney 2009).

Within international organizational attachments and in the configurations of normative instruments the political ecology of the cultural heritage rights is now tied to membership in specific communities rather than to national citizenship (Coombe 2017, p. 390). For example, I have been following the representational practices by and for the Sámi in Northern Europe for a longer period (see Kuutma 2006), where the indigenous Sámi have held so far quite a cautious distance from the state-monitored UNESCO initiatives. This contrasts with their long-term active independent participation in other UN agencies like UNPFII or WIPO, the World Intellectual Property Organization. What complicates the situation is that Sápmi, the area traditionally inhabited by the Sámi, is divided by the borders of the four nation-states, Finland, Sweden, Norway, and Russia. Thus, the expedient task has been to uphold a common Sámi political agenda, which is furthered by the Sámi Parliamentary Council (SPC), which is the co-operational body for the Sámi parliaments in Finland, Norway, and Sweden, participating actively in the UN agencies (see Kulonen et al. 2005, pp. 50, 141, 148, 350, 354). The most instrumental In Sámi politics has been the concept of indigeneity as it is defined in the International Labour Organization (ILO) Convention on Indigenous and Tribal Peoples (No. 169) of 1989 and enforces the practical recognition of the UN Declaration on the Rights of Indigenous Peoples (UNDRIP) from 2007 with the ICH framework significantly missing (see, e.g., Seurujärvi-Kari and Virtanen 2019; Seurujärvi-Kari 2011; UNDRIP 2008). In their promotion of self-government, the Sámi Parliament (Sámediggi) documentation declares the paramount position of their own terms in handling intangible heritage references (see, e.g., *Remissvar* . . . 2010; *Immateriella* . . . 2022). Noteworthily, a certain shift has occurred since 2018 with Sámi representatives attending Intergovernmental Committee meetings of the 2003 Convention as part of the Norwegian delegation, and with a couple of targeted promotional conferences and seminars taking place recently, with effectual input from the designated heritage agencies in Finland and Norway (see, respectively, *#urbánbeaivvit* 2018; *webinar* 2022, hosted by the Sámi Parliament and Arts Council Norway).[14] Ultimately, a productive visionary approach to the issue of group rights for Indigenous Peoples acknowledges "the endemic form of accountability that restricts the larger society on its sovereignty" (Kymlicka 2009, p. 67).

In the alternative and non-discriminative representative structure, "the politics of the possible" entails spaces (re)created from below under the conditions where transnational regimes animate and provide incentives for cultural collectives to assemble, multiply resources, and ways to claim agency (see Clifford 2013). To give another case of bottom-up activism in search for an effective platform for indigenous rights and control of resources, the organization Maasai Cultural Heritage (M.H.C.) representing the Laikipiak Maasai in Northern Kenya has been accredited already for two rounds to provide advisory services to the Intergovernmental Committee and participate in the NGO Forum (Maasai report 2021). It is a community-based organization dedicated to documenting and preserving knowledge resources while representing the Maasai desperate in their fight for pastoralist land use and rights to access traditional resources. What proves my point above, the M.H.C. has collaborated already for over a decade with the Traditional Knowledge Division at WIPO on cultural heritage protection, the latter being so far a much more receptive organizational partner for indigenous recognition.[15]

These instances draw attention to the power and disputed politics of representation where the historical experience defines imaginaries in the present, molds the current dynamics and positionalities, or constrains the redistribution of agency (see Cowan 2009). Self-representational agency and the consecutive resource command imply the empowering recognition of and practical implementation of cultural and social rights also in the ICH framework that is dependent on the state-monitored system.

4.6. Conclusion

To conclude this chapter on ownership and rights for self-determination in resource management, let me return to the observations that Isar (2017) made when analyzing SD from the perspective of cultural policy-making: The major cultural challenge would be to engage with the ecological on the local level. That, in turn, requires enhanced parity by acknowledging grassroots agency in ecosystem management, exploring the potentials and possibilities in heritage-focused practices and livelihoods to generate sustainable existential measures, the empowerment through endorsed sociocultural change. His take likewise calls for a new political economy that enhances local solutions, or in other words, small-scale interventions that respond to global challenges.

Consequently, it urges to profoundly rethink policies and normative activities in the global or national heritage governance: how to attain reduction of inequalities in a meaningful way while encompassing the issues of empowering communities, gender equality, endorsing livelihoods by engaging more directly with economic configurations and affordances on offer. Heritage designation in the UNESCO system transubstantiates a cultural expression or condition into a political and socioeconomic asset, favoring national interests and representational agendas. National ICH governance infrastructure, though, has usually been established to administrate historically significant cultural phenomena, which are also promoted for international listing in the form of fixed descriptions. Hence, that framework targets inscriptions of cultural expressions with retrospective appraisal and nurtures safeguarding initiatives that correspond to the national governmental perspective on resource management.

The various examples introduced in this chapter have aimed to illustrate how heritage policy-making on different levels entails eventually a redistribution of power relations in the process of installing the national heritage framework, and subsequently, access to resources for local actors becomes constrained. The concurrent political and economic implications as well as contested agency in the context of national heritage governance effectuate permissive conditions for appropriation and dismissive dominance over autonomous cultural rights. State-monitored ICH regulatory system signals a representational malfunction and a continued contestation of resource command that goes against the principle of reducing inequalities and the acknowledgement of a dynamic resource. By contrast, the politics of recognition of rights and affordances would generate access to networks, infrastructures, and knowledge that effectuate self-representation as well as instigate a change in positionality also in heritage governance for indigenous and minority groups. Agency in resource command denotes participatory parity where heritage can serve as a vehicle for finding strength through embracing change.

Notes

1 Such problematic unidirectional understanding of sustainability prevails, for example, in Schreiber 2017. The instructive promotional materials published by the designated unit in the field, the UNESCO Living Heritage Entity has nevertheless sought to incorporate the economic, social, and environmental dimensions in synergy when highlighting the requisite of 'holistic approaches to policies' (see UNESCO 2015, p. 3).
2 I have elaborated further on those fieldwork settings in Kuutma 2018.
3 The pertinent informative literature in the ICH field analyses the historical trajectory of references to SDGs and the issue of rights in the UNESCO standard-setting instruments (Blake 2017), the community involvement extending to the ICH – rights – SD formula (Blake 2019), plus intellectual property contingencies (see Deacon 2018; Deacon and Smeets 2018). The studies debating the World Heritage Convention take on sustainability, rights, and economic affordances revolve significantly around the sphere of archaeological heritage and/or representation (e.g., Labadi and Gould 2015; Meskell 2016). The concurrent conservation ideals run up against complex infringements (cf. Logan et al 2010), whereas ICH configuration has instigated a paradigmatic reorientation for WH, accentuating rights-based heritage practice of identification and management, with special focus on Indigenous Peoples (see, e.g., Logan 2012; Disko 2016); local enabling moments for indigenous rights have been studied, e.g., in the museum setting (Mugabowagahunde 2016), or in heritage tourism (Ndoro 2016; Keitumetse and Nthoi 2009), to name just a few.
4 For the anthropological debate on equality that distinguishes the "culture" concept as an ideational realm while being embedded in the issue of rights, see, e.g., Cowan 2009; Benhabib 2002; Cowan, Dembour & Wilson 2001.
5 I have discussed this in greater detail in Kuutma 2018.
6 For a more detailed analysis of the Seto – Suiti collaboration see Kuutma and Vaivade 2021.
7 This event was part of workshops arranged in the EHESS UNESCO frictions project, led by Chiara Bortolotto.
8 An admissive case of shortcomings in state-monitored crafting of "national ICH" may be given in Eritrea, where I attended a promotional ICH-focused meeting in April 2009, and the 2003 Convention was ratified the next year, but a national governance infrastructure with representatives from the nine ethno-linguistic groups was established only in 2018.
9 See Bortolotto 2020.
10 My comments advocated the agency of the local community in any relevant negotiations, and their prerogative to find and debate ways for adapting to the changing living conditions. Interview for the programme *Plekktrumm*, October 4, 2021 https://arhiiv.err.ee/vaata/plekktrumm-kristin-kuutma
11 Personal communication by a community leader, September 30, 2021.
12 Exchange by the Athens seminar participants in September 2019.
13 See the publication "Living Heritage and Indigenous Peoples' https://ich.unesco.org/en/indigenous-peoples
14 The situational and representational parameters vary, here are included instances from Finland, Norway, and Sweden.
15 It should be acknowledged, however, that gender equality and rights remain a highly contested claim in the context of traditional practices in the region (see, e.g., Laher and Sing'Oei 2014).

References

Alivizatou, M. (2021). *Intangible Heritage and Participation: Encounters with Safeguarding Practices*. London–New York: Routledge.

Arantes, A. A. (2013) 'Beyond tradition: Cultural mediation in the safeguarding of intangible cultural heritage.' In: Arizpe, L. (ed.) *Anthropological Perspectives on Intangible Cultural Heritage*. New York: Springer, pp. 39–56.

Bendix, R. F., Eggert, A. and Peselmann, A. (eds.) (2012) *Heritage Regimes and the State*. Göttingen: Göttingen University Press.

Benhabib, S. (2002) *The Claims of Culture: Equality and Diversity in the Global Era*. Princeton–Oxford: Princeton University Press.

Blake, J. (2017) 'Development of UNESCO's 2003 Convention: Creating a new heritage protection paradigm?' In: Stefano, M. L. and Davis, P. (eds.) *Safeguarding Intangible Heritage: Practices and Politics*. London–New York: Routledge, pp. 11–21.

Blake, J. (2019) 'Further reflections on community involvement in safeguarding intangible cultural heritage.' In: Akagawa, N. and Smith, L. (eds.) *The Routledge Companion to Intangible Cultural Heritage*. London–New York: Routledge, pp. 17–35.

Bortolotto, C. (2020) 'Commercialization without over-commercialization: Normative conundrums across heritage rationalities.' *International Journal of Heritage Studies* 27(9), pp. 857–868.

Brightman, M. and Lewis, J. (eds.) (2017) *The Anthropology of Sustainability: Beyond Development and Progress*. London: Palgrave McMillan.

Brown, H., Reed, A. and Yarrow, T. (2017) 'Introduction: Towards an ethnography of meeting.' In: Brown, H., Reed, A. and Yarrow, T. (eds.). Special Issue: Meetings: Ethnographies of Organizational Process, Bureaucracy, and Assembly. *Journal of the Royal Anthropological Institute* 23(S1), pp. 10–26.

Clifford, J. (2013) *Returns: Becoming Indigenous in the Twenty-First Century*. Cambridge, MA: Harvard University Press.

Coombe, R. J. (2017) 'Cultural property's futures and frontiers in the global South.' In: Geismar, H. and Anderson, J. (eds.) *The Routledge Companion to Cultural Property*. London: Routledge, pp. 374–400.

Coombe, R. J. and Weiss L. M. (2015) 'Neoliberalism, heritage regimes, and cultural rights.' In: Meskell, L. (ed.) *Global Heritage: A Reader*. Hoboken–NJ: Wiley-Blackwell, pp. 43–69.

Cowan, J. K. (2009) 'Culture and Rights After Culture and Rights.' In: Goodale, M. (ed.) *Human Rights: An Anthropological Reader*. London: Wiley Blackwell, pp. 305–331.

Cowan, J. K., Dembour, M.-B. and Wilson, R. A. (2001) 'Introduction.' In: Cowan, J., Dembour, M. and Wilson, R. (eds.) *Culture and Rights: Anthropological Perspectives*. Cambridge: Cambridge University Press, pp. 1–26.

Deacon, H. (2018) 'Safeguarding the art of pizza making: Parallel use of the traditional specialities guaranteed scheme and the UNESCO intangible heritage convention.' *International Journal of Cultural Property* 25(4), pp. 515–542.

Deacon, H. and Smeets, R. (2018) 'Intangible heritage safeguarding and intellectual property protection in the context of implementing the UNESCO ICH Convention.' In: Akagawa, N. and Smith, L. (eds.) *Safeguarding Intangible Heritage: Practices and Politics*. London–New York: Routledge, pp. 36–53.

Disko, S. (2016) 'Indigenous peoples' rights and the world heritage convention.' In: Logan, W., NicCraith, M. and Kockel, U. (eds.) *A Companion to Heritage Studies*. London: Wiley-Blackwell, pp. 355–372.

Fotopoulou, S.-V. (2016) 'Notes on the Greek Experience in the Implementation of the Convention for the Safeguarding of the Intangible Cultural Heritage', in Ivanova, M. (ed.) *The Contribution of UNESCO Member States of South-Eastern Europe to the Implementation of the Convention for the Safeguarding of the Intangible Cultural Heritage*. Sofia: RC ICH (Regional Centre UNESCO), pp. 129–141.

Gellner, D. N. and Hirsch, E. (eds.) 2001. *Inside Organizations: Anthropologists at Work*. Oxford: Berg.

Goodale, M. (2009) 'Introduction: Human rights and anthropology.' In: Goodale, M. (ed.). *Human Rights: An Anthropological Reader*. London: Wiley Blackwell, pp. 1–19.

Hafstein, V. Tr. (2018) *Making Intangible Heritage: El Condor Pasa and Other Stories From UNESCO*. Bloomington–IN: Indiana University Press.

Isar, Y. R. (2017) 'Culture, "sustainable development" and cultural policy: A contrarian view.' *International Journal of Cultural Policy* 23(2), pp. 148–158.

Kangas, A., Duxbury, N. and De Beukelaer, C. (2017) 'Introduction: cultural policies for sustainable development.' *International Journal of Cultural Policy* 23(2), pp. 129–132.

Karampampas, P. (2021) '(Re)inventing intangible cultural heritage through the market in Greece.' *International Journal of Heritage Studies* 27(6), pp. 654–667.

Kearney, A. (2009) 'Intangible cultural heritage: Global awareness and local interest.' In: Smith L. and Akagawa N. (eds.) *Intangible Heritage*. Abingdon: Routledge, pp. 209–225.

Keitumetse, S. O. and Nthoi, O. (2009) 'Investigating the impact of world heritage site tourism on the intangible heritage of a community: Tsodilo hills world heritage site, Botswana.' *International Journal of Intangible Heritage* 4, pp. 144–149.

Kulonen, U.-M., Seurujärvi-Kari, I. and Pulkkinen, R. (eds.) (2005) *The Saami: A Cultural Encyclopaedia*. Vammala: Suomalaisen Kirjallisuuden Seura (SKS).

Kuutma, K. (2006) *Collaborative Representations: Interpreting the Creation of a Sámi Ethnography and a Seto Epic*. FF Communications, No. 289. Helsinki: Academia Scientiarum Fennica.

Kuutma, K. (2018) 'Inside the UNESCO apparatus: From intangible representations to tangible effects.' In: Akagawa, N. and Smith, L. (eds.) *Safeguarding Intangible Heritage: Practices and Politics*. London–New York: Routledge, pp. 68–83.

Kuutma, K. and Vaivade, A. (2021). 'Political Imperatives in the Heritage Regime and the Emergent Collaborative Scenarios on the Ground: Case Studies from the Baltics.' *Slovenský národopis/Slovak Ethnology* 69(4), pp. 519–533.

Kymlicka, W. (2009) The good, the bad, and the intolerable: Minority group rights.' In: Goodale, M. (ed.). *Human Rights: An Anthropological Reader*. London: Wiley Blackwell, pp. 58–67.

Labadi, S. and Gould, P. G. (2015) 'Sustainable development: Heritage, community, economics.' In: Meskell, L. (ed.) *Global Heritage: A Reader*. London: Wiley-Blackwell, pp. 196–216.

Laher, R. and Sing'Oei, K. (eds.) (2014) *Indigenous People in Africa: Contestations, Empowerment and Group Rights*. Pretoria: Africa Institute of South Africa.

Logan, W. (2012) 'Cultural diversity, cultural heritage and human rights: Towards heritage management as human rights-based cultural practice.' *International Journal of Heritage Studies* 18(3), pp. 231–244.

Logan, W., Langfield, M. and Nic Craith, M. (2010) 'Intersecting concepts and practices.' In: Langfield, M., Logan, W. and Nic Craith, M. (eds.) *Cultural Diversity, Heritage and Human Rights: Intersections in Theory and Practice*. London: Routledge, pp. 3–20.

Meissner, M. (2021) *Intangible Cultural Heritage and Sustainable Development: The Valorisation of Heritage Practices*. Heritage Studies–Cham: Springer.

Meskell, L. (2016) 'Heritage and cosmopolitanism.' In: Logan, W., Nic Craith, M. and Kockel, U. (eds.) *A Companion to Heritage Studies*. London: Wiley Blackwell, pp. 479–490.

Minde, H. (ed.) (2003) *Indigenous Peoples: Resource Management and Global Rights*. Delft: Eburon Academic Publishers.

Mosse, D. (2005) *Cultivating Development: An Ethnography of Aid Policy and Practice*. London–Ann Arbor: Pluto Press.

Mugabowagahunde, M. (2016) 'African indigenous heritage in colonial and postcolonial museums: The case of the batwa of Africa's great lakes region.' In: Logan, W., Nic Craith, M. and Kockel, U. (eds.) *A Companion to Heritage Studies*. London: Wiley Blackwell, pp. 146–159.

Müller, B. (2013) *The Gloss of Harmony: The Politics of Policy-Making in Multilateral Organisations*. Anthropology, Culture and Society series. New York: Pluto Press.
Ndoro, W. (2016) 'World heritage sites in Africa: What are the benefits of nomination and inscription?' In: Logan, W., Nic Craith, M. and Kockel, U. (eds.) *A Companion to Heritage Studies*. London: Wiley Blackwell, pp. 392–409.
Schreiber, H. (ed.) (2017) *Intangible Cultural Heritage: Safeguarding Experiences in Central and Eastern European Countries and China: 10th Anniversary of the Entry into Force of the 2003 Convention through the Prism of Sustainable Development*. Warszawa: National Heritage Board of Poland.
Seurujärvi-Kari, I. (2011) 'Alkuperäiskansatutkimus; alkuperäiskansaliike ja saamelaiset.' In: Seurujärvi-Kari, I., Halinen, P. and Pulkkinen, R. (eds.) *Saamentutkimus tänään*. Helsinki: Finnish Literature Society.
Seurujärvi-Kari, I. and Virtanen, P. K. (2019) 'Sámi reconciliation in practice: Long and ongoing process.' In: Datta, R. (ed.) *Reconciliation in Practice: A Cross-Cultural Perspective*. Winnipeg: Fernwood Publishing.
Shore, C. and Wright, S. (1997) 'Policy: A new field of anthropology.' In: Shore, C. and Wright, S. (eds.) *Anthropology of Policy: Critical Perspectives on Governance and Power*. London: Routledge, pp. 3–39.
Skounti, A. (2009) 'The authentic illusion: Humanity's intangible cultural heritage, the Moroccan experience.' In: Smith, L. and Akagawa, N. (eds.) *Intangible Heritage*. London: Routledge, pp. 74–92.
Smith, L. and Waterton, E. (2009) *Heritage, Communities and Archaeology*. London: Duckworth Publishers.
Wiktor-Mach, D. (2020) 'What role for culture in the age of sustainable development? UNESCO's advocacy in the 2030 agenda negotiations.' *International Journal of Cultural Policy* 26(3), pp. 312–327.
Yarrow, T. (2017) "'Where knowledge meets: Heritage expertise at the intersection of people, perspective, and place." In: Brown, H., Reed, A. and Yarrow, T. (eds.) Special Issue: Meetings: Ethnographies of Organizational Process, Bureaucracy, and Assembly.' *Journal of the Royal Anthropological Institute* 23(S1), pp. 95–109.

Documents and websites

Immateriella . . . 2022 = Immateriella kulturarv www.sametinget.se/163873 (Accessed: 27 August 2022)
Maasai report 2021 = *Maasai Cultural Heritage–M.C.H Activity Report* https://ich.unesco.org/doc/src/52821-EN.pdf (Accessed: 15 December 2022)
Remissvar . . . 2010 = *Remissvar Immateriellt kulturarv [PDF] 2010–08–09*www.sametinget.se/14571 (Accessed: 27 August 2022)
UNESCO 2015 = *Intangible Cultural Heritage and Sustainable Development*. Paris: UNESCO 2015 (kit #8). https://ich.unesco.org/en/kit#8; https://ich.unesco.org/doc/src/34299-EN.pdf (Accessed: 05 September 2022)
UNDRIP 2008. *United Nations Declaration on the Rights of Indigenous Peoples*. United Nations. https://www.un.org/esa/socdev/unpfii/documents/DRIPS_en.pdf
#urbánbeaivvit = Sámi Cultural Intangible Heritage Conference May 23rd–24th, Sajos #urbánbeaivvit 17–5–2018 www.samediggi.fi/2018/05/17/sami-njalmmalas-arbevieruid-konfereansa-23-24-5-2018-sajosis-urbanbeaivvit/?lang=en
webinar 2022 = hosted by the Sámi Parliament and Arts Council Norway = Webinar *Practitioners Experiences in the Traditional Arts Economy*, June 9 www.kulturradet.no/kalender/hendelse/-/practitioners-experiences-in-the-traditional-arts-economy

5

MISAPPROPRIATION, INTELLECTUAL PROPERTY, AND ETHICS

Benedetta Ubertazzi

5.1. Introduction

Misappropriations occur when practicing communities consider individual members of the community, the State, tour operators, researchers, or other outside persons to have inappropriately obtained unjust rewards through the exploitation of intangible cultural heritage (ICH). Misappropriations of ICH can consist of wide-scale copying of traditional designs, motifs, symbols, and artworks for commercial gain without the knowledge or permission of communities.

The Brundtland Report (1987) defined sustainable development as "development that meets the needs of the present without compromising the ability of future generations to meet their own needs." The sustainable development paradigm is composed of three "integrated and indivisible" dimensions: social, environmental, and economic. Misappropriation, which consists of obtaining unjust rewards through exploitation, although often framed as primarily an economic challenge, may have profound implications for all three dimensions of sustainable development.

Misappropriations pose many challenges to sustainable development and cultural heritage. Approached from an economic perspective, sustainable development depends upon stable, equitable, and inclusive economic growth, as based on sustainable patterns of production and consumption. Rosati (2020, p. 26). Alteration of traditional practices and products may result from commercialization, which can lead to the adaptation of such practices and products to fit the taste of potential consumers, whether that be tourists or the general public (Petrillo, 2019, p. 14). This can damage the sustainability of heritage in both the present and the future. Therefore, a major concern for indigenous artists and communities is the integrity of their creations. As such, the obstacles in the preservation of ICH today

DOI:10.4324/9781003244158-8

are not only the result of disuse or abandonment by members of the communities concerned but also the result of abuse or misappropriation by third parties. This chapter will begin by analyzing examples of misappropriations relating to elements that are already inscribed in UNESCO ICH Lists. Next, an evaluation of the capacity of cease-and-desist mechanisms and ethical principles to prevent misappropriations is offered. Finally, this chapter will examine the extent to which intellectual property rights (IPRs) can help communities prevent and fight against misappropriations. Throughout, this chapter will engage with cases in which the author has been directly involved, to demonstrate that while no measure in isolation can be a "silver bullet" against misappropriation, the more legal measures that are adopted, the stronger the position of the community to protect cultural heritage from the threat of misappropriation.

5.2. Misappropriation and safeguarding measures

One example of misappropriation arose in relation to the ICH element *Chhau dance* inscribed on the Representative List of the Intangible Cultural Heritage of Humanity in 2010.[1] *Chhau dance* is a "tradition from eastern India that enacts episodes from epics including the Mahabharata and Ramayana, local folklore and abstract themes" (UNESCO, *Chhau Dance*, 2010) which I engaged with through my work for the Heritage Sensitive Intellectual Property and Marketing Strategies (HIPAMS) Project.[2] The purpose of the HIPAMS Project is "to investigate how developing 'heritage-sensitive' intellectual property protection strategies can give communities greater control over the commercialization of their heritage while contributing to its safeguarding and viability" (HIPAMS, no date). As an academic, intellectual property lawyer and UNESCO facilitator, the Project was therefore well-suited to my personal areas of expertise. The purpose of the HIPAMS project is also consistent with the approach of the UNESCO (2003) Convention for the safeguarding of intangible cultural heritage (ICHC), and specifically with the Overall Results Framework of the ICHC Guidance Note 14.1 of the Framework states that "Forms of legal protection, such as intellectual property rights and privacy rights, [should be] provided to ICH practitioners, bearers and their communities when their ICH is exploited by others for commercial or other purposes." The purpose of HIPAMS is to develop "heritage-sensitive" intellectual property protection strategies that can give communities greater control over the commercialization of their heritage, therefore correlating closely with Guidance Note 14.1, and by extension, the approach of the ICHC.

Returning to the element of *Chhau dance*, the "vocabulary of movement" of the dance "includes mock combat techniques, stylized gaits of birds and animals and movements modeled on the chores of village housewives" and the dance "is performed at night in an open space to traditional and folk melodies" (UNESCO, *Chhau Dance*, 2010). Additionally, *Chhau dance* plays an integral role in binding together "people from different social strata and ethnic backgrounds with diverse social practices, beliefs, professions and languages" (UNESCO, *Chhau Dance*, 2010). For over 200 years, the dance has been performed only by men (UNESCO Office New Delhi, 2020). The Bengali film *Jobordokhol*,[3] streamed by Zee5 in 2019, used Mousumi Choudhury's story; a key character in the film is Mita, who is the leader of an all-female Chhau dance group. The film used footage of Mousumi (and other dancers from her all-female group) dancing in a mask. Mousumi's face is never revealed, however; when she removes the mask at the end of her performance, it is Mita's face that is revealed. At no stage does the film credit or mention Mousumi or her fellow dancers. Due to the lack of official recognition of the use of her story and footage of her performing *Chhau dance* for the film, the filmmakers inappropriately obtained unjust rewards through the exploitation of Mousumi Choudhury. Moreover, the absence of any recognition of Mousumi and her fellow dancers has denied her and her community the possibility of using recognition arising from the film to support *Chhau dance* (HIPAMS, *Chhau Dance*, 2019)

A further example, which I worked on as a lawyer is misappropriation relating to the *Ceremonial Ritual de los Voladores*. This ceremonial ritual, which was registered on the Representative List of the Intangible Cultural Heritage of Humanity by Mexico in 2009,[4] constitutes a dance associated with fertility. It is performed by ethnic groups of Mexico and Central America, in particular the Totonac people of the Mexican state of Veracruz. The objective of the ceremony is to express profound respect for nature and the spiritual universe, as well as the living harmony between both. Beer companies Heineken (based in the Netherlands) and its daughter company Cerveceria Moctezuma (based in Mexico) included images alluding to the ceremony in their labels of the beer "cervezaIndio." The community understood this as trivializing their cultural expressions and violating the recognition given by UNESCO and its status of intangible cultural heritage (Camacho, 2017). The community, therefore, brought a legal case against Cerveceria Moctezuma in Mexico, which ultimately resulted in the Mexican National Commission on Human Rights enacting a general recommendation on the protection of the cultural heritage of indigenous people and communities of the Mexican Republic.[5] This recommendation recognized two key points regarding ICH. First, it described in detail all cases of misappropriation of ICH in Mexico by multinational companies and concluded by characterizing these misappropriations as human rights violations, enforceable before courts. Second, it recognized the role of sui generis IPRs in protecting ICH (Bahar, 2016).

A third and final example of third-party misappropriation with which I engaged as a lawyer arose in relation to Mevleviye.[6] The Mevleviye community considers that Rumi vodka inappropriately exploits their cultural heritage due to the use of the name "Rumi" alongside the use of an image of a Mevleviye dancer on bottles of vodka. The Mevleviye is an ancient ascetic Sufi order and today can be found in many Turkish communities throughout the world. Traditionally, dancers used to receive 1,001 days of reclusive training within the Mevlevi houses (*mevlevihane*), where they learned about ethics, codes of behavior, and beliefs by practicing prayer, religious music, poetry, and dance. The Mevlevi Sema ceremony, which is of great cultural, spiritual, and religious significance to the Mevleviye community, has been inscribed on the Representative List of the Intangible Cultural Heritage of Humanity since 2008.[7] This ceremony is one of the oldest rituals of the Mevlevi Order, founded in 1273 in Konya (Turkey) by Mevlâna Celâleddin-I Rûmi.[8] The community, therefore, feels that the use of the name "Rumi," coupled with the use of the image of a Mevleviye dancer, without asking for or receiving permission to use the image, amounts to misappropriation.

5.2.1. Codes of ethics and cease and desist letters

Communities typically try to safeguard their ICH element against misappropriation through mechanisms like codes of ethics and cease and desist letters. Cease and desist letters can be sent by communities to misappropriators to make them "cease and desist" the acts of misappropriation. In the case of the misappropriation of the Ritual Ceremony of the Voladores by Cerveceria Moctezuma and Heineken (its Dutch parent company), the ICH-practicing community sent a cease-and-desist letter to both the Mexican and Dutch companies. This letter emphasized that the ceremony has been considered to be an intangible cultural heritage by UNESCO since its registration on the Representative List of the Intangible Cultural Heritage of Humanity by Mexico in 2009. Thus, the community required the beer companies to immediately cease their misappropriations and indemnify community representatives. The letter was based upon the community's petition under the relevant Mexican law on sui generis copyright, as well as under other international human rights instruments. Despite this letter, and the strong reaction of support from the community against the beer companies, these companies did not behave in the expected manner and perpetrated their infringement and the community had to start legal proceedings in Mexico.[9]

In the case of the misappropriation of the Mevlevi Sema ceremony by "Rumi vodka," the 22nd Descendant of the Mevlâna Celâleddin-i Rûmi and the community, with my support among others, the community sent a letter[10] to Wijnhandel De filosoof (the company that advertises and distributes Rumi vodka) alleging that its commercial behavior infringed several legal provisions. The letter emphasized that, *inter alia*, "Wijnhandel De filosoof's use of our sign and name is a culturally insensitive misappropriation of the Mevleviye community's intangible cultural heritage and has caused distress, discomfort and offence to the community" and "Wijnhandel De filosoof's use of the sign constitutes a violation of the Mevleviye community's fundamental human right to intangible cultural heritage that is recognised and guaranteed under international and European Union law." The liquor company included images of the "Whirling Dervish" in their labels of the liquor "Rumi Vodka with Persian spices." The community understood this as trivializing their cultural expressions and violating the recognition given by UNESCO and its status of intangible cultural heritage. Thus, in the letter, the community required the liquor companies to immediately cease and desist their misappropriation. Further, the letter from the community reserved the right to take appropriate legal action against Wijnhandel De filosoof. The community also notified their intention of bringing this matter to the attention of the Turkish Government to gain the support of the Government for community action. However, Wijnhandel De filosoof did not reply and instead posted the cease-and-desist letter on social media in a very disrespectful manner.

With particular regard to ethical codes, in 2015 the Intergovernmental Committee endorsed 12 ethical principles for safeguarding ICH. These principles "represent a set of overarching aspirational principles" and "are intended to serve as a basis for the development of specific codes of ethics . . . adapted to local and sectoral conditions" (UNESCO, no date). One context in which codes of ethics have been used relates to the misappropriation of Mousumi Choudhury's story discussed earlier in this chapter. Following the misappropriation, the Chhau community worked alongside the HIPAMS team to develop a Chhau Dance Code. This Code contains several principles that are embedded in Indian law, such as the right of attribution for performers, and several other principles that emanate from general human rights norms, such as the right to culture. The Code lays out the hopes and expectations of the members of the *Chhau dance* community in their dealings with these different groups who draw on and often profit from their dance. The Chhau Dance Code was distributed among these groups generally, and each time that Chhau dancers interacted with one of these groups for a particular project or event, the organizers are individually given a copy of this Code. The aim is that through this process, respect will be shown for the Chhau dancers and their intangible heritage, and they will be given due acknowledgment and remuneration to ensure that their heritage continues.

From a legal perspective, codes of ethics are characterized as guidelines. Guidelines function in much the same way as contracts; they are binding on those who voluntarily accept to be bound by them. Thus, they can only be partially enforced since in legal terms, "guidelines, no matter how good they are, are just guidelines. They are seldom legally enforced, and they often only apply within a certain context" (Tunón, Kvarnström, and Lerner, 2016, p. 76). The partially enforceable nature of codes of ethics (and codes of conduct) is evident in the examples of such codes provided by UNESCO.[11] One such example states that "codes that are not complied with *can* also have legal implications for code adherents and others" who voluntarily accept to follow them.

Ultimately, ethical guidelines and protocols and cease-and-desist letters can provide a degree of protection against misappropriation for ICH. However, as ethical guidelines and protocols only apply to those who agree to be bound by them and cease-and-desist letters are not in themselves legally binding, they leave misappropriators with the power to choose whether or not to carry out or continue their misappropriation.

5.2.2. Consumer campaigns and policy briefs

One factor that can affect the choice made by misappropriators – particularly when they misappropriate for commercial gain – are campaigns by consumers, such as boycotting. In one case of cultural appropriation consumer campaigns successfully led to the misappropriator publicly acknowledging and seeking to rectify their misappropriation. In this case, Papercut Patterns, a New Zealand company of pattern creators, labeled a new pattern of jackets as "Kochi Kimono." The pattern of the jacket labeled as "Kochi Kimono" "was a square-cut short jacket, with optional side ties" (Wahlquist, 2019). Influenced by the creation and advertisement of "Kochi Kimono" jackets on social media, the Instagram followers of Papercut Patterns, specifically inexpert seamstresses, started creating their own patterns for jackets and shared their results on Instagram, by using the hashtag #Kochikimono, comprising the name of a traditional Japanese dress, "Kimono." Kimono is considered the national dress of Japan with loose long sleeves and is typically tied with a sash. This popularity, of tagging a particular design of jacket as "#kochikimono" continued for 18 months until Helen Kim, an Asian American woman, pointed out that labeling any design of jacket as "Kimono," a name of a Japanese traditional dress, "without any connection beyond a certain boxiness about the sleeves to the traditional Japanese dress, was cultural appropriation" (BBC, 2019). There was much debate on the topic of cultural appropriation on social media regarding "Kimono" as well as an interview of Helen Kim, who initiated awareness raising of the cultural significance behind the design of the traditional Japanese dress, "Kimono" through a leading newspaper company, the Guardian. Following this awareness campaign on social media as well as in print media, Papercut Patterns promised to rename the pattern of the jacket in question to "kochi" and also publicly thanked everyone "who let [them] know the mistake [they] made in giving one of [their] patterns a culturally sensitive name" (Wahlquist, 2019).

A further approach that can be employed to prevent the misappropriation of cultural heritage is the use of policy briefs, which I explored in relation to the *Chhau Dance* as part of the HIPAMS Project. "A policy brief is a concise summary of a particular issue, the policy options to deal with it, and some recommendations on the best option" and is "aimed at government policymakers and others who are interested in formulating or influencing policy" (UN FAO, 2011). Policy briefs, therefore, provide communities with the opportunity to engage with policymakers and play an active role in identifying how existing policy frameworks can be adapted to better safeguard cultural heritage.[12]

As the case studies of cease-and-desist letters, codes of ethics, and consumer campaigns indicate, these mechanisms can prevent misappropriation, but they are not a guarantee that misappropriations will not occur. An additional consideration, with specific regard to consumer campaigns, is that even when such campaigns are successful, the group that effectively combats the misappropriation is not (solely) the community that has suffered the misappropriation, but rather the consumers who make the choice to support them. Similarly, while policy briefs enable communities to play a more active role in identifying how misappropriation can be prevented, the power to achieve change is held by the policymakers to whom policy briefs are addressed. ICH-practicing communities, groups, or individuals, therefore, need legally binding mechanisms that can be enforced in court to complement the measures discussed earlier and give them an active role in preventing misappropriations.

5.3. Intellectual property and other rights as protective safeguarding measures

One set of mechanisms that can be enforced in court and used to help communities fight misappropriations are intellectual property rights (IPRs).[13] IPRs can help communities combat misappropriation in two ways. First, they can provide positive protection by being adopted on intellectual creations that derive from ICH. Second, they can provide defensive protection by allowing communities to challenge third parties that register IPRs on intellectual creations that violate ICH.

5.3.1. Positive protection

Positive protection of ICH occurs when communities register IPRs to protect their own ICH (Ubertazzi, 2010). Examples, with which I have been directly involved as a legal advisor is of positive protection in action, are the collective trademark registered on *Traditional violin craftsmanship in Cremona* (Italy); the individual trademark registered on *Mediterranean Diet* (Italy); geographical indications (GIs) registered in relation to food products which form part of *Alpine Food Heritage* (which is currently being nominated to the UNESCO Lists); and the Traditional Speciality Guaranteed (TSG) registered on *The Art of Neapolitan "Pizzaiuolo"* (Italy). Where IPRs are registered on ICH, they enable practicing communities to enforce the IPR before a court and thereby achieve legal protection for ICH.

However, the positive protection of ICH through IPRs can be problematic. The case study of *Traditional violin craftsmanship in Cremona* demonstrates that sometimes communities may decide that the positive protection already afforded by the registered IPR is not sufficient to protect against misappropriation. In this case, the violin-making community of Cremona is considering revising the IPR already granted (a collective trademark) and adding a new IPR protection strategy. The existing collective trademark has positive impacts on Cremona violinmakers from a misappropriation perspective. It protects artisanal characteristics since to be part of the Consortium that registered the trademark,[14] a violinmaker must produce the instrument entirely by hand according to the ethical principles dictated by the specification. The trademark also establishes a system of controls to verify that "Cremona Liuteria" trademarked instruments are made in full compliance with the trademark regulation.

Nonetheless, the trademark may allow misappropriations to occur even though an IPR has been registered. Although the trademark establishes a system of controls to ensure compliance with the trademark regulation, the body responsible for enforcing the system of controls is a Controlling Body formed mainly by the Directive Council of the Consortium. Clearly, the Controlling Body is not an entirely impartial body. A further problem with the existing trademark is its lack of representativeness; the Consortium that registered the trademark represents only 55 out of the 167 violinmakers operating in Cremona. Another problematic feature of the "Cremona Liuteria" trademark is that it does not establish a minimum level of production. At the time of writing, approximately 7% of violins are produced respecting the regulation. This low percentage is not, in and of itself a problem, since "the beauty of violin making is that . . . almost every craftsman has a particular way of understanding the work" (Sora et al., 2020) and the plurality of understandings of the craft is part of the community's rich heritage. However, violin makers can use generic terms such as "violin makers" (Liuteria) and "Cremona" in relation to violins that have not been made in line with the regulation. This may create confusion with the trademark "Cremona Liuteria." Indeed, this second problem, of no minimum production of instruments, contributes to the first problem (lack of representativeness). Many of the violinmakers who are not members of the consortium dislike the trademark and are not members, precisely because the trademark establishes no minimum production of violins that must be made according to the trademark specification. This, they feel, opens the door to internal competition among violinmakers. As such, in Cremona, there is a desire among members of the community for violin makers to "openly declare" the "different types of violin making" used in the creation of each violin to ensure it is clear how each violin has been made and which violins produced in Cremona have been made in line with the processes safeguarded by UNESCO.

The community would therefore like to register a GI, which they believe would offer a broader protection than that offered by the existing collective trademark.[15] GIs establish protection that is more closely related to a territory as far as both geographical origin and tradition are concerned than that offered by trademarks. This is because the quality standards of European Union (EU) GIs are attributable to the place of origin of the product and to the long-standing traditional knowledge developed by the local people, which are fixed in the relevant specifications. This contrasts with the quality standards of collective trademarks, which, as shown in the previous paragraph, are fixed by regulations, which are essentially acts of private autonomy. Furthermore, GIs allow the monopolization of a specific geographical name in relation to the specific good on which the GI is registered. Hence, the registration of a GI means that all products using the registered geographic name would have to comply with the GI specification. Consequently, GIs can offer a greater level of security as well as facilitate more binding controls to be carried out by the entire community. The registration of a GI could therefore resolve many of the loopholes that allow for misappropriation under the protection currently offered by the "Cremona Liuteria" trademark.

While the registration of GI protection may be beneficial for the community of Cremona violinmakers, it must be noted that the registration of GI protection is not in itself a guarantee against misappropriation. Indeed, the case study of Bitto Cheese, which I engaged with in my work creating intellectual property guidelines for the element *Alpine Food Heritage*, provides a perfect example of the risks that may arise from the registration of GIs. Specifically, this case study reveals the problems that may arise when GIs are registered without the participation of the whole ICH-practicing community and are consequently registered with specifications that do not accurately reflect the practices of that community.

Bitto cheese has been produced since at least the fifteenth century and is a product of the Bitto Valleys in Valtellina in Lombardy (Rinallo and Pitardi, 2019). In April 1995, Bitto cheese obtained a Protected Designation of Origin (PDO); as a result, the new Consortium of Valtellina Casera and Bitto was founded. The approved product specification introduced significant changes to traditional Bitto-making processes. First, the PDO specification enlarged the production area to the entire Sondrio province, promoting the transfer of knowledge related to Bitto production to other areas of the province where Bitto-like cheese had never previously been produced. Second, the specification removed distinctions previously made between Bitto cheese and other cheeses from the province. Third, the production process mandated by the PDO specification did not require that the cheese must be produced in Alpine pastures during the summer. Finally, the percentage of goat milk allowed was reduced from the traditional 20–30 % to only 10 %, with an option of not using goat milk at all. The PDO specifications also permitted the use of animal fodder and enzymes and introduced various other provisions that overall, represented a remarkable deviation from tradition. Rather than protecting Bitto cheese and the communities that had traditionally produced it, the PDO caused division, with some Bitto Valleys producers founding a Bitto Committee to safeguard the historical production method and area in 1994. Unable to use the Bitto name due to the presence of the PDO, producers making cheese according to traditional Bitto-making methods and located in the Bitto Valley were no longer allowed to use the Bitto name for their product. In the years since the registration of the PDO, there have been multiple conflicts between the PDO Consortium and cheese producers from the Bitto Valley.[16]

As is shown by the earlier analysis of GIs in relation to violinmaking in Cremona, GIs have the capacity to provide positive protection of ICH. However, the goods that can benefit from such protection are limited, as EU GIs cannot be registered on non-agricultural goods. Despite the desire of the violinmakers of Cremona to use such protection, at the time of writing, they are unable to do so. The example of Bitto Cheese highlights further challenges that are raised by using EU GIs for positive protection of ICH, including the need for the engagement of the full ICH-practicing community and accuracy in the specifications of the GI if such IPRs are to provide an effective safeguard against misappropriation.

5.3.2. Defensive protection

IPRs can help communities combat misappropriation not only through positive protection, by being adopted on intellectual creations that derive from ICH, but also through defensive protection, namely by allowing communities to challenge third parties that register IPRs on intellectual creations that would be determinantal to the ICH practice. An example of defensive protection arose in a case surrounding a three-dimensional trademark registered by Lindt. The European Community trademark registered by Lindt was of a gold-colored chocolate bunny in a sitting position, wearing a red ribbon with a bell attached, with the words Lindt GOLDHASE in brown lettering. Lindt claimed local manufacturers were infringing the trademark by producing products similar to the trademarked Lindt bunny. Small producers successfully counter-argued, however, claiming that "Lindt knew that in both Austria and Germany, a tradition existed from at least 1930 of marketing chocolate bunnies, commonly called Osterhasen (Easter bunnies), in shape and colour very similar to the one represented by the Lindt three-dimensional mark" (Ubertazzi, 2010. Thus, Austrian and German communities who bear the traditional heritage of chocolate Easter bunnies were able to argue that the trademark lacked the "distinctive character" that trademarks must possess. Communities were able to protect that heritage, through an IPR registered by a third party on a product that misappropriated their cultural heritage.

Defensive protection of ICH can also be associated with complementary rights that communities could enforce together with IPRs. A first complementary right is that of contractual approaches aimed at providing communities with access and benefit-sharing legal mechanisms. A contractual approach to safeguarding allows communities to give prior and informed consent to uses of their cultural heritage by allowing the ICH-practicing community to define clauses for both access and benefit-sharing. By defining access, communities can determine what the other party is entitled to access and on what terms. In defining benefit-sharing, communities can determine not only how financial gains should be shared (where relevant), but also key issues that sometimes are crucial to communities, such as acknowledgments and credits. Hence, a contractual approach aims to give "the owners of the culture the right to control it and its uses" (Lixinski, 2020).

Access and benefit-sharing agreements have several qualities that are valuable in the context of protecting ICH. As contracts, they can recognize and work in concert with other existing safeguarding measures (such as IPRs). Furthermore, they can be tailored to the specific interests of communities, and unlike IPRs (which can normally be enforced only in their country of registration), contracts can state a choice of law and a choice of forum (Lixinski, 2020). This last quality is particularly valuable given the often-multinational nature of misappropriation. Contractual arrangements do have their disadvantages, however. Contracts, as discussed earlier in relation to ethical protocols and guidelines, are only binding on the parties that consent to the terms of the contract. Additionally, communities can be at a disadvantage in negotiating contracts, as such negotiations can give the other, stronger party the opportunity to use the contract to abuse the ICH-practicing community.[17] To avoid this happening, codes of ethics and cultural protocols may be used to help regulate how ICH-bearing communities are approached by those who are interested in negotiating with them.

One type of contract is a Creative Commons (CC) license.[18] These licenses allow creative material to be shared and reused under terms that are flexible and legally sound.[19] All CC licenses "require that users provide attribution . . . to the creator when the material is used and shared." CC licenses are non-exclusive, allowing creators and owners to enter dual or multi-licensing arrangements. In other words, they "can enter into additional, different licensing arrangements for the same material at any time." Once granted, CC licenses are non-revocable, with the exception of the breach, in which case the license is only terminated for the licensee in breach. CC may be combined with one or more of three additional license elements: NonCommercial, which prohibits commercial use of the material; NoDerivatives, which prohibits the sharing of adaptations of the material; and ShareAlike, which requires adaptations of the material be released under the same license. CC licenses may be applied to many categories of material, such as educational resources, databases, and public sector information. However, it is recommended that CC licenses not be applied to computer software and hardware, as well as to materials that are no longer copyright protected "or are otherwise in the public domain." CC licenses operate only when applied to copyrighted material, and furthermore, "only when a particular use would otherwise not be permitted by copyright." CC licenses also apply to neighboring rights and sui generis database rights. Thus, CC licenses' terms and conditions do not apply to elements of licensed public domain works or permitted uses under applicable copyright exceptions and limitations. Similarly, CC licenses cannot impose contractual restrictions on the uses of materials unless there is an underlying copyright. Various judicial decisions enforcing CC licenses reflect their enforceability around the world. The "severability" clause contained in CC licenses allows courts to invalidate unenforceable provisions, thereby deeming the remaining provisions enforceable.[20]

CC licenses seek to "forge a balance inside the traditional 'all rights reserved' setting that copyright law creates" and create a 'standardized way' for creators 'to grant copyright permissions to their creative work' (CC Licenses, no date). As such, these licenses may be useful in many situations where copyright applies, and consequently, they may have a very broad application in the heritage sector. One use of CC licenses that I have been directly involved in, relates to the outputs of the HIPAMS Project. Many of the Project outputs were original works to which copyright applies. The purpose of this Project, as previously cited, was to "investigate how developing 'heritage-sensitive' intellectual property protection strategies can give communities greater control over the commercialization of their heritage, while contributing to its safeguarding and viability." It was therefore the desire of the Project that many of the Project outputs, including, inter alia, the HIPAMS toolkit, should be shared and used with greater freedom than traditional copyright allows. The Project team, therefore, used CC licenses to allow the outputs of the Project to be shared and reused, hopefully for the benefit of ICH communities in India and other countries.

5.4. Conclusions

Misappropriations occur when an unjust reward is gained by a party from the inappropriate exploitation of ICH. Engaging with misappropriation sheds light on the ways in which heritage sustains communities, is sustained by communities, and how fragile that process of mutual sustenance can be. Misappropriation also reflects how making information about their heritage widely available can be important for communities, and how this can contribute to keeping the heritage alive. At the same time, for this to work, communities need to be able to protect their heritage against misappropriation, which can threaten their livelihoods and prevent them from practicing their heritage, thereby preventing sustainable development of the community.

Communities can guard against misappropriation through mechanisms like codes of ethics and cease and desist letters. However, these mechanisms do not always provide effective protection against misappropriation. Consumer campaigns and policy briefs can provide further mechanisms to combat misappropriation, but again, these are not always effective in an ICH framework and give ICH-practicing communities themselves at best, limited capacity to actively combat misappropriation. Legal tools like contractual rights and IPRs are therefore important for communities, as they provide additional protection and give communities a legal basis upon which to prevent misappropriation. IPRs can provide both positive and defensive protection for ICH. Positive protection involves communities registering IPRs on their own ICH to achieve the desired protection. Although IPRs can provide effective legal protection for ICH, examination of both the "Cremona Liuteria" trademark and the PDO registered on Bitto Cheese reveals that to achieve positive protection of ICH through IPRs, the correct IPR(s) must be selected to provide the type of protection the ICH-practicing community desires. Additionally, IPRs must be drafted with full community participation, as well as exceptional care and accuracy, if they are to provide protection against misappropriation. Defensive protection entails communities defending their ICH through IPRs that infringe on their ICH. Other legal rights complementary to IPRs can also be implemented to provide defensive protection for ICH-practicing communities. Image and personality rights provide a means through which ICH can be protected. Contractual rights provide a means for communities to give prior, informed consent to certain uses of their culture and access benefits. Finally, AI can be adopted together with IPRs and contractual access and benefit-sharing agreements, to foster ethical and community values. Digitization, AI, and contractual rights can all be implemented together with IPRs to offer protection for ICH against misappropriations. To conclude, no one measure can be a complete solution to the challenge of misappropriation. However, it is contented here that, when implemented with full participation and inclusivity, the more legal measures are adopted, the stronger the position of the community to protect their cultural heritage from the threat of misappropriation, transmit the practice to future generations, and sustain themselves.

Notes

1 Chhau Dance was inscribed in 2010 by the Intergovernmental Committee for the Safeguarding of the Intangible Cultural Heritage, Fifth Session, Nairobi, Kenya, November 15 to 19, 2010, Decision 5.COM 6.15 [Online]. Available at: https://ich.unesco.org/en/decisions/5.COM/6.15/. (Accessed 10 April 2020)

2 See HIPAMS, 'HIPAMS India' [Online]. Available at: https://hipamsindia.org/. (Accessed 18 July 2021)

3 For a trailer of the film, see ZeeBanglaCinema (2019), "Jobordokhol" [Film]. Trailer available at: https://youtu.be/rhN-PcLmqRw/. (Accessed February 14, 2020)

4 For a description of the "Ceremonial Ritual de los Voladores," see UNESCO, "Report of the Intergovernmental Committee for the Safeguarding of the Intangible Cultural Heritage," 4th session (Abu Dhabi, September 28, 2009, to October 2, 2009) RL09 No. 00175; UNESCO, "Ritual ceremony of the Voladores" [Online]. Available at: https://ich.unesco.org/en/RL/ritual-ceremony-of-the-voladores-00175/. (Accessed July 27, 2019)

5 See Comisión Nacional de los Derechos Humanos de México, *Recomendación general no 35 sobre la protección del patrimonio cultural de los pueblos y comunidades indígenas de la república mexicana*. Ciudad de México, January 28, 2019, www.cndh.org.mx/documento/recomendacion-general-352019/. (Accessed 10 April 2020)

6 There are numerous examples of misappropriations beyond the three discussed at the start of this chapter. For a recent example of the misappropriation of music, see Ommy Dallah, "Kenyan Musician In Trouble With Tuku Music Over 'Todii' Song" (April 22, 2020) [Online]. Available at: https://ommydalla.co.ke/buzz/item/1489-kenyan-musician-in-trouble-with-tuku-music-over-todii/. (Accessed April 30, 2020)

7 Mevlevi Sema Ceremony was inscribed in 2008 by the Intergovernmental Committee for the Safeguarding of the Intangible Cultural Heritage, Third session, Istanbul, Turkey, November 4 to 8, 2008, Decision 3.COM 1 [Online]. Available at: https://ich.unesco.org/en/decisions/3.COM/1/. (Accessed 10 April 2020)

8 For more information on the ceremony see UNESCO, "Mevlevi Sema ceremony" [Online]. Available at: https://ich.unesco.org/en/RL/mevlevi-sema-ceremony-00100/. (Accessed April 10, 2020)

9 This legal proceeding in Mexico could not stop the Dutch Heineken from perpetrating the infringement.

10 I saw the letter, and I was one of the counselors of the community together with Prof. Scovazzi, Professor of International Law at the University of Milano-Bicocca, Milan.

11 To view these examples, see UNESCO, "Examples of Codes of Ethics" [Online]. Available at: https://ich.unesco.org/en/examples-of-codes-of-ethics-00868/. (Accessed April 10, 2020)

12 As an example, HIPAMS has developed a policy brief alongside communities in India in relation to the Ministry of Culture, Government of India's June 2015 initiative to set up a National Mission on Intangible Heritage of India.

13 IPRs and cease and desist letters are particularly compatible as when IPRs are present, such letters can incentivize misappropriators to comply with the terms of the cease-and-desist letter, by promising legal proceedings on the grounds of infringement of the registered IPR should the misappropriator fail to comply with the letter.

14 For general information regarding the Consortium, see Consorzio Liutai "Antonio Stradivari," "The Consortium" [Online]. Available at: www.cremonaviolins.com/en/the-consortium/. (Accessed April 20, 2021)

15 The community is particularly interested in registering a non-agricultural EU GI. At the time of writing however, this is not possible, as EU GIs cannot be registered on non-agricultural goods.

16 For a full account of these conflicts, see *Rinallo and Pitardi* (n 47).

17 In the context of Traditional Knowledge, WIPO has also recognized this risk and has encouraged assistance for 'the holders and users of TK and TCEs in formulating mutually agreed terms and conditions governing access and benefit-sharing arising from the commercial application of TK' (See, World Intellectual Property Organisation, Traditional Knowledge Division and the Department for Transition and Developed Countries, "Intellectual Property, Traditional Knowledge and Traditional Cultural Expressions/Folklore a Guide for Countries in Transition" [Online]. Available at: https://www.wipo.int/edocs/pubdocs/en/wipo_pub_transition_9.pdf. (Accessed 29 April 2020, 2013).

18 The use of these licenses forms an important pillar of the HIPAMS digital media strategy for Baul, Chau, and Patachitra cultural practices. The use of such licenses is seen by the relevant culture-bearing communities as a way to underpin their marketing strategy by making digital content available. Such licenses also allow the communities a degree of control and the capacity to enforce the license in court, while also encouraging the re-use of digital content for non-commercial purposes. Thus, such licenses enable communities to protect their cultural heritage while also providing the freedom for evolution inherent in intangible cultural heritage as laid out by the ICHC.

19 For more information on CC licenses, see. Creative Commons, "Frequently Asked Questions"

20 For example, Decisions enforcing Creative Commons Licenses include the following: *Lichôdmapwa v L'asbl Festival de Theatre de Spa* Case no 09–1684-A (Le Tribunal de Premiere Instance de Nivelles, October 28, 2010); *Äventyrsgruvan i Tuna Hästberg v Gunnarsson* (Svea hovrätt, February 25, 2016); *Chang v Virgin Mobile* (Northern District of Texas, January 16, 2009); *Curry v Audax* Case no. 334492 / KG 06–176 SR (District Court of Amsterdam, March 9, 2006); *Drauglis v Kappa Map Group, LLC* (D.C. District Court, August 18, 2015); *Gerlach v DVU* Case no 16 O 458/10 (District Court of Berlin, October 8, 2010); *Jacobsen v. Katzer* case no. 06-CV-1905 (United States Court of Appeals for the Federal Circuit, August 13, 2008); *SGAE v Fernandez* Case no 15 / 2.006

Bibliography

Bahar, A. (2016), 'The politics of intangible heritage and food fights in Western Asia', *International Journal of Heritage Studies* 22(10).

BBC News (2019), *Kim Kardashian West's Kimono underwear Meets Japanese Backlash* [Online]. Available at: www.bbc.com/news/world-asia-48767678/. (Accessed: 20 July 2019)

Beijing Academy of Artificial Intelligence (2019), *Beijing AI Principles* [Online]. Available at: www.baai.ac.cn/news/beijing-ai-principles-en.html/. (Accessed: 10 April 2020)

Camacho, Z. (2017), *Voladores de Papantla acusan "daño moral" de cervecería Cuauhtémoc-Moctezuma* [Online]. Available at: Contralínea.com.mx/, www.contralinea.com.mx/archivo-revista/2017/03/30/voladores-de-papantla-acusan-dano-moral-de-cerveceria-cuauhtemoc-moctezuma/. (Accessed: 27 July 2019)

Consorzio Liutai (no date), *Antonio Stradivari, The Consortium* [Online]. Available at: www.cremonaviolins.com/en/the-consortium/. (Accessed: 20 April 2021)

Creative Commons (2020), *About the Licenses* [Online]. Available at: https://creativecommons.org/licenses/. (Accessed: 14 April 2021)

Creative Commons (2020), *Frequently Asked Questions* [Online]. Available at: https://creativecommons.org/faq/#can-i-offer-material-under-a-cc-license-that-has-my-trademark-on-it-without-also-licensing-or-affecting-rights-in-the-trademark/. (Accessed: 29 April 2020)

Dallah, O. (2020), *Kenyan Musician in Trouble with Tuku Music Over 'Todii' Song* [Online]. Available at: https://ommydalla.co.ke/buzz/item/1489-kenyan-musician-in-trouble-with-tuku-music-over-todii/. (Accessed: 30 April 2020)

Deacon, H. (2020), 'A patent on the Sámi sun: Ethics, intellectual property and commercialization of cultural heritage', *Pravovedenie* 64(1): 93–111.

De Anda Corral, J. F. (2021), *Secretaría de Cultura defiende el Ritual de Los Voladores, El Economista*, [Online]. Available at: www.eleconomista.com.mx/arteseideas/-Secretaria-de-Cultura-defiende-el-Ritual-de-Los-Voladores-20210628-0018.html/. (Accessed: 28 July 2021)

desInformémonos (2017), *Voladores de Papantla denuncian que la cervecera Cuauhtémoc-Moctezuma profana su ceremonia ritual* [Online]. Available at: https://desinformemonos.org/voladores-papantla-denuncian-la-cervecera-cuauhtemoc-moctezuma-profana-ceremonia-ritual/. (Accessed: 20 July 2019)

Food and Agriculture Organization of the United Nations (2011), *Agriculture and Economic Development Analysis Division (2011) Food Security Communications Toolkit* [Online]. Available at: www.fao.org/3/i2195e/i2195e03.pdf/. (Accessed: 17 June 2020)

Government of Canada Office of Consumer Affairs, Industry Canada, and the Regulatory Affairs Division, Treasury Board Secretariat. Ottawa, ON: Distribution Services Communications Branch (2016), *Voluntary Codes: A Guide for their Development and Use* [Online]. Available at: https://ich.unesco.org/doc/src/Example_guidance_document-Canada-EN.pdf/. (Accessed: 12 April 2020)

Heritage Sensitive Intellectual Property and Marketing Strategies (2020), *About* [Online]. Available at: https://hipamsindia.org/about/. (Accessed: 20 December 2020)

HIPAMS (2019), *Chau Dance Art Code: Treating Chau Dance Artists Fairly: Code of Ethics and Practical Guidelines for Performance Organisers, the Media and Researchers* [Online]. Available at: https://india.org/wp-content/uploads/2019/01/Chau-Dance-Art-Code.pdf. (Accessed: 29 August 2022)

HIPAMS India (no date), *Heritage-Sensitive Intellectual Property & Marketing Strategies* [Online]. Available at: https://hipamsindia.org/research-output/code-of-ethics/. (Accessed: 20 October 2020)

Intergovernmental Committee for the Safeguarding of the Intangible Cultural Heritage, Fifth Session (2010), *Decision 5.COM 6.15* [Online]. Available at: https://ich.unesco.org/en/decisions/5.COM/6.15/. (Accessed: 10 April 2020)

Intergovernmental Committee for the Safeguarding of the Intangible Cultural Heritage, Tenth session (2015), *Decision 10.COM 15* [Online]. Available at: https://ich.unesco.org/en/decisions/10.COM/15.A/. (Accessed: 20 September 2020)

Intergovernmental Committee for the Safeguarding of the Intangible Cultural Heritage, Third session (2008), *Decision 3.COM 1* [Online]. Available at: https://ich.unesco.org/en/decisions/3.COM/1/. (Accessed: 10 April 2020)

Le Gall, S. and Deacon, H. (2020), *Draft Issues Paper on Intellectual Property Policy and Artificial Intelligence*, WIPO Conversation on Intellectual Property (IP) and Artificial Intelligence (AI) Second Session WIPO/IP/AI/2/GE/20/1 [Online]. Available at: www.

wipo.int/export/sites/www/about-ip/en/artificial_intelligence/call_for_comments/pdf/ind_deacon_gall.pdf/. (Accessed: 20 December 2020)

Lixinski, L. (2020), *Commercializing Traditional Culture: Promises and Pitfalls in the Convergence of Intellectual Property Law and Cultural Heritage Law*, AIDA [Online]. Available at: SSRN: https://ssrn.com/abstract=3607658/. (Accessed: 20 December 2020)

Petrillo, P. L. (2019), *The Legal Protection of Intangible Cultural Heritage*, Springer.

Rinallo, D. and Pitardi, V. (2019), 'Open conflict as differentiation strategy in geographical indications: The Bitto Rebels case', *British Food Journal* 121(12): 3102.

Rogers, S. (2019), *Should Non-Inuit Performers Be Allowed to Throat Sing?* Nunatsiaq News [Online]. Available at: https://nunatsiaq.com/stories/article/should-non-inuit-performers-be-allowed-to-throat-sing/. (Accessed: 14 May 2020)

Rosati, M. (2020), 'Intangible cultural heritage as a driver and enabler for sustainable development: The UNESCO perspective'. In: Sinibaldi, E. (ed.) *UNESCO and the Intangible Cultural Heritage: Patrimonialization and Safeguarding*. Rome: UNESCO Office, Italian Ministry for Cultural Heritage and Activities and for Tourism.

Sora, D., Menta, A., Bardella, E. and Jost, M. (2020), *Contemporary Cremonese Violin Making: Testimonies and Perspectives*, Cited in: Sinibaldi, E. (no date) *UNESCO and the Intangible Cultural Heritage: Patrimonialization and Safeguarding*, Ufficio UNESCO, MiBACT, Rome [Online]. Available at: www.unesco.beniculturali.it/pdf/ICH_2509.pdf/. (Accessed: 20 December 2020)

Tunón, H., Kvarnström, M. and Lerner, H. (2016), *Ethical Codes of Conduct for Research Shall also Be Developed Related to Indigenous Peoples and Local Communities–Core Principles, Challenges and Opportunities*, In: Drugge, A. L. (no date), *Ethics in Indigenous Research: Past Experiences–Future Challenges, Vaartoe*, Centre for Sami Research, Umeå [Online]. Available at: https://pub.epsilon.slu.se/14401/11/tunon_h_etal_171116.pdf/. (Accessed: 11 April 2020)

Ubertazzi, B. (2010), 'Territorial and universal protection of intangible cultural heritage from misappropriation', *New Zealand Yearbook of International Law* 8(3): 81.UN (1987), *Report of the World Commission on Environment and Development: Our Common Future*, Annex to UN doc A/42/427 (Brundtland Report).

UNESCO (2008), *Mevlevi Sema Ceremony* [Online]. Available at: https://ich.unesco.org/en/RL/mevlevi-sema-ceremony-00100/. (Accessed: 10 April 2020)

UNESCO (2009), Report of intergovernmental committee for the safeguarding of the intangible cultural heritage, Fourth session Abu Dhabi, United Arab Emirates, RL09 No. 00175

UNESCO (2010), *Chhau Dance* [Online]. Available at: https://ich.unesco.org/en/RL/chhau-dance-00337/. (Accessed: 10 April 2020)

UNESCO (2015), *Ethics and Intangible Cultural Heritage* [Online]. Available at: https://ich.unesco.org/en/ethics-and-ich-00866/. (Accessed: 18 July 2021)

UNESCO Office New Delhi (2020), *Chau Dancing Is for Women too!*, In: UNESCO Office New Delhi, Youth in Action with UNESCO: Stories of Youth Engagement in India, p. 2 [Online]. Available at: https://unesdoc.unesco.org/ark:/48223/pf0000372622/. (Accessed: 10 April 2020)

UNESCO (no date), *Basic Texts of the 2003 Convention for the Safeguarding of the Intangible Cultural Heritage*, CLT-2018/WS/15.

UNESCO (no date), *Examples of Codes of Ethics* [Online]. Available at: https://ich.unesco.org/en/examples-of-codes-of-ethics-00868/. (Accessed: 10 April 2020)

Wahlquist, C. (2019), 'Stitch-up: Online sewing community at war over cultural appropriation', *The Guardian* [Online]. Available at: www.theguardian.com/lifeandstyle/2019/jun/01/stitch-up-online-sewing-community-at-war-over-cultural-appropriation/. (Accessed: 20 July 2019)

WIPO, Traditional Knowledge Division and the Department for Transition and Developed Countries, *Intellectual Property, Traditional Knowledge and Traditional Cultural Expressions/Folklore a Guide for Countries in Transition* [Online]. Available at: www.wipo.int/edocs/pubdocs/en/wipo_pub_transition_9.pdf/. (accessed: 15 June 2021)

Zee Bangla Cinema (2018), *Jobordokhol* [Film]. Trailer available at: https://youtu.be/rhN-PcLmqRw/. (Accessed: 14 February 2020)

6

GOVERNING INTANGIBLE CULTURAL HERITAGE COMMONS[1]

Hanna Schreiber

6.1. Introduction

The discourse on intangible cultural heritage (ICH) has involved matters concerning its nature and governance since the adoption of the 2003 UNESCO Convention. Little reflection has been done, however, on the nature of diverse ICH elements as shared resources and as goods – even though "sharing" is essential for ICH transmission and existence. Thus, this chapter aims to analyze ICH elements by approaching them through the lens of "the commons," typology of goods, and, in particular, through the concept of "polycentric governance" developed by the Nobel laureate Elinor Ostrom. The research question of this chapter is as follows: How might Ostrom's key concepts on the governance of the commons be useful in understanding the nature of ICH as commons, and in overcoming the challenges of governing ICH?

6.2. The wall of sovereignty

"Establishing institutional arrangements in which diverse types of collective actors can engage . . . remains a difficult challenge, particularly when these actors include national governments jealously guarding their sovereignty" (McGinnis and Ostrom, 1992, p. 31). Indeed, whenever civil society push "too much" to be present, heard, and taken into account in the international ICH system, it is often reiterated that the Convention belongs to the States.[2] Having observed UNESCO's intangible heritage arena for almost a decade, I have to agree that "on the international level, the wall of sovereignty seems to be impassable" (Skounti, 2017). However, the voice of communities is getting audibly louder. The participatory bottom-top

DOI:10.4324/9781003244158-9

approach paradigm and the need to share governance tasks between state and non-state actors are changing the discourse surrounding the 2003 Convention.

> It has become increasingly clear that we are poised between an old world that no longer works and a new one struggling to be born. Surrounded by an archaic order of centralized hierarchies on the one hand and predatory markets on the other, presided over by a state committed to planet-destroying economic growth, people around the world are searching for alternatives. . . . People want to emancipate themselves not just from poverty and shrinking opportunities, **but from governance systems that do not allow them meaningful voice and responsibility**.
>
> *(Bollier and Helfrich, 2012)*

As a heritage scholar and practitioner, engaged in the glocal[3] field of the 2003 UNESCO Convention for the safeguarding of the intangible cultural heritage (the 2003 Convention), I became intrigued and practically challenged by the tension related to the choice of the most suitable mode of governance that should be applied to such complex, identity-driven resource.

I have engaged in the implementation of the 2003 Convention in Poland since 2011 sitting for five – years (2013–2018) in the Polish Intangible Cultural Heritage Council. This experience allowed me to taste policy-making dilemmas, also by crafting concrete heritage governance guidelines at the national level (e.g., drafting the rules for the Polish ICH List, the Polish Register of Best Practices in Safeguarding ICH, or the Rules of Procedure for the Polish ICH Council). At the same time, as an expert of the national delegation, I was closely following meetings of experts and the organs of the 2003 Convention. Being a coordinator and co-author of the first Polish nomination to the Representative List (The Nativity Scene [szopka] tradition in Krakow) and following the life of the *szopka* community after their successful inscription in 2018 made me sensitive to the complex and context-based problems related to the ICH governance on different levels. This knowledge and experience have been further enriched by my engagement with the Intangible Cultural Heritage Council of the Capital City of Warsaw. This was an experience of "observant participation" (Mosse, 2005) in the dilemmas underpinning the governance of ICH on all levels: local, national, and international. This also made me look for theoretical and methodological frameworks that would offer a different language from the one developed in critical heritage studies.

6.3. Governing the commons

Research on cultural heritage has focused on governance for quite some time (Leask and Fyall, 2006; Karpati, 2008; Schmitt, 2009; Bertacchini, Saccone, and Santagata, 2011; Bendix, Eggert, and Peselmann, 2012; Florea, Mirea, and Susu,

2020).[4] Questions asked by heritage scholars include the following: How does a given community approach, define, and engage with its heritage resources? How should a given community govern heritage resources? What are the criteria for effective and ethical heritage governance? What will be the most appropriate methodology to address these issues? This discussion has also recently entered the field of ICH (Farah and Tremolada, 2015; Skounti, 2017; Kuutma and Vaivade, 2021).[5]

The ambitious idea to pursue safeguarding efforts on all levels of ICH governance (bilateral, subregional, regional, and international) is expressed in Article 19 of the 2003 Convention. The question, however, of *how* to govern ICH on all these levels (taking into account the necessary connection to local and national ones as stipulated in Article 1c[6]) and in cooperation with the communities concerned, is not answered by the Convention itself. It must be sought in other related instruments, such as the Operational Directives for the implementation of the Convention,[7] the Ethical Principles for the safeguarding of the intangible cultural heritage,[8] and national and local regulations (Cornu et al., 2020) – and is still not clear at all. Principle 12 of the Ethical Principles for the Safeguarding of the ICH states simply: "The safeguarding of intangible cultural heritage . . . should therefore be undertaken through cooperation among bilateral, subregional, regional and international parties."

In order to show the interconnectedness of all levels of ICH governance, which are at play after the inscription of an element on the Lists, let us call the sphere of ICH governing practices a "glocal field": one that reflects the processes whereby institutional arrangements shift from the national scale both upward to global scales and downward to the scale of local, urban, or regional configurations.[9]

It might seem surprising that the literature analyzing the interrelated questions of *how* and *when* heritage is conceptualized as a "shared resource," *what* is shared with *whom*, and *how* to govern ICH as a *shared* resource remains in its infancy (Cominelli, 2011; Bortolotto, 2020; Debarbieux et al., 2021).

Elinor Ostrom offered an empirically based analysis of the dilemma of how to govern resources shared by diverse communities effectively in the long term in her book *Governing the Commons: The Evolution of Institutions for Collective Action* (Ostrom, 1990). Based on wide ethnographic fieldwork (e.g., in the Philippines, Sri Lanka, Spain, Scotland, and Switzerland), she identified a set of eight institutional design principles for sustainable community-based commons management (Ostrom, 1990, pp. 90–102): (1) Clearly defined boundaries should be in place (effective exclusion of external unentitled parties); (2) Rules in use are well matched to local needs and conditions[10]; (3) Individuals affected by these rules can usually participate in modifying the rules; (4) A system for self-monitoring members' behavior has been established[11]; (5) A graduated system of sanctions is available[12]; (6) Community members have access to low-cost conflict-resolution mechanisms[13]; (7) The right of community members to devise their own rules is respected by external authorities; (8) Nested enterprises – that is, appropriation, provision, monitoring and sanctioning, conflict resolution, and other governance activities – are organized in a nested structure with multiple layers of activities.

The community of scholars that use her concepts and methods has been steadily growing, and since the 1990s (McGinnis and Ostrom, 1992) more research has been focusing on the possibility of applying these principles to international regimes and global problems, for example, climate change or cybersecurity (Haller et al., 2019; Shackelford, 2020).

6.4. From natural to cultural and heritage commons

Commons is "a resource shared by a group of people that is subject to social dilemmas" (Hess and Ostrom, 2007, p. 6, see more below). This, however, is not the only definition of the commons existing in the abundant literature on this topic. While commons were classically regarded as environmental, encompassing fisheries, forests, pastures, and irrigation systems (Hardin, 1968; Ostrom, 1990; Bollier and Helfrich, 2012), concepts of human-made "new commons" have been introduced to refer to knowledge commons, digital commons, cultural commons, urban commons, etc. (Hess, 2008; Foster and Iaione, 2019). Knowledge commons were considered by Hess and Ostrom (2007), as having a dual function: of a human need and an economic good (Hess, 2012, p. 15). This dual function is also a characteristic of ICH.

Among the "new commons," the concept of "cultural commons" (Bertacchini et al., 2012) and "cultural heritage commons" has emerged recently (Zhang, 2012; Gould, 2017; Lekakis, 2020). A "cultural commons" is characterized as "a cultural resource shared by a group, which can generate one or more social dilemmas and is defined by the confluence of three dimensions: culture, space and community" (Bertacchini et al., 2012). According to Bertacchini, Bravo, Marrelli, and Santagata, cultural commons matter because culture and creativity play an increasing role in economic, social, and environmental development. Within such a broad definition, the ideas, knowledge, beliefs, rites, customs, and shared and participated productive techniques contribute to the making of a cultural commons (Bertacchini et al., 2012, pp. 1–5). This definition of a cultural commons seems very close to the definition of ICH due to the centrality of ideas of sharing, collaboration, and transmission. What is new for ICH scholarship here, however, is the focus on social dilemmas (Hess, 2012).

The authors point to two main classes of social dilemmas. The first social dilemma is labeled as the "free riding problem," in which individuals can try to exploit the commons without contributing to their maintenance, for example, producing imitations of cultural products. The second social dilemma specific to cultural commons relates to the decision on whether and how to reproduce cultural resource, creating uncertainty in the transmission of the commons to the next generation (compare: Bertacchini et al., 2012, pp. 3, 13). This is also the central issue of safeguarding ICH as "cultural maintenance" and the decisions on how to transmit ICH are of paramount importance. It is precisely this key social dilemma that distinguishes "cultural commons" from any other commons as it is linked to cultural dynamics and may imply a struggle between "innovators and traditionalists" inside a given culture (Bertacchini et al., 2012, p. 7). As noted by Zhang (2012, p. 154), "Even if cultural heritage may suffer from social dilemmas leading to over-exploitation and the destruction of its cultural values, this 'tragic' destiny is not inevitable as strong and cohesive relationships among communities make self-governing institutional arrangements possible and especially important." He also considers "heritage commons" as belonging to "cultural commons" and not need a separate definition. In order to make the definition of "ICH commons" operational and close to the ICH definition from the 2003 Convention I nevertheless propose to define that *ICH commons is a cultural resource shared and transmitted within communities, groups or individuals which can generate one or more social dilemmas.*

Concepts of "sharing" and "shared resource" are particularly relevant for our understanding of ICH (Bortolotto, 2020; Debarbieux et al., 2021). Summary records from the meetings of the Intergovernmental Committee reveal that in 2012, the debate on this topic was particularly interesting. The experts suggested "it was preferable not to refer to 'similar' elements given that each manifestation was specific and unique to a given community" (UNESCO, 2012, pp. 134–136). Instead, it was stressed that a reference was to be made to "shared heritage" and to "elements with shared characteristics"; others invoked the notion of "family" as a potentially useful one. Certain experts argued that multinational files should be further promoted to highlight "shared ICH" (ibidem). Some delegations supported the notion of "shared heritage," which in their opinion had a huge potential to create new platforms for building intercultural dialogue among countries that go beyond making lists (ibidem). The topic came back in 2017 when the delegation of Hungary commented on the work done by the Evaluation Body. The delegation wished to highlight that the inscription mechanism should in no way be used to appropriate intangible cultural heritage or as a means to authenticate such practice in a specific country. Intangible cultural heritage is shared among countries; this is the norm. It lives in the exchange and interaction between communities, and the boundaries of States do not respect those interactions. (UNESCO, 2017, p. 83).

Sharing is here a defining element of ICH intended as a concept aimed at building bridges across nations and communities. However, the act of sharing always involves problems and dilemmas. Therefore, framing ICH elements as shared resources and goods – that is in terms of institutional economics – helps us to analyze the problems and dilemmas underpinning the governance of these elements.

6.5. Typology of intangible cultural heritage goods

Elinor Ostrom's work and that of the researchers identifying with her research program (the Bloomington School of Institutional Analysis) are linked with the so-called new institutional economics (McGinnis, 2021). The goods typology is a part of its disciplinary language.

Goods were classified by Ostrom and her husband Vincent into four categories: public, private, club/toll goods, or common-pool resources (CPR) depending on the extent of their excludability and subtractability. Excludability refers to the ease or the difficulty with which goods can be protected from their use by others. Subtractability, in turn, evokes the sharable nature of the goods and varies on a low to high scale: If one person uses the good and thereby subtracts from the pool of available goods that can be used by others, then it is said for this resource to have a high subtractability (Shackelford, 2020, p. 12).

Hess and Ostrom encountered a problem with subtractability, as high subtractability, which is usually a key characteristic of common-pool resources, does not apply to many knowledge (and heritage) commons that are traditionally relatively non-subtractive. "The more people who share useful knowledge, the greater the common good" (Hess and Ostrom, 2007, p. 5). This seems to apply to ICH as well: Despite existing exceptions, it is usually believed that the wider the tradition and practice are shared, the more vibrant, vivid, and resistant to extinction they are. Hess and Ostrom even concluded that "Consideration of knowledge as a commons, therefore, suggests that the unifying thread in all commons resources is that they are jointly used, managed by groups of varying sizes and interests" (ibidem).

However, the reality is more complex. The joint use of a commons by various groups with various interests may also make a commons more vulnerable or even subject to radical deterioration, decontextualization, or damage. This applies to ICH as well as to many other heritage commons. The abuse of heritage elements due to their over-commercialization and transformation into sheer touristic products that may eventually even lead to the loss of their initial purpose and meaning are well-known phenomena (Hulubas, 2017). Appropriation of heritage practices by powerful actors is so frequent that it is a key concern for UNESCO and is regarded as one of the main threats to ICH (Bortolotto, 2021). UNESCO lists are regarded as responsible for this phenomenon, which was aptly called "UNESCO-cide" (Ruttkowski, 2017).

Some of the elements inscribed on the UNESCO lists, for example, yoga or tango, could be considered as belonging to the category of a classic public good (Hess and Ostrom, 2003, p. 120, but also see the original source: Ostrom and Ostrom, 1977). It is highly difficult to exclude anyone from exercising yoga or dancing tango and practicing them does not "diminish" yoga or tango remaining for others. However, yoga studios and yoga lessons are very much excludable (studios have doors) and subtractable (limited space). The ideas or knowledge of yoga or tango could thus be considered public goods, but the yoga or tango lessons as a service could be considered club goods. The same applies, for example, to the sauna culture in Finland (inscribed in 2020). As the nomination claims: "With 3.3 million saunas in a country of 5.5 million inhabitants, the element is readily accessible to all"[14] (unless they all decide to enter the sauna at the very same moment). Thus, on the one hand, the *knowledge* about sauna tradition is a public good that can be enjoyed by everyone in the world. On the other hand, concrete saunas in Finland have rather limited space. A similar consideration will apply to the Mediterranean diet or reggae music of Jamaica: It is highly unlikely that we will ever be able to exclude people from eating such food if they only wish to eat according to Mediterranean diet principles (including extra virgin olive oil, fresh vegetables, and fruits, whole grains, low amounts of meat) or ban listening, singing, and dancing to reggae music of Jamaica. However, access to the food itself is a challenge in many parts of the globe, and similarly, access to music could be dependent on the access to the technology that transmits it.

Some other ICH elements could be classified as belonging to the category of common-pool resources (CPR), such as the Beer culture in Belgium or the traditions related to the date palm: it is difficult to exclude anyone, but at the same time, one person's consumption at some point may subtract from the quantity available

		SUBTRACTABILITY	
		Low	High
EXCLUDABILITY	Difficult	**PUBLIC GOODS** Tango Mediterranean diet Yoga Reggae music of Jamaica Sauna culture in Finland	**COMMON-POOL RESOURCES** Irrigation systems in Murcia and Valencia Beer culture in Belgium Date palm: knowledge, skills, traditions and practices
	Easy	**CLUB GOODS** Falconry	**PRIVATE GOODS as sub-elements of ICH goods** Gloves (Falconry) Clothes (Yoga) Towels (Sauna culture in Finland) Shoes (Tango) Crops (Irrigation system in Murcia and Valencia) Greek salad (Mediterranean diet) Bottle of beer (Beer culture in Belgium)

FIGURE 6.1 Typology of intangible cultural heritage as goods based on the proposed classification of the chosen ICH elements inscribed into the Representative List of the Intangible Cultural Heritage of Humanity. Own elaboration based on (Hess and Ostrom, 2003, p. 120).

Note: The dashed line between the squares intends to visualize the porous character of borders between these four categories and the possibility that many of them may find themselves somewhere in the middle between "difficult" and "easy" excludability, or "low" and "high" subtractability. It is also important to note that the institutional arrangements developed to govern particular ICH elements might change in time and thus goods considered club in one particular setting might subsequently turn into public or the other way around. So, placing any ICH good in any of those pools should be regarded as subject to change.

for others. Interestingly, among the current 529 inscriptions on the Representative List, there is one famous CPR that has been studied by Elinor Ostrom (Ostrom, 1990, p. 71): the irrigation system in Valencia and Murcia (Spain), inscribed into the UNESCO list in 2009 as Irrigators' tribunals of the Spanish Mediterranean coast: the Council of Wise Men of the plain of Murcia and the Water Tribunal of the plain of Valencia.[15]

Some inscribed ICH elements would belong to the category of club goods, such as Falconry: It is quite easy to exclude others from practicing it, as the practice itself is highly specific and takes years of preparation. Falconers use their specific language and rituals and are often involved in making the necessary equipment (hoods, gloves, jesses, bells, etc.). They are also required to comply with applicable legislation, falconry tradition, and ethics.[16] Joining falconers is much harder than joining a global group of yoga practitioners. The level of subtractability in Falconry is also quite low.

There are no private goods inscribed on UNESCO Lists as such. It would be against the definition of ICH which is always shared, "transmitted," "recreated," and "providing the sense of identity," therefore linked to a social group and a broader cultural context. However, private goods constitute important subelements of the inscribed ICH elements. For instance, when approaching the Beer culture in Belgium that is based on the brewing tradition, one cannot ignore the fact that a bottle of beer, which is bought and consumed, constitutes a private good (same as a towel brought to a sauna in Finland). The same relates to dates: Tangible elements of much broader knowledge, skills, and practices related to the date palm know-how or the irrigation system, which, taken as a complex social eco-system, constitute rather common-pool resources.

The Ostroms' goods typology makes it possible to introduce more clarity into thinking about different heritage elements if we see them as types of goods. It shows that different goods (ICH elements) are associated with different types of rules and norms and represent different governance challenges: to production, consumption, management, and other collective or social dilemmas, which are likely to be associated with different types of property regimes or management schemes (i.e., different configurations of rules and norms). Different types of goods pose different social dilemmas which are best approached through specific policy instruments. Very few regimes include rules for dealing with only one type of good. What is far more common are situations where the governance regime has to establish rules, norms, and strategies that are suited to the dilemmas posed by the production, consumption, and management of all types of shared resources.

It is also important to note that classifying the good into a category cannot be taken for granted. The character of ICH goods is dynamic and transformative, and the borders between categories should be regarded rather as "porous," not "impermeable." Many of them may also find themselves somewhere in the middle between "difficult" and "easy" excludability or "low" and "high" subtractability, depending on the particular context. Thus, in a different institutional setting with different rules, ICH goods may change their very nature.

Therefore, it is clear that ICH commons consist of multiple types of goods and regimes. Different goods will certainly have different governance regimes. The governance of beer culture in the whole of Belgium will differ from the governance of traditions related to the date palm in several countries. But they both will also differ (change or transform) in time: The beer culture in Belgium or the date palm traditions in the nineteenth century were governed differently than they are governed in the twenty-first century. This opens up new research paths for heritage scholars to really "dive into"[17] ICH and search for patterns used to govern – that is safeguard – these ICH elements.

6.6. Safeguarding is governing

"Safeguarding" is the main objective of the Convention. It is defined in Article 2 (3) as "measures aimed at ensuring the viability of the intangible cultural heritage." The governing bodies of the Convention are guided by this definition in their activities, and all rules, norms, and strategies are subordinated to this principle. The whole governance system of the Convention is aimed at determining which organ of the Convention shall have what kind of functions in order to ensure that the idea of safeguarding is enforced. The functions of the General Assembly of States Parties, the Intergovernmental Committee, and the Secretariat are also defined and listed according to the "safeguarding" definition in Article 2(3). Governing intangible cultural heritage, according to the Convention's regime, therefore means safeguarding ICH. All safeguarding measures and activities proposed are in fact also governing measures: Even if governing can be understood as a broad task that involves creating regulations or institutions whose effects may in practice be far from safeguarding, the very existence of those regulations and institutions would not be possible if the "safeguarding principle" was ignored. This means that the term "governance" might be equated with "safeguarding" in the context of the 2003 Convention. As proposed by McGinnis: "governance is the process through which the repertoire of rules, norms, and strategies relevant to a given realm of policy interactions are made, implemented, interpreted, and reformed" or subsequently: "governance determines who can do what to whom, and on whose authority" (McGinnis, Baldwin, and Thiel 2020, p. 6).

As a consequence of equating "governance" with "safeguarding," a closer analysis of ethical principles for safeguarding ICH is needed, as they were adopted with the aim of guiding the governance of ICH.

6.7. Ethical principles as a toolbox with polycentric governance rules

The Ethical Principles for the safeguarding of the intangible cultural heritage, adopted in 2015, have been elaborated in the spirit of the 2003 Convention and existing international normative instruments protecting human rights and the rights of indigenous peoples.[18] However, although the document does not contain any of Ostrom's key terms, its careful reading proves that they are integral as guiding governance ideas, starting with Principle 1: "Communities, groups and, where applicable, individuals should have the primary role in safeguarding their own intangible cultural heritage". Taken to heart, this first principle should result in the creation of rules allowing for the voices of communities to be heard at the international level. "Primary" means "not the only one" but "the one that cannot be replaced by anyone else." An additional explanation of the "spirit" of this governance is to be found in Principle 3. "Mutual respect as well as a respect for and mutual appreciation of intangible cultural heritage, should prevail in interactions between States and between communities, groups and, where applicable, individuals". Respect between States and communities can only be introduced if both sides are "sitting at the same table" as equal partners; respect means that they listen to each other, affirm each other's rights to hold different opinions, can empathize and search for solutions in which both sides are treated as *subjects*, not *objects* of the governance. In this way, both sides develop trust. More concrete suggestions on how to interact, cooperate, and collectively govern ICH are provided in Principle 4: "All interactions with the communities, groups and, where applicable, individuals . . . should be characterized by transparent collaboration, dialogue, negotiation and consultation, and contingent upon their free, prior, sustained and informed consent".

At first glance, it might seem astonishing that these principles, despite being created and adopted by UNESCO and States Parties, are undermined when it comes to discussions on concrete solutions securing the practical involvement of communities at the international level. Their practical invisibility is also noted in the UNESCO Internal Oversight Service's (IOS's) report, which states that

> there is little data regarding ethical behaviour beyond the inclusion of communities, groups, and individuals. . . . there is very little other information that provides indications of other aspects of ethical behaviour as described in Ethical Principles. . . . Similarly, most reporting to date does not effectively document the quality and extent of community engagement in projects.[19]

This observation resulted in IOS Recommendation 6 directed to the Secretariat of the 2003 Convention to include "sections in all project proposals and reports on ethical behaviour, especially the active participation of tradition bearers, the links with sustainable development and the consideration of rights-based approaches including gender equality."[20]

The Recommendation proves the challenge of glocal governance: without adequate mechanisms, institutions, and procedures that could monitor the implementation of Ethical Principles, they will remain on the margins of, or even out of the governance system. Principle 7 insists that

> the communities, groups, and individuals who create intangible cultural heritage should benefit from the protection of the moral and material interests resulting

> from such heritage, and particularly from its use, research, documentation, promotion or adaptation by members of the communities or others.

It is important to note in this regard that the rules on the use of a shared resource are the key components of Ostrom's sustainable governance principles. Collective decisions concerning the viability of ICH as well as of the communities who practice it are also a common denominator for both sustainable governance and Ethical Principle 9.

The pinnacle of all Ethical Principles is contained in Principle 12.

> The safeguarding of intangible cultural heritage is of general interest to humanity and should therefore be undertaken through cooperation among bilateral, sub-regional, regional and international parties; *nevertheless, communities, groups and, where applicable, individuals should never be alienated from their own intangible cultural heritage.* (emphasis added)

This warning about the threat of community alienation from their heritage evokes the famous words of Elinor Ostrom:

> Trust is the most important resource. If a community has been forbidden from managing its resources for a long time, the main obstacle to overcome is the lack of trust and the effort to get organized in the first place. It's not a trivial matter.
>
> *(after Escotet, 2010)*

If trust exists, common resources are capable of being collectively managed by users in ways that support their needs yet sustain the resource over the long run (Foster and Iaione, 2019). Ostrom and McGinnis found that sustainable and effective governance of commonly shared resources is based on polycentricity.[21] This was called "polycentric governance" (see later; McGinnis, 1999a, 1999b; Ostrom, 2005, 2009). The relationship between the nature of the resource shared within a community and the mode of its governance (polycentric) remains inseparable; they are not only "tied" but rather "glued."

According to McGinnis, Baldwin, and Thiel (2020):

> In a system of polycentric governance, *a diverse array of communities and public and private authorities with overlapping domains of responsibility* interact in complex and ever-changing ways, and out of these seemingly uncoordinated processes of mutual adjustment emerges a persistent system of social ordering that can support and sustain capacities for individual liberty, group autonomy, and *community self-governance* (emphasis added).

This concept was originally introduced by Vincent Ostrom, Tiebout, and Warren (1961) but the best-known application of polycentricity to real-world settings remains the pioneering research of Elinor Ostrom (1990, 2010) on community-based collective management of natural resources.

The definition itself shall "ring a bell" for any ICH scholar analyzing the community participation principle. The idea of participatory, collaborative, and community-based governance is a credo for the safeguarding of ICH and is widely discussed in the whole heritage research community (García et al., 2021; Sokka et al., 2021; Bortolotto, 2015).[22] Thus, Ostrom's focus on the agency of local communities is another important bridge to the 2003 Convention: the involvement of communities (groups and individuals) is at the center of all safeguarding practices (Article 15 of the 2003 Convention; Lixinski, 2019); as it is the communities that are to be "the heart" of this Convention.[23] This principle brings us closer to the question on the characteristics of polycentric governance.

There are eight characteristics that scholars have associated with the concept of polycentric governance, which I cite hereafter McGinnis, Baldwin, and Thiel (2020, p. 10). However, as they note – and contrary to the need to cumulatively meet the 8 principles of sustainable governance of the commons – here characteristics 1–4 seem to be of crucial importance:

1. Multiple decision centers (which may be of varying sizes and types).
2. De jure independence or de facto autonomy of decision-making authority for each decision center.
3. Overlapping jurisdictions in the range of authority for different decision centers (in addition to spillover effects of outcomes).
4. Multiple processes of mutual adjustment among decision centers (taking each other into account).

The precise relationship chosen is an empirical matter and depends on many factors such as the nature of collective action problems or the type of goods and services to be produced or provided, the legal-political landscape, cultural norms, and so on (Ostrom, Tiebout, and Warren, 1961). Moreover, the specific ways in which polycentricity will manifest in different contexts depending on a host of factors: objectives and motivations of agents, background conditions, technological and political constraints, choice of rules at various decision centers across levels, and the resulting emergent processes (Rayamajhee and Paniagua, 2021).

6.8. Conclusion

"Successful commons governance requires that rules evolve," argued Ostrom (Dietz, Ostrom, and Stern, 2003). Indeed, her research confirms that the most sustainable and effective governance system is adaptive (Dietz et al., 2003), especially in the case of dynamically changing cultural and heritage commons. The adaptive character of the complex, multi-level ICH governance regime is reflected by regular amendments to the Operational Directives.

However, the analysis presented earlier proves that effective and sustainable multi-level systems have to be based on the constant development of methods that assess the benefits and costs of particular strategies, the strong commitment to finding ways of embracing diverse actors (from local to global level) and their needs, as well as never-ending efforts aimed at building the trust and consensus around the understanding of the nature of the shared resource and of the values associated with that resource, which the international ICH community (embracing states and non-state actors) considers crucial for the sustainable existence of this regime.

The governance of ICH seems to be destined to sharing and to "commoning"; otherwise, it cannot retain its credibility. This has been the real essence – and the real sense – of the 2003 Convention from the very beginning. However, existing dilemmas and tensions also prove that the ICH regime, in order to remain sustainable and adaptive, must be at the same time inclusive, and governed in a polycentric manner – because people want "governance systems that allow them meaningful voice and responsibility."[24] And this is still an important "work in progress,' 20 years after the Convention was adopted.

Notes

1 The author wishes to acknowledge that her work on this paper was funded by the National Science Centre of Poland research grant Sonata 15, no 2019/35/D/HS5/04247: *Between the heritage of the world and the heritage of humanity: researching international heritage regimes through the lens of Elinor Ostrom's Institutional Analysis and Development (IAD) framework*. The author would like to express her gratitude for the very helpful remarks received from Scott Shackelford, Michael McGinnis, Peter Gould, Veeshan Rayamajhee, Bartosz Pieliński, and the editors of this volume to this paper.

2 2nd meeting of the open-ended intergovernmental working group on the Global reflection on the listing mechanisms of the 2003 Convention (UNESCO 2022).

3 "Glocalisation" refers to the twin process whereby, firstly, institutional/regulatory arrangements shift from the national scale both upwards to supra-national or global scales and downwards to the scale of the individual body or local, urban, or regional configurations and, secondly, economic activities and inter-firm networks are becoming simultaneously more localized/regionalized and transnational (Swyngedouw, 2004, p. 24).

4 See also the website of the Global Political Economy of Cultural Heritage group at the Max Planck Institute for Social Anthropology: www.eth.mpg.de/3534616/heritage.

5 See also the website of the UNESCO Frictions: Heritage-making Across Global Governance project: https://frictions.hypotheses.org.

6 The purposes of this Convention are as follows: (. . .) (c) to raise awareness at the local, national and international levels of the importance of the intangible cultural heritage, and of ensuring mutual appreciation thereof. (. . .)

7 https://ich.unesco.org/en/directives.

8 https://ich.unesco.org/en/ethics-and-ich-00866.

9 See footnote 4.

10 Appropriation rules restricting time, place, technology, and/or quantity of resource units are related to local conditions and to provision rules requiring labor, materials, and/or money (McGinnis and Ostrom, 1992, p. 9).
11 Monitors, who actively audit CPR conditions and participant behavior, are accountable to the participants or are the participants (McGinnis and Ostrom, 1992, p. 9).
12 Participants who violate operational rules are likely to be assessed graduated sanctions (depending on the seriousness and context of the offense) from other participants, by officials accountable to these participants, or by both (McGinnis and Ostrom, 1992, p. 9).
13 Participants and their officials have rapid access to low-cost, local arenas to resolve conflict among participants or between participants and officials (McGinnis and Ostrom, 1992, p. 9).
14 https://ich.unesco.org/en/RL/sauna-culture-in-finland-01596.
15 https://ich.unesco.org/en/RL/irrigators-tribunals-of-the-spanish-mediterranean-coast-the-council-of-wise-men-of-the-plain-of-murcia-and-the-water-tribunal-of-the-plain-of-valencia-00171. Interestingly, this CPR has also been inscribed in 2019 under the name Historical Irrigation System at l'Horta de València into Globally Important Agricultural Heritage Systems (GIAHS), the new heritage list under the auspices of FAO, the driving ideas of which evoke great similarity to Ostrom's concepts and approaches, see: the www.fao.org/giahs/giahsaroundtheworld/designated-sites/europe-and-central-asia/historical-waterscape-of-lhorta-de-valencia/en/.
16 See nomination file available at: https://ich.unesco.org/en/RL/falconry-a-living-human-heritage-01708.
17 https://ich.unesco.org/en/dive.
18 Ethical Principles Preamble, UNESCO 2015.
19 UNESCO, 2021, p. 24, repeated at p. 68.
20 UNESCO, 2021, p. 47.
21 More on these concepts: Stephan, Marshall and McGinnis (2019).
22 As noted by Jakubowski:

> In such context, it worth to mention that the International Law Association (ILA), the largest international law non-profit organization worldwide, established in 2017 the Committee on Participation in Global Cultural Heritage Governance (ILA Committee). Within its four-year mandate this body has sought to explore the engagement of communities and, derivatively, individuals in the governance of cultural heritage, including an examination of how community governance operates in other contexts not directly related to heritage.

See more: Jakubowski (forthcoming).
23 UNESCO 2008, par. 36.
24 See Bollier, Helfrich 2012 as cited in the introduction to this chapter.

References

Bendix, R.F., Eggert, A., and Peselmann, A. (eds.) (2012) *Heritage Regimes and the State*. Göttingen: Universitätsverlag Göttingen.

Bertacchini, E., Bravo, G., Marrelli, M., and Santagata, W. (eds.) (2012) *Cultural Commons: A New Perspective on the Production and Evolution of Cultures*. Cheltenham: Edward Elgar Publishing.

Bertacchini, E., Saccone, D., and Santagata, W. (2011) 'Embracing diversity, correcting inequalities: Towards a new global governance for the UNESCO world heritage', *International Journal of Cultural Policy*, 17(3), pp. 278–288.

Bollier, D., and Helfrich, S. (eds.) (2012) *The Wealth of the Commons: A World Beyond Market and State*. Amherst: Levellers Press.

Bortolotto, C. (2015) 'UNESCO and heritage self-determination: Negotiating meaning in the Intergovernmental Committee for the Safeguarding of the ICH', in Adell, N., Bendix, R.F., Bortolotto, C., and Tauschek, M. (eds.) *Between Imagined Communities and Communities of Practice. Participation, Territory and the Making of Heritage*. Göttingen: Göttingen University Press, pp. 249–272.

Bortolotto, C. (2020) 'The making of shared heritage between bureaucratization of utopia and utopianization of bureaucracy', *L'Espace géographique*, 49(4), pp. 319–336.

Bortolotto, C. (2021) 'Commercialization without over-commercialization: Normative conundrums across heritage rationalities', *International Journal of Heritage Studies*, 27(9), pp. 857–868.

Cominelli, F. (2011) *Governance of Cultural Commons: The Case of Traditional Craftsmanship in France* [online]. Available at: https://hal-paris1.archives-ouvertes.fr/hal-00645244 (Accessed: 11 February 2022).

Cornu, M., Vaivade, A., Martinet, L., and Hance, C. (2020) *Intangible Cultural Heritage Under National and International Law*. Cheltenham: Edward Elgar Publishing.

Debarbieux, B., Bortolotto, C., Munz, H., and Raziano, C. (2021) 'Sharing heritage? Politics and territoriality in UNESCO's heritage lists', *Territory, Politics, Governance*, pp. 1–16.

Dietz, T., Ostrom, E., and Stern, P.C. (2003) 'The struggle to govern the commons', *Science*, 302, pp. 1907–1912.

Escotet, M. (2010) *Interview with the Nobel Laureate Elinor Ostrom*. Available at: https://escotet.org/2010/11/interview-with-nobel-laureate-elinor-ostrom/

Farah, P.D., and Tremolada, R. (2015) 'Global governance and intangible cultural heritage in the information society: At the crossroads of IPRs and innovation', in Archibugi, D. and Filippetti, A. (eds.) *The Handbook of Global Science, Technology, and Innovation*. Chichester: John Wiley & Sons.

Florea, I.M., Mirea, M., and Susu, C. (2020) 'Public governance and cultural heritage: Exploring the links between culture and social indicators with the principal component analysis', in Turcanu-Carutiu, D. (ed.) *Heritage*. London: IntechOpen [online]. Available at: www.intechopen.com/chapters/70968 (Accessed: 11 February 2022).

Foster, S.R., and Iaione, C. (2019) 'Ostrom in the city: Design principles and practices for the urban commons', in Hudson, B., Rosenbloom, J., and Cole, D. (eds.) *Routledge Handbook of the Study of the Commons*. Abingdon: Routledge, pp. 53–62.

García, G., Vandesande, A., Cardoso, F., and Van Balen, K. (eds.) (2021) *The Future of the Past: Paths towards Participatory Governance for Cultural Heritage*. London, New York: Routledge.

Gould, P.G. (2017) 'Considerations on governing heritage as a commons resource', in Gould, P.G. and Pyburn, K.A. (eds.) *Collision or Collaboration: Archaeology Encounters Economic Development*. Cham: Springer International Publishing, pp. 171–187.

Haller, T., Breu, T., De Moor, T., Rohr, C., and Znoj, H. (eds.) (2019) *The Commons in a Glocal World: Global Connections and Local Responses*. London, New York: Routledge.

Hardin, G. (1968) 'The tragedy of the commons', *Science*, 162(3859), pp. 1243–1248.

Hess, C. (2008, July 14–18) *Mapping the new commons*. Paper presented at the Governing Shared Resources: Connecting Local Experience to Global Challenges, 12th Biennial Conference of the International Association for the Study of the Commons, University of Gloucestershire, Cheltenham [online]. Available at: https://dlc.dlib.indiana.edu/dlc/bitstream/handle/10535/304/Mapping_the_NewCommons.pdf (Accessed: 11 February 2022).

Hess, C. (2012) 'The unfolding of the knowledge commons', *St Anthony's International Review*, 8(1), pp. 13–24.

Hess, C., and Ostrom, E. (2003) 'Ideas, artifacts and facilities: Information as a common-pool resource', *Law and Contemporary Problems*, 66, pp. 111–145.

Hess, C., and Ostrom, E. (eds.) (2007) *Understanding Knowledge as a Commons: From Theory to Practice*. Cambridge, MA: MIT Press.

Hulubaş, A. (2017) 'Securing the future of intangible cultural heritage in Romania in a sustainable way: Benefits and subsequent risks', in Schreiber, H. (ed.) *Intangible Cultural Heritage: 10th Anniversary of the Entry into Force of the 2003 UNESCO Convention Through the Prism of Sustainable Development*. Warsaw: National Heritage Board, pp. 412–421.

Jakubowski, A. (forthcoming) 'Cultural heritage and human rights', in Morriset, L. and Lixinski, L. (eds.) *Routledge Handbook on Heritage and Law*.

Karpati, T.H. (2008) *Management of World Heritage Sites*. Saarbrücken: VDM Verlag Dr. Mueller E.K.

Kuutma, K., and Vaivade, A. (2021) 'Academic and research engagements alongside professional or public entanglements in the field of intangible cultural heritage', *Slovenský národopis*, 69(4), pp. 466–472.

Leask, A., and Fyall, A. (2006) *Managing World Heritage Sites*. Oxford: Butterworth-Heinemann.

Lekakis, S. (ed.) (2020) *Cultural Heritage in the Realm of the Commons: Conversations on the Case of Greece*. London: Ubiquity Press.

Lixinski, L. (2019) *International Heritage Law for Communities: Exclusion and Re-Imagination*. Oxford: Oxford University Press.

McGinnis, M.D. (ed.) (1999a) *Polycentric Governance and Development: Readings From the Workshop in Political Theory and Policy Analysis*. Ann Arbor: University of Michigan Press.

McGinnis, M.D. (ed.) (1999b) *Polycentricity and Local Public Economies: Readings From the Workshop in Political Theory and Policy Analysis*. Ann Arbor: University of Michigan Press.

McGinnis, M.D. (2021) 'New institutional economics: Building from shared foundations', in Lemke, J.S. and Tarko, V. (eds.) *Elinor Ostrom and the Bloomington School: Building a New Approach to Policy and the Social Sciences*. Montreal–Kingston–Chicago: McGill-Queen's University Press, pp. 25–46.

McGinnis, M.D., Baldwin, E.B., and Thiel, A. (2020, September 14) *When is polycentric governance sustainable? Using institutional theory to identify endogenous drivers of dysfunctional dynamics*. Paper prepared for presentation at The Ostrom Workshop, Indiana University, Bloomington [online]. Available at: https://ostromworkshop.indiana.edu/pdf/seriespapers/2020fall-colloq/mcginnis.pdf (Accessed: 11 February 2022).

McGinnis, M., and Ostrom, E. (1992, April 23–25) *Design principles for local and global commons*. Paper prepared for presentation at a Conference on "Linking Local and Global Commons", Harvard Center for International Affairs, Cambridge, Massachusetts [online]. Available at: https://dlc.dlib.indiana.edu/dlc/bitstream/handle/10535/5460/design%20principles%20for%20local%20and%20global%20commons.pdf (Accessed: 11 February 2022).

McGinnis M.D. (2020) *Updated Guide to IAD and the Language of the Ostrom Workshop: A Simplified Overview of a Complex Framework for the Analysis of Institutions and their Development*. Available at:
https://mcginnis.pages.iu.edu/iad_guide.pdf.

Mosse, D. (2005) *Cultivating Development: An Ethnography of Aid Policy and Practice*. London: Pluto Press.
Ostrom, E. (1990) *Governing the Commons: The Evolution of Institutions for Collective Action*. Cambridge: Cambridge University Press.
Ostrom, E. (2005) *Understanding Institutional Diversity*. Princeton: Princeton University Press.
Ostrom, E. (2009) 'A polycentric approach for coping with climate change: Background paper to the 2010 world development report', *The World Bank: Policy Research Working Paper*, 5095, pp. 2–54.
Ostrom, E. (2010) 'Beyond markets and states: Polycentric governance of complex economic systems', *American Economic Review*, 100, pp. 641–672.
Ostrom, V., and Ostrom, E. (1977) 'Public goods and public choices', in Savas, E.S. (ed.) *Alternatives for Delivering Public Services: Toward Improved Performance*. New York: Routledge.
Ostrom, V., Tiebout, C.M., and Warren, R. (1961) 'The organization of government in metropolitan areas: A theoretical inquiry', *American Political Science Review*, 55, pp. 831–842.
Rayamajhee, V., and Paniagua, P. (2021) 'The ostroms and the contestable nature of goods: Beyond taxonomies and toward institutional polycentricity', *Journal of Institutional Economics*, 17, pp. 71–89.
Ruttkowski, S. (2017, August 30) 'Unesco-cide: Does world heritage status do cities more harm than good?' *The Guardian* www.theguardian.com/cities/2017/aug/30/unescocide-world-heritage-status-hurt-help-tourism.
Schmitt, T.M. (2009) 'Global cultural governance: Decision-making concerning world heritage between politics and science', *Erdkunde*, 63(2), pp. 103–121.
Shackelford, S.J. (2020) *Governing New Frontiers in the Information Age*. Cambridge: Cambridge University Press.
Skounti, A. (2017) 'The intangible cultural heritage system: Many challenges, few proposals', *Santander Art and Culture Law Review*, 2(3), pp. 61–76.
Sokka, S., Badia, F., Kangas, A., and Donato, F. (2021) 'Governance of cultural heritage: Towards participatory approaches', *European Journal of Cultural Management & Policy*, 11(1), pp. 4–19.
Stephan, M., Marshall, G., and McGinnis, M. (2019) 'An introduction to polycentricity and governance', in Thiel, A., Blomquist, W., and Garrick, D. (eds.) *Governing Complexity*. New York: Cambridge University Press, pp. 21–44.
Swyngedouw, E. (2004) 'Globalisation or "glocalisation"? Networks, territories and rescaling', *Cambridge Review of International Affairs*, 17(1), pp. 25–48.
UNESCO (2008) *Summary Records of the Second Extraordinary Session (Sofia, Bulgaria, 18–22 February 2008) and the Third Extraordinary Session (Paris, 16 June 2008) of the Intergovernmental Committee for the Safeguarding of the Intangible Cultural Heritage*, ITH/08/3.COM/CONF.203/5.
UNESCO (2012) *Summary Records of the Seventh Session of the Intergovernmental Committee for the Safeguarding of the Intangible Cultural Heritage, held in UNESCO Headquarters, Paris, from 3 to 7 December 2012*, ITH/13/8.COM/4.
UNESCO (2015) *Ethical Principles for the Safeguarding of the Intangible Cultural Heritage* 10. COM 15.A.
UNESCO (2017) *Summary Records of the Twelfth Session of the Intergovernmental Committee for the Safeguarding of the Intangible Cultural Heritage held in Jeju Island, Republic of Korea, from 4 December to 9 December 2017*, ITH-18–13.COM-4-EN.

UNESCO (2021, November) *Evaluation of UNESCO's Action in the Framework of the 2003 Convention for the Safeguarding of the Intangible Cultural Heritage*, IOS/EVS/PI/100.

UNESCO (2021) *Reflection on the Listing Mechanisms of the Convention and Proposal for Related Revisions to the Operational Directives*, LHE/21/16.COM/14, Annex.

UNESCO (2022) *Global Reflection on the Listing Mechanisms of the 2003 Convention* [online]. Available at: https://ich.unesco.org/en/global-reflection-on-the-listing-mechanisms-01164 (Accessed: 11 February 2022).

Zhang, Y. (2012) 'Heritage as cultural commons: Towards an institutional approach of self-governance', in Bertacchini, E., Bravo, G., Marelli, M., and Santagata, W. (eds) *Cultural commons*. Cheltenham, UK: Edward Elgar.

PART III

Negotiating inclusiveness

7

NO SUSTAINABILITY WITHOUT MATERIALITY

Complex paths to good practices in Switzerland

*Julien Vuilleumier and Ellen Hertz**

7.1. Introduction

While the principle of sustainable development has played a role in the conceptual framework of the UNESCO ICH Convention since its beginnings, it is increasingly being called on to shape the evolution of the Convention going forward, and even to serve as a criterion for distinguishing "good" ICH from "bad." As discussed in depth in various chapters in this book, this has resulted in a plethora of declarations, recommendations, indicators, and tools designed to facilitate the integration of these two powerful normative frameworks, discursive work that necessarily takes place at a high level of abstraction. In our chapter, we focus on a particular national setting – Switzerland – and one of the three pillars of sustainability – the environment – to highlight both the tensions raised by this process of integration and its innovative potential.

Specifically, we examine in detail two sets of recognized ICH practices in Switzerland – collecting and cultivating wild plants and traditional irrigation schemes – that carry important implications for environmental sustainability, notably for sustainable development goals ("SDGs") 6 ("Clean water and sanitation"), 12 ("Responsible consumption and production"), 13 ("Climate Action"), 15 ("Life on land"), and 17 ("Partnership for the goals"). Historical analysis of the constitution of these elements demonstrates that their safeguarding has involved significant political, legal, scientific, cultural, and economic investments, ranging from the creation of research centers, to reworking zoning regulations, to promotion through tourism marketing, implemented through coordinated efforts by different national and cantonal programs and offices. With these examples in mind, we argue that highlighting the benefits of ICH for sustainability (and vice versa) requires a more thorough consideration of the material conditions and infrastructures that underpin

DOI: 10.4324/9781003244158-11

intangible heritage (Harrison, 2018). Put more provocatively, taking environmental sustainability seriously as a facet of ICH may require revisiting the long-contested divide between the material and the immaterial at the heart of the 2003 Convention (see Kirshenblatt-Gimblett, 2014).

This demonstration echoes current research in critical heritage studies that "focus[es] attention on the range of heterogeneous elements – objects, people, places, practices, pronouncements, bureaucratic apparatuses – that are brought together in 'heritage assemblages'" (Harrison, 2018, p. 1370). Indeed, as the international community pays increasing attention to the relationship between ICH and SD, it would do well to remember the heated debates that marked the creation of the Convention itself, many of which turned on how best to recognize the deep interconnection between material, natural, and intangible heritage (see Aikawa, 2004; Hertz et al., 2018, pp. 35–59). Then as today, if we wish to guarantee the sustainability of the intangible heritage of humanity, we must work to preserve the sustainability of the ecosystems, infrastructures, transactions, skills, and knowledge that are its preconditions. Reflecting on the complex relationship between heritage and the various environmental crises we are currently experiencing necessarily takes us beyond official definitions and lists to a reconsideration of "what we care about" (Tornatore, 2014). It also requires confronting the question of who is "we," an inevitably political question that involves choices, tradeoffs, and value judgments.

We come to these questions from different backgrounds, and this accounts for differences in emphasis and tone in our article. Julien is a federal employee who has been involved in the implementation of the ICH Convention with the Swiss Federal Office for Culture ("FOC") since 2017. Ellen is an academic anthropologist who has carried out research on the implementation of the 2003 Convention in Switzerland since 2008, and who has found herself criticizing its conceptual framework while simultaneously recommending elements for inclusion in cantonal and national inventories. Joining our different perspectives, we propose a critique of critique; we seek to understand how linking SD and ICH, despite the contradictions and incoherencies this may involve, can nonetheless help administrative and civil society actors develop creative proposals for addressing current environmental crises. Our hope is that by scrutinizing the trajectories of certain ICH elements in Switzerland, we can interrogate the material, political, economic, and administrative conditions that make this linkage possible, but also the resistance that it inevitably runs up against, thereby encouraging a more open discussion of the political project it represents.

7.2. The rise of sustainable development as a framework for conceptualizing ICH

The basic principles of sustainable development, with its three "pillars" (economic, social, and environmental), have inspired efforts to conceptualize and safeguard intangible cultural heritage for decades (see chapters by Janet Blake and Marc Jacobs in this volume). However, as multiple environmental crises make themselves felt with growing urgency, sustainability has increasingly become the master motif guiding the evolution of the Convention. This is an encouraging development, as it highlights the relevance of ICH policy for addressing issues of global concern such as climate change, biodiversity preservation, maintenance of ecosystem services, and future generations' access to critical natural resources. However, operationalizing this linkage brings ICH administrations up against SD's notoriously flexible and ambiguous contours. Environmental activists in particular have long pointed out that SD's three pillars frequently enter into tension, even direct contradiction, in ways that fundamentally weaken their ability to help decision-makers choose between contested political options (see Sachs, 1993).

We might presume that this situation was clarified by the establishment of the 17 specific goals set forth in the U.N.'s 2030 Agenda for sustainable development. However, this is not the case, and in some ways, the proliferation of specific goals only further complicates an already fuzzy picture. Policymakers now have potentially more rather than less leeway to decide which of these goals they wish to promote and which they choose to ignore, widening the possibilities for trade-offs, compromises (both useful and dangerous), and greenwashing. As anthropologists Larsen and colleagues argue, the problem is not the articulation of specific goals *per* se, but rather the "depoliticized critique" which focuses on lack of implementation through "win-win language" that decontextualizes sociopolitical circumstances and avoids "questioning . . . structural challenges" (Larsen et al., 2022, p. 21). More troublesome still is the SDGs' neglect of the cultural field, an absence that has been frequently criticized by cultural and political actors worldwide (see Marc Jacobs's contribution to this volume).

UNESCO, as a UN agency, has followed this general trend and thoroughly integrated the 2030 SDGs into its different policy instruments. In the area of education, it has highlighted the complexity of the SDG framework, foregrounding the urgent need to promote key competencies in the areas of systems thinking, anticipation, strategy, collaboration, critical thinking, self-awareness, integrated problem solving, and, perhaps most importantly, normative trade-offs and judgment calls.[1] In the area of intangible heritage, various instruments have been promulgated to align the 2003 Convention with the SDGs, such as the Overall Results Framework ("ORF") adopted in 2018.[2]

While these new measures are promising, they are also highly technical, even technocratic, as illustrated by the new Periodic Reporting System for the 2003 Convention, launched in 2020. Based on the ORF, periodic reporting now takes the form of an online tool[3] of unprecedented complexity, involving 26 indicators and nearly 100 questions formulated in highly abstract terms. While the intention – widely shared by member states – is to produce a finer and more analytical monitoring of the implementation of the 2003 Convention, its format has given rise to some skepticism and criticism, notably that its conceptual apparatus requires multiple interpretations and reformulations in order to render it comprehensible to communities, tradition bearers, and local authorities and allow them to contribute by providing information about their safeguarding activities. This perplexity was palpable for Julien when he oversaw the preparation of Switzerland's 2021 Periodic Report. One representative of the ICH element "Art of dry-stone walling," for example, mentioned ironically during an online meeting that it would be far more sustainable for him and others to limit the time spent in front of a computer filling in forms. This example demonstrates the risk of user disconnect that this type of administrative mechanism can generate, creating a distance between safeguarding practices, their meaning for their bearers, and the abstract formulations that are produced over the course of the reporting process, especially with its extra focus on SD. Nonetheless, these arrangements have placed ICH within the framework of the SDGs at the international level and prompt State Parties to seek ways to consider this linkage nationally. Various initiatives have been launched, notably in Switzerland.

7.3. SD's special role in the new Swiss ICH framework

In Switzerland, the Federal Office for Culture has articulated a series of reflections intended to guide cantonal authorities in their selection and treatment of elements of ICH to be included in the national inventory. In 2022, the FOC launched a new process for updating the national inventory (called "List of Living Traditions in Switzerland"[4]) and introduced "contribution to sustainable development" as an additional criterion for new proposals,[5] echoing UNESCO guidelines. Reflecting the considerations discussed earlier, the SDG framework was judged too complex and abstract and was not adopted as such. Rather, the FOC spelled out a general understanding of sustainable development in four dimensions, the fourth of which is culture.

To give concrete expression to this approach, it chose the "Wheel Chart of Sustainability and ICH,"[6] developed in Finland, which it transmitted to bearers of ICH elements, public authorities in charge of culture, and partners in the field of cultural heritage. This chart makes it possible to question the sustainability of an element so as to provide incentives for the promotion of SD. Its purpose is to encourage cultural actors to critically examine their proposals by asking simple questions such as "How does the activity impact nature?" or "What economic opportunities are generated through the activity?" Following this approach, the introduction of the sustainability criterion is conceived of as a form of awareness-raising and an incentive for self-reflection on the part of the bearers of ICH nominations. Favoring voluntary engagement over obligations, the guidelines also encourage applicants to reflect on possible conflicts to be resolved. In short, the FOC has set itself politically realistic though modest goals, promoting a "flexible" understanding of the sustainability framework for ICH.

A second measure adopted to encourage bearers of ICH to integrate SD into their thinking was the new call for financial support for projects to safeguard intangible cultural heritage launched by the FOC in 2022.[7] This support scheme allows tradition bearers to apply for monetary assistance for ICH safeguarding projects, something that Swiss cultural policy had thus far excluded. This incentive to promote safeguarding projects at different scales and to articulate sustainability as a "bonus" is coupled with the decision to identify and monitor elements (best practices) that exemplify the federal encouragement scheme and demonstrate that ICH bearers adhere to it. Thus, sustainability has been placed alongside the classic concept of safeguarding as a criterion for receiving funding from the Confederation.

The desire to adopt a modest, voluntary approach to integrating SD within the Swiss ICH framework was motivated by a number of considerations: fear of controversy, certainly, but also of the non-inclusion (or even exclusion) of elements that do not satisfy the criteria of environmental sustainability but are nonetheless of considerable social importance for their bearers. In so doing, the FOC took a position in favor of maintaining another balance, that of the regional, cultural, and linguistic representativeness of the inventory which is central to maintaining popular acceptance of ICH policy in the Swiss context (Hertz et al., 2018).

Echoing the critiques of SD mentioned earlier, this "flexible" approach is of course marked by a certain number of incoherencies and contradictions. A charming example of this is the "Bikers' meeting in Hauenstein,"[8] an ICH element that the canton of Solothurn proposed for inclusion in the national inventory in the first round of applications. This social practice involves the weekly meeting of "several hundred motorbike enthusiasts" at an inn at the top of a mountain pass, and as such emphatically does not pass muster as an environmentally sustainable practice. However, it is clearly also an important social ritual for hundreds of men and women, bringing together a community of practice around motorbiking with its own social, cultural, and perhaps even spiritual significance. It is thus both socially and economically sustainable. Banning practices such as these from what is considered to be the legitimate intangible heritage of Switzerland could cause more harm than good, by creating sociocultural exclusion, alienating parts of the population from the concept of ICH, and reinforcing stereotypes about elite "green" Bernese bureaucrats disconnected from popular culture.

In sum, Switzerland's cautious and "flexible" approach to introducing the sustainability criterion is a reflection of SD's complexity. This is particularly true in the area of environmental sustainability, as the direct and indirect relations between ICH and environmental concerns are multiple and difficult to assess. More difficult still, however, is the problem of the environment's fundamental materiality. Public policy that aims to use ICH to promote environmental sustainability must take into account other measures and political-legal frameworks, embedding cultural practices in their socio-ecological contexts. This is the case, for example, for know-how related to food production, such as the Alpine pasture season,[9] which concerns cheese-making in mountain areas. These practices are inseparable from the sustainable management of high-altitude meadows, the effects of climate change, cohabitation with large predators, or the maintenance of biodiversity, all of which are themselves subject to controversy, regulation, and normative prescriptions. Thus, placing a focus on environmental sustainability represents a challenge for public administrations, which generally operate in silos and have notorious difficulties integrating transversal and systemic approaches. In this context, raising awareness and providing carrots rather than sticks to promote the integration of environmental sustainability into intangible heritage policy would seem to provide a pragmatic way forward for both authorities and tradition bearers.

At the time of this writing, the FOC's new philosophy and measures linking intangible heritage to SD are at their very beginnings. At this stage and this level of analysis, we have therefore chosen to take a step backward, analyzing past experiences to draw attention to considerations that we consider fundamental for creating a workable and meaningful linkage between ICH and SD.

7.4. Before and beyond "best practices"

The two sets of ICH elements we will examine would seem to represent very successful convergences between intangible heritage safeguarding and environmental sustainability. Both involve socio-environmental knowledge and practices that trace their roots back for centuries, and both symbolize the ingenuity and *débrouillardise* of mountain communities facing the constraints of their geo-political situations. From a purely environmental point of view, both promote practices, respectively, of horticulture and water management, that have (potentially!) positive impacts in the areas of carbon emissions and biodiversity. While both sets of practices were listed as ICH *before* Switzerland officially adopted its new "linkage" philosophy, they would appear to be perfect candidates to showcase the shift that the FOC wishes to accomplish.

Key to our understanding here is the fact that this linkage did not operate at the discursive or conceptual level. Rather, these eco-friendly traditions were kept alive and promoted through massive, multi-sectorial investments by politicians, cultural actors, scientists, urban planners, and entrepreneurs (notably in the tourist industry). The rationales, institutions, and people behind these investments take us very far from the imagined world of resilient mountain peasants inventing environmentally sustainable solutions to the constraints under which they labor. To the contrary, as with ICH generally, the safeguarding of these traditional practices, knowledge, and value systems reflects urban imaginaries, policies, and attachments more than it does those of the inhabitants of the regions being "safeguarded." They represent modernizing projects that need to be examined in their own right for their important role in promoting sustainability.

7.4.1.a. Swiss medicinal mountain herbs – "culturalizing" natural remedies

Three items related to medicinal mountain herbs, wild or cultivated, are recognized by the national inventory of ICH in Switzerland: "Herbal knowledge in the convents of Central Switzerland,"[10] "Collecting and cultivating of wild plants,"[11] and "Natural healing in Appenzell Ausserrhoden."[12] Each of these has its historical roots, its long-term practitioners and promoters, its cultural, health-related, and spiritual significations, and its socio-economic organizational base, and there is no doubt that each makes reference to, and is to a certain extent based on, traditional practices, values, and knowledge regimes that fully warrant the attention of heritage experts. However, none of these traditional practices would have been recognized as ICH without the multi-million-dollar industry in plant-based natural medicines, dietary supplements, beauty products, and comestibles that was created through relatively recent development projects and made economically sustainable through considerable amounts of financial and political resources.

In her dissertation entitled *Soigner la Patrie. La fabrique des plantes médicinales suisses* (2017), Julie Perrin describes the "heritage careers" of each of these three items and places them within the larger context of the national project to promote the image of folkloric mountain Switzerland that emerged in urban centers over the course of the 19th and 20th centuries. She focuses on the creation and institutionalization of a specific product line: that of "Swiss medicinal plants" which, contrary to what we might imagine, did not exist as such before the 1980s. With this background in mind, her study "examines 'Swiss medicinal plants' as the product of a wide variety of public policies (agricultural, regional, health, cultural, commercial and for the promotion of innovation)" (Perrin, 2017, p. 5, *EH translation*). This involved both the (re)qualification of these plants to bring to light the full diversity of their properties (culinary, dietary, therapeutic, cosmetic, spiritual, and for pest-management) and the creation of a market niche, with its attendant market targets. It further involved the creation of legal and regulatory norms to guarantee that the market differentiation that these actors wished to establish was backed up by institutional enforcement powers, creating a price differential that compensated for the higher costs of production in Switzerland. Finally, it involved the very materiality of these plants themselves, as they become the object of research and development aimed at selecting the best varieties, organizing production sites, and standardizing agronomic techniques and procedures.

Perhaps the most surprising of Perrin's findings is the discovery that the creation and promotion of "Swiss medicinal plants" as a specific market niche had little to do with Swiss medicinal plants at all, but was rather motivated by the desire of a group of engineers from Graubunden canton to fight the progressive loss of wealth and population of Poschiavo, the region they hailed from and loved. This project was thus born as a response to the depopulation of the Swiss mountains and addressed through the Federal Law on Aid for Investments in Mountain Regions. In the words of one of the main protagonists of this enterprise, an agronomist with a degree from the prestigious Swiss Federal Institute of Technology in Zurich:

> In the beginning, they didn't know that they wanted to do something for medicinal plants, they wanted to do something for Poschiavo. Then, in 1976, they went to see the [local government] authorities, of course. They asked them whether they had any ideas for what could be interesting [to develop]. And exactly at this

> moment, the authorities were busy creating the first-ever concept of regional development. It was completely new in Switzerland at the time, and they based their work on the Federal Law on Aid for Investments in Mountain Regions of 1974. You could say that this was the beginning of regional policy planning in Switzerland.
>
> *(p. 68,* EH translation*)*

To develop their project, this group of young engineers solicited the help of a Zurich consulting firm specializing in urban development, for whom "development" was essentially conceived in economic terms. They hit upon the idea of developing a new economic sector, appropriate to the rural economy of the region: the market for medicinal plants. To convince local, cantonal, and federal authorities of the viability of this project, the promoters had simultaneously to argue for its innovative character and to anchor their discourse in a rhetoric that made sense for this mountain valley, where tobacco and vegetables were well-known regional products. They did this by highlighting the "special character" of the valley, rich in biodiversity, and the existence of a convent that had cultivated medicinal herbs in the region for centuries. Thus, while environmental sustainability and safeguarding of traditional know-how were central elements of the project design, the principal reasons for its existence were commercial and political. Ecological preconditions were combined with cultural traditions to create a sense of the *naturalness* of this innovation, which was in fact the first of its kind. In Perrin's analysis: "This operation of conceptualization was the first step in the qualification of the future economic sector of Swiss medicinal plants, a conceptualization that depended on the progressive singularization of this product" (p. 72, *EH translation*).

While this conceptual framework served to legitimate the project, it did little to move it forward to realization. The project developers soon discovered that both scientific knowledge about the properties of these plants and the agronomical know-how necessary to create a commercial product line were, in the words of Perrin's key informant, "basically inexistant." To fill these gaps, the group mandated a study from the cantonal Center for agronomical vulgarization, which led them to another surprising discovery: the small number of Swiss firms active in this sector, including Ricola, the famous Swiss brand, depended on foreign imports for their production! Furthermore, much of the transformation of these herbs into ingredients fit for commercialization took place outside of Switzerland.

Taking stock, the developers launched an entirely new phase of the project to convince federal authorities and the major commercial actors in this market of the advantages of developing a domestic product line. They pointed out that importing herbs internationally placed Swiss firms in a dependency relation with respect to supply, reduced their quality, and limited Swiss research capacity in this area. These general economic arguments were then accompanied by a detailed analysis of the best qualification of the product line with respect to current Swiss legislation in the areas of medicinal products (focused on quantitative analysis of active medicinal substances), environmental security (which covered risks of contamination from pesticides), and food production. From these analyses, it emerged that the most advantageous positioning for this new product line was neither as a medicine nor as foodstuff, but rather as a "health-related natural stimulant" (p. 80, *EH translation*). This characterization connoted closeness with well-being and nature without entangling this production in the complex regulatory frameworks that governed pharmaceuticals and agriculture, all the while highlighting the advantages of locally based production for health and food security.

Most interesting for our argument is the fact that the final and crucial addition to this mixture of economic, regulatory, and political logics came from the cultural sphere. It soon became apparent that reference to the highly charged Swiss symbol that are mountains would lend extra credibility and appeal to a production line that had up until then taken place essentially at lower altitudes. While production over a certain altitude in fact reduced the active properties of certain plants, it provided the necessary association with the historically invested images of Swiss mountains as places of purity, innocence, and authenticity, and with a non-industrial imaginary thought to be healthier and more respectful of the environment. Drawing on this set of cultural connotations, the project developers successfully lobbied for a regulated category of "mountain herbs," produced at an altitude of 800 meters or above.

In sum, underlying the recognition and safeguarding of the living traditions of herbal mountain remedies was an immense political, economic, and scientific infrastructure that integrated Alpine farmers' traditional activities within a modernizing project to create an agro-industrial sector with high added value. The result is a form of ICH that corresponds in many respects with the goals of SD[13]: It promotes knowledge and know-how around biodiversity in mountain regions, it provides farmers with a market for their agricultural activities, allowing them to survive economically in these peripheral regions, and it further cultivates awareness about the importance of mountain ecosystems for the environmental well-being of the country. However, heritage policy alone could never have brought this about: politics, economics, law, and science are necessarily part of this picture.

7.4.2.b. Traditional irrigation: infrastructures before practices

Two living traditions concerning water and irrigation management are listed in the national inventory: the Wässermatten[14] (irrigated meadows) in the Oberaargau region and the "Consortage in the Valais."[15] These two examples, inscribed separately in 2012 on the national inventory, are currently the subject of a multinational nomination file for the Representative List of the Intangible Cultural Heritage of Humanity, submitted in March of 2022. Entitled "Traditional irrigation in Europe: knowledge, technique and organization,"[16] this nomination brings together six countries led by Austria, the result of pre-existing collaborations between these different regions that were initiated by a network of academics and practitioners to recognize and safeguard traditional irrigation practices in Europe (Leibundgut and Vonderstrass, 2016). In the process, the initial approach focusing on irrigation systems, their development, and structure has been transformed into an approach focused on the intangible dimensions of techniques and knowledge related to the construction, maintenance, and collective management of irrigation. This shift from irrigation itself, as a technical, landscape, and agricultural infrastructure to be protected and valued, to the know-how, techniques, and organization of irrigation is a shift in focus from the tangible to the intangible. As we will see, this rearrangement reveals issues in terms of trajectories, support, and understanding of this heritage. How is the link between environmental sustainability and ICH reflected in these two cases? How are environmental contributions recognized and supported by public policies?

The Wässermatten is primarily described as a surviving agro-cultural landscape: "The Wässermatten in the Langete, Oenz and Rot River valleys of Oberaargau are the last remaining examples of a cultural practice of cooperative meadow irrigation and fertilization that was once widespread in the Swiss Central Plateau" (Rieder, 2022, p. 1, *JV translation*). This understanding is accompanied by a historical narrative that legitimizes the need for conservation: "The practice was promoted in the 13th century by the Cistercian monks of the St. Urban monastery as part of a soil enrichment campaign" (*id.*). The historical trajectory of this irrigation system, and even more so of the associated mode of social organization allowing for the construction, maintenance, and use of a complex network of main and secondary canals, locks and dams, has been well documented (Leibundgut, 1993). This research shows that after the closure of the Convent of St. Urban in 1848, it was public authorities (cantons and municipalities) that took up the preservation of this heritage. From the middle of the twentieth century, interest in irrigation declined as artificial fertilizers replaced natural fertilization systems using water from the river. In addition, the canal system was an obstacle to mechanized agriculture. Thus, intensive agriculture, mechanization, and the use of artificial fertilizers threatened the survival of these traditional practices. It is in this context that awareness grew, in the 1970s, of the need to maintain these irrigated meadows, in particular among environmentalists who demanded the protection of wetlands in virtue of their biological and landscape qualities.

In 1983, the irrigated meadows of the Langete, Rot, and Oenz valleys were included in the Federal Inventory of Landscapes, Sites, and Natural Monuments.[17] However, this legal classification was not sufficient to keep these structures functional, as they require specific forms of agricultural exploitation and maintenance. It is at this stage that the recognition of know-how and techniques came into play through the implementation of financial support measures for farmers. In 1991, the canton of Bern adopted the legal and financial basis for the conservation of several typical areas, granting credit to certain farmers and establishing a foundation, the Wässermatten Stiftung, that concluded contracts with farmers to compensate them for their extra work and loss of income. This legal and financial structure is thus the keystone of the site protection and know-how safeguarding system, and its role is central to the coordination and representation of the Wässermatten model. As this historical trajectory shows, it is the combination of growing awareness of the ecological benefits of water-based fertilization with legal mechanisms for the protection of territory and the environment, themselves associated with financial mechanisms for compensation, that have promoted the local knowledge and know-how that allow this traditional irrigation model to be recognized as intangible heritage.

Our second example comes from the canton of Valais, where "*bisses*" (irrigation channels) are emblematic elements of the territory and landscape. The *bisses* have been developed into a tourist attraction through organized walking tours and represent an important element of local agricultural infrastructure in a region known for its vineyards and orchards. In recognition of this, a drawing of the famous Bisse d'Ayent features on the Swiss 100 francs bill, issued in 2019. The attachment to these water channels as infrastructure is also reflected in public financial support provided by the canton for their maintenance, conservation, improvement, and even revitalization. The *bisses* are therefore recognized as important regional heritage, mainly material and infrastructural in nature, as evidenced by the initiative led by the Association des Bisses du Valais between 2012 and 2014 to nominate the *bisses* for inscription on the World Heritage List.[18] While this proposal was not retained at the national level, following an unfavorable technical analysis (related to the integrity of the material heritage) by federal authorities, it left a mark on the various social actors involved in creating this nomination.

What is important here is how this form of material heritage was reformulated in terms of intangible cultural heritage and became the subject of a new nomination in the framework of the 2003 Convention. In 2012, "Consortages in Valais" (translated in English as "cooperatives") was inscribed as a living tradition in the Swiss inventory of ICH. They are defined as follows:

> A cooperative is a working or ownership collective in which the members have rights and duties as set down in statutes and regulations. While members' duties include participating in the work of the cooperative and assuming official functions, their rights include the use of goods and facilities owned by the cooperative.
>
> (*Antonietti, 2022, p. 1,* JV translation)

These cooperatives collectively manage common goods such as mountain pastures, forests, and irrigation canals. Thus, it is through their model for governance of a common good (water) and through the contributions of this model to sustainability through collective responsibility and optimized resource management (Schweizer et al., 2014) that the *bisses* cooperatives came to be recognized as an element of Swiss ICH.

Following this listing, the traditional irrigation model, using *bisses* but also involving runoff techniques based solely on the principles of gravity, raised awareness, especially in the Oberwalliser Sonnenberge region. Considered a *Bewässerungslandschaft* (an "irrigated landscape"), the landscape and ecological value of traditionally irrigated meadows has increasingly been valued (Stiftung Landschaftsschutz Schweiz, 2020), as evidenced by the Landschaftsschutz Schweiz Foundation's Landscape of the Year Award for the Oberwalliser Sonnenberge in 2020. These irrigated meadows and pastures are also recognized by a local planning act as "protected agricultural zones," and some of them are also located inside the UNESCO World Heritage Site "Swiss Alps Jungfrau-Aletsch." This protected landscape is managed by a commission bringing together the communes and organizations active in the environmental field, with the aim to ensure the support and maintenance of traditional irrigation. Here again, the recognition of the irrigation system as a contribution to the landscape and as a tool for maintaining and promoting biodiversity and the sustainable management of resources precedes its framing as an intangible cultural heritage.

Sustainable development is placed at the center of the multi-state ICH application project for traditional irrigation, presented as an exemplary or even emblematic case of sustainable management of a natural resource. The application form mentions the following contributions:

> Traditional irrigation techniques can make an important contribution to the availability, sustainable management and natural purification of water; they can be an inspiration in finding solutions to the increasing problems related to the Sustainable Development Goals of 2030 (in short SDGs), e.g., of floods and droughts (SDG 6 Clean water and sanitation), as this irrigation form helps to raise ground water levels and uses available, flowing water resources in a sustainable way. . . . They also contribute to mitigating the effects of climate change at the local level (SDG 13 Climate action) and make a positive contribution to increasing biodiversity (SDG 15 Life on land)).[19]

This description provides the keys to understanding the assembly of different rationalities and discourses on these techniques, associating them with the SDGs for environmental sustainability (water, climate action, or biodiversity). In light of these two Swiss examples, we see that the environmental sustainability of these irrigation systems enhances their recognition and support through different public policies (agriculture, environment, culture, tourism). This recognition precedes that of intangible cultural heritage, which represents an innovative framing and creates new potential for support, by involving the know-how, techniques, and socio-economical organization necessary for the maintenance of these agro-environmental infrastructures.

7.5. Conclusion

The integration of sustainable development, in particular environmental sustainability, represents an important challenge for heritage policy in general, and for ICH in particular. At the international level, the interpretative framework and monitoring mechanisms stemming from the 2030 Agenda walk a delicate administrative tightrope: While they raise awareness and promote analysis of the relationship between ICH and sustainability, they can also create a disconnect between community practices and real-life situations. At the domestic level in Switzerland, recent efforts to promote sustainability in heritage policy are still in their infancy and reflect the felt need to adopt a flexible and politically sensitive approach, aimed primarily at maintaining regional and linguistic representativity. As we have pointed out, this philosophy runs the risk that "flexibility" will render these measures toothless, providing easy outs or occasions for greenwashing that contradict the spirit and the letter of the UN's 2030 Agenda.

Rather than approach these questions purely as matters of principle, our article focuses on concrete examples to highlight how environmental sustainability has been promoted by linking ICH with other sectors and government policies: agricultural and environmental policy, economic development of mountain regions, promotion of biodiversity, and support for scientific research. These cases demonstrate that the combination of different public policies with a potential impact in terms of economic and territorial development can indeed establish certain linkages between environmental sustainability and so-called traditional practices. Taking these insights a step further, we conclude that if ICH is to contribute to SD in a meaningful way, it must be thoroughly integrated into planning in all policy sectors – agricultural, commercial, scientific, educational, infrastructural as well as cultural – at the local, national, and regional levels. Echoing Marx, we would like to insist that the superstructure that is culture – intangible heritage with its ideals and values – be grounded in the worldly infrastructures of power, money, and policy: no sustainability without materiality!

We are aware that this formulation implies re-opening the Pandora's box of political considerations and conflicting national priorities that marked the Convention from its beginnings (Aikawa, 2004). We believe these conceptual and normative battles, which take place within the ethereal spheres of international policy formulation, are crucially important, not only in and of themselves but also because they illustrate the importance of the heritage domain as an arena for thinking about humanity's diverse pasts in relation to our necessarily common futures (Harrison, 2018). However, we also believe that we can and should anchor these general and abstract reflections by examining the concrete contexts in which solutions, trade-offs, and failures actually occur. The case studies we have presented represent different configurations in which multiple policy frameworks and constraints, but also opportunities and resources, have combined to create plausible linkages between elements of Swiss ICH and environmental sustainability. The FOC has launched a long-term reflection on the best means for promotion and monitoring these linkages, with the ambition to remain as pragmatically rooted and critically alert as possible. Such an engagement must include an honest examination of those instances in which ICH comes into direct conflict with SD, and vice versa.[20] It must also include attempts to create linkages not with SD in the abstract but with the specific departments and ministries that have the economic, legal, and political resources to promote sustainability, in particular, those responsible for environmental and agricultural policy.

Anne-Sophie Haeringer and Jean-Louis Tornatore (2022) title their recent edited volume *Héritage et anthropocène* with the provocative (and untranslatable) subtitle: "Shall we get rid of heritage altogether?" ("En finir avec le patrimoine?", *EH translation*). While this is not the position we defend, we do argue that linking ICH and SD in meaningful ways can and will alter the very nature of ICH itself. As with other important normative revolutions, we cannot just "add sustainability and stir." In order to create a sustainable linkage between the two, both concepts must be subtly but profoundly transformed.

Notes

* We would like to extend our warm thanks to Julie Perrin for her critical comments, and to Chiara Bortolotto and Ahmed Skounti for their expertise and patience throughout the publication process.

1 See https://unesdoc.unesco.org/ark:/48223/pf0000247444.

2 The Overall Results Framework for the 2003 Convention was adopted in 2018 by the 7th General Assembly. It establishes 26 indicators, themselves classified into eight thematic areas: institutional and human capacities, transmission and education, inventorying and research, policies and legal and administrative measures, the role of intangible cultural heritage and its safeguarding in society, awareness-raising, engagement of communities, groups and individuals as well as other stakeholders, and international engagement. See https://ich.unesco.org/en/overall-results-framework-00984.

3 See https://ich.unesco.org/en/perioding-reporting-ich-10-2020-01081?edit_form=764#1.

4 See www.lebendige-traditionen.ch/tradition/en/home.html.

5 The following criteria are taken into account for the evaluation of a nomination for inscription on Switzerland's List of Living Traditions: 1. completeness and comprehensibility of the application, 2. right to apply, 3. belonging to the ICH domains as defined in the 2003 Convention, 4. continuity, 5. social anchorage, 6. participation and agreement of the bearers, 7. uniqueness and exemplary character, and finally 8. contribution to sustainable development.

6 See www.aineetonkulttuuriperinto.fi/en/julkaisut/wheelchart.

7 See the call for projects at www.bak.admin.ch/bak/fr/home/patrimoine-culturel/immaterielles-kulturerbe-unesco-lebendige-traditionen/foerderung-des-immateriellen-kulturerbes.html.

8 See www.lebendige-traditionen.ch/tradition/en/home/traditionen/toefftreff-hauenstein.html.

9 See www.lebendige-traditionen.ch/tradition/en/home/traditions/summer-grazing-season-in-the-alps.html.

10 See www.lebendige-traditionen.ch/tradition/en/home/traditions/herbal-knowledge-in-the-convents-of-central-switzerland.html.

11 See www.lebendige-traditionen.ch/tradition/en/home/traditions/foraging.html.

12 See www.lebendige-traditionen.ch/tradition/en/home/traditions/natural-healing-in-appenzell-ausserrhoden.html.

13 In hindsight, as Perrin argues, it may be necessary to relativize the success of this extraordinary experiment in invented tradition. While limiting the production of medicinal herbs to these mountain areas made good cultural sense, allowing for the higher prices that made this product line economically viable, it created a series of secondary effects that should be evaluated. Some mountain farmers were induced or obliged to sell their small

parcels of land to larger enterprises seeking economies of scale under an industrialized model of production. Semi-industrial production in turn both contradicted certain precepts of traditional agriculture and blocked the development of alternative agroecological paradigms that better protect biodiversity. Cultivating in hilly regions also required the presence of productive and hardy plants that could meet commercial quantity requirements. Agronomical research institutes thus developed new "traditional" mountain varieties, to be grown rather than gathered, even introducing species that had never been cultivated in these areas. It is too soon to tell what effects these new plants will have on mountain ecosystems, but we know that they were often patented, requiring farmers to purchase the seeds that they had previously produced autonomously. In sum, many of the historical divisions of labor, power, and authority between urban-trained agronomists and mountain farmers have been reproduced: Farmers have been conscripted into a national project in which they figured more as symbols than as beneficiaries within a semi-industrial paradigm for biodiversity protection that has triumphed over alternatives.

14 See www.lebendige-traditionen.ch/tradition/en/home/traditions/waessermatten.html.

15 See www.lebendige-traditionen.ch/tradition/en/home/traditions/cooperatives-in-valais.html.

16 See www.bak.admin.ch/bak/fr/home/patrimoine-culturel/immaterielles-kulturerbe-unesco-lebendige-traditionen/immaterielles-kulturerbe-unesco-in-der-schweiz/liste-indicative-du-patrimoine-culturel-immateriel-en-suisse/traditionnelle-bewaesserung.html.

17 Object 1312 of the Federal Inventory of Landscapes, Sites and Natural Monuments, see description: https://data.geo.admin.ch/ch.bafu.bundesinventare-bln/objectsheets/2017revision/nr1312.pdf.

18 See https://bisses-valais.ch/app/uploads/2019/09/Synthese-Site-internet.pdf.

19 Nomination form ICH-02 "Traditional irrigation in Europe: knowledge, technique and organization," https://ich.unesco.org/doc/download.php?versionID=66560.

20 For a detailed description of an outright clash between bearers of ICH and government regulators aiming to protect biodiversity in Switzerland, see Aebi and Hertz (2022).

References

Aebi, A. and Hertz, E. (2022) "La santé des châtaigniers comme cause patrimoniale: Bioterrorisme amateur, assouplissement administrative et 'neutralité active' des sciences citoyennes", In (A.-S. Haeringer and J.-L. Tornatore, eds.), *Héritage et anthropocène. En finir avec le patrimoine*, pp. 51–77. Nancy: Éditions Arbre bleu.

Aikawa, N. (2004) "An Historical Overview of the Preparation of the UNESCO International Convention for the Safeguarding of the Intangible Cultural Heritage", *Museum International*, 56(1–2): 137–149.

Antonietti, T. (2022) "Les consortages en Valais", *List of Living Traditions in Switzerland* (online) (www.lebendige-traditionen.ch/dam/tradition/fr/dokumente/tradition/vs/geteilschaften_imwallis.pdf.download.pdf/les_consortages_envalais.pdf).

Haeringer, A.-S. and Tornatore, J.-L. (2022) *Héritage et anthropocène. En finir avec le patrimoine*. Nancy: Éditions Arbre bleu.

Harrison, R. (2018) "On Heritage Ontologies: Rethinking the Material Worlds of Heritage", *Anthropological Quarterly* 91(4): 1365–1383.

Hertz, E., Graezer Bideau, F., Leimgruber, W. and Munz, H. (2018) *Politiques de la tradition. Le patrimoine culturel immatériel*. Savoir suisse, pp. 131. Lausanne: Presses polytechniques et universitaires romandes.

Kirshenblatt-Gimblett, B. (2014) "Intangible Heritage as Metacultural Production", *Museum* 66: 163–174.

Larsen, P.B., Haller, T. and Kothari, A. (2022) "Sanctioning Disciplined Grabs (SDGs): From SDGs as Green Anti-Politics Machine to Radical Alternatives?", *Geoforum* 131: 20–26.

Leibundgut, C. (1993) "Wiesenbewässerungssysteme im Langetental–6 Kartenblätter mit Erläuterungen", *Geographica Bernensia G 41*.

Leibundgut, C. and Vonderstrass, I. (2016) *Traditionelle Bewässerung–ein Kulturerbe Europas*. Langenthal: Merkur Druck AG.

Perrin, J. (2017) *Soigner la Patrie. La fabrique des plantes médicinales suisses*. Ph.D. Thesis, University of Neuchâtel (https://libra.unine.ch/Publications/Personne/P/Julie_Perrin/37735).

Rieder, K. (2022) "Wässermatten", *List of living traditions in Switzerland* (online) (www.lebendige-traditionen.ch/tradition/fr/home/traditions/prairies-irriguees.html).

Sachs, W. (ed.). (1993) *Global Ecology: A New Arena of Political Conflict*. New York: ZED Books.

Schweizer, R., Rodewald, R., Liechti, K. and Knoepfel, P. (2014) Des systèmes d'irrigation alpins entre gouvernance communautaire et étatique–Alpine Bewässerungssysteme zwischen Genossenschaft und Staat, Rüegger Verlag, Ökologie & Gesellschaft 24, Zürich, 405.

Stiftung Landschaftsschutz Schweiz (2020) *Die Hangbewässerungslandschaft der Oberwalliser Sonnenberge–ein Kulturgut von europäischer Bedeutung, SL-FP, Bern* (www.sl-fp.ch/de/stiftung-landschaftsschutz-schweiz/landschaft-des-jahres/2020-oberwalliser-hangbewaesserungslandschaft-126.html).

Tornatore, J.-L. (2014) "Words for Expressing What We Care About: The Continuity and the Exteriority of the Heritage Experience", In (J. Bondaz, F. Graezer Bideau, C. Isnart, and A. Leblon, eds.), *Les vocabulaires locaux du "patrimoine". Traductions, négociations, transformations*, pp. 31–54. Berlin: LIT Verlag.

8

SAFEGUARDING THE INTANGIBLE HERITAGE OF INDIGENOUS PEOPLES

A conceptual distance in intergovernmental discourses[1]

Anita Vaivade

8.1. Introduction

At the end of 2019, the International Decade of Indigenous Languages 2022–2032 was proclaimed by Resolution 74/135 "Rights of indigenous peoples," adopted by the General Assembly of the United Nations (UN) on December 18, 2019 (United Nations, 2019). UNESCO was invited to serve as the lead agency for it. In this same Resolution, the UN General Assembly recalled the 2030 Agenda for sustainable development (United Nations, 2015) and encouraged Member States "to give due consideration to all the rights of indigenous peoples in fulfilling the commitments undertaken in the 2030 Agenda" (Point 12). The 2019 Resolution speaks of the "transmission of traditional knowledge, languages, spiritual and religious traditions and practices." Interestingly and despite UNESCO's extensive action in the field of heritage, no reference is given to heritage in the Resolution, and thus neither to intangible cultural heritage. This evokes a question about possible explanations as well as prospective consequences of such a conceptual absence. Prior to addressing that, I wish to begin with a personal discursive encounter.

A decade after the UNESCO Convention for the Safeguarding of the Intangible Cultural Heritage (hereafter: Convention) was adopted in 2003, the Intergovernmental Committee for the Safeguarding of the Intangible Cultural Heritage (hereafter: Committee), established on the grounds of the Convention, met for its eighth session. In addition to examining numerous nominations to the recently established international lists, the Committee examined reports submitted by States Parties to the Convention on the status of inscribed elements. That year, a discussion took place on the first and extraordinary[2] periodic report submitted by Brazil on the "Yaokwa, the Enawene Nawe people's ritual for the maintenance of social and cosmic order," inscribed in 2011 on the UNESCO List of Intangible Cultural Heritage in

DOI:10.4324/9781003244158-12

Need of Urgent Safeguarding. That was one of the rare occasions at the Committee's discussions that the intangible cultural heritage (ICH) of Indigenous peoples[3] was discussed explicitly and was given particular attention. In 2013, Latvia was one of the 24 Committee members being elected for a four-year period (2012–2016) and that year I was invited to join the Latvian delegation and to contribute to its work at the Committee.[4] This was my initial personal experience of this intergovernmental setting of collaboration. The discussion on the Enawene Nawe heritage safeguarding became a memorable one in particular because of the striking distance that could be observed between government representatives involved in the discussion and the people concerned, the Enawene Nawe people. This distance was described in geographical and also relational terms. As we could read in the 2013 report of Brazil on the inscribed element,

> To reach the indigenous lands it is necessary to fly an hour and a half from Cuiabá, capital of Mato Grosso to the city of Juina, in the interior of the state, from there it is an hour by car to the mooring point on the river with a further eight hours by boat to the village of the Enawenê Nawê. . . . Even today there is almost no contact between this ethnic group and society surrounding their territories, a fact that makes their participation in the planning and implementing of safeguarding actions difficult. However, it is worth noting that the Enawenê Nawê leaders make weekly telephone contact with the local office of IPHAN [Instituto do Patrimônio Histórico e Artístico Nacional] in Mato Grosso state and, despite their poor Portuguese, an exchange of information takes place regarding the actions carried out by both parties.
>
> *(Brazil, 2013, pp. 6–7)*[5]

The Enawene Nawe people were explained to be almost unreachable, despite the governmental efforts to contact them, and their participation in preparing the report was deemed impossible. Thus, we, the members of the Committee, were discussing their heritage and taking decisions with advice for its safeguarding without any Enawene Nawe people being present, heard, or in any way actively involved in the discussion process (UNESCO, 2014, pp. 44–46). As we may now learn from a retrospective scholarly account, grounded on personal involvement in the research and inventorying processes carried out in collaboration with the Enawene Nawe people, "(u)ntil the start of the 2000s, they (Enawene Nawe) made very few incursions into the small nearby towns or into non-indigenous lands in general," and interdisciplinary scholarly studies on Enawene Nawe culture were undertaken only in 2007, with gradually built trust and consent from the people concerned (Lima Rodgers et al., 2016, pp. 98–99). Enawene Nawe heritage became inscribed on the national ICH inventory in 2010, followed by an international inscription in 2011. This has thus been a dramatic change for the Enawene Nawe people in terms of their external relations, and this all happened within a time span of only about a decade.

This experience of an intergovernmental debate and decision-making (Decision 8.COM 6.B of the Committee), accompanied by the absence of the Indigenous people concerned, the Enawene Nawe people, and witnessing also a geographical and relational distance between the Indigenous people and their government, raises further question about the attention paid internationally to the safeguarding of Indigenous cultures and heritage. Taking this example as a starting point, while acknowledging that geographical and relational distances may not be considered equally characteristic to all Indigenous peoples, this chapter will embark on more generic discursive grounds. It will follow a historical as well as prospective approach and explore the presences and absences of the concerns about Indigenous intangible heritage safeguarding within intergovernmental debates and decisions at UNESCO, and beyond, their dynamics in relation to the sustainable development discourse, conceptual connections and distances that may be observed, and their present and potential consequences.

8.2. The UNESCO 2003 Convention: "a missed opportunity"?

The Convention for the Safeguarding of the Intangible Cultural Heritage was adopted by the UNESCO General Assembly for several purposes, above all – to safeguard intangible cultural heritage, and also to ensure respect for it, raise awareness of its importance, and provide for international cooperation. As recognized in its Preamble[6]: "communities, in particular indigenous communities, groups and, in some cases, individuals, play an important role in the production, safeguarding, maintenance and re-creation of the intangible cultural heritage, thus helping to enrich cultural diversity and human creativity" (UNESCO, 2003a).

This is the only place within the text of the Convention where Indigenous communities are mentioned. As Paul Kuruk, one of the legal experts involved in the drafting of the Convention, has recognized,

> the failure to provide specific rules governing the access to and use of intangible cultural heritage coupled with the reference to the State's obligations in rather exhortatory terms weakens the ICH Convention as an instrument for tackling cases of misappropriation and unauthorized use of cultural heritage. To this extent, the ICH Convention may come to be viewed as a missed opportunity to enhance the protection of indigenous knowledge.
>
> *(Kuruk, 2004, Introduction)*

As later recognized by Janet Blake, a legal scholar whose contribution was crucial to the drafting of the Convention, this turned out to be a point where a "compromise position" was adopted, although not without debates on this issue during the drafting process (Blake, 2020, p. 30).

Potential difficulties to come to an intergovernmental agreement with regard to the protection of Indigenous heritage were acknowledged already prior to undertaking the drafting process. The major reason for that was seen in the difficulty of separating heritage protection from the question of land rights and the self-determination of Indigenous peoples (Daes, 1997, p. 77, para. 4, cited in Blake, 2001, p. 61). As was recognized at the time, addressing this connection could have become problematic for many States that might be "generally interested in developing protection for intangible heritage" (Blake, 2001, p. 61).[7] The problematic side of this was indeed expressed, once reaching the stage of drafting the Convention and receiving general comments and proposals for amendments by UNESCO Member States on the initial draft prepared by legal scholars and other experts.

As the documents compiling Member States' positions witness (UNESCO, 2003b, 2003c; see Smeets, 2021, p. 13), there were only a few countries who explicitly defended a need to emphasize the intangible heritage of Indigenous peoples, communities, and groups, and those were Bolivia and Vanuatu. However, there was also a strong opposition to this idea. India objected to having an emphasis on certain communities, including the Indigenous (UNESCO, 2003c, p. 32), and stated, "many countries, including India, [at the First Meeting of Intergovernmental Experts] were opposed to allowing any special emphasis to be given to 'indigenous people'" (UNESCO, 2003b, p. 15). In a more moderate way, Sweden proposed that

> (t)he convention's use of the intangible cultural heritage concept should be kept as general as possible so that while there may be an urgent need to emphasize such matters as the difficult plight of indigenous peoples, the intangible cultural heritage should not refer to this area alone.
>
> *(Ibid., p. 19)*

There were also more generic reflections, partly on already existing national regulations and policies, as by Australia, or on procedural and participatory issues regarding the drafting process, as by Canada. As we may read:

> Canada regrets the almost complete absence of observers from communities and organizations representing Aboriginal peoples at the recent First Intergovernmental Meeting of Experts. We encourage the Director-General to explore possible mechanisms, such as the Permanent Forum on Indigenous Issues, to provide a voice for Aboriginal peoples in the current dialogue.
>
> *(UNESCO, 2003c, pp. 17–18)*

The non-governmental sector present was also willing to integrate a clear connection to the United Nations Permanent Forum on Indigenous Issues (UNPFII) within the Convention's text, however unsuccessfully. Apart from these written positions and compiled amendment proposals, there is no record of a debate on safeguarding the heritage of Indigenous peoples in the reports on the three sessions of the Intergovernmental Meeting of Experts who discussed the advancement while drafting the Convention.

However, prior to drafting the Convention particular attention was paid within UNESCO to Indigenous and minority heritage. For instance,

> (t)o promote the Recommendation [on the Safeguarding of Traditional Culture and Folklore, 1989] UNESCO further focused a part of its culture programme on the establishment of inventories and safeguarding plans, as well as the revitalisation of ICH of minority and indigenous groups.
>
> *(UNESCO, 2013, p. 4)*

As former Secretary of the Convention Rieks Smeets highlights, it was during an expert meeting, titled "International consultation on new perspectives for UNESCO's programme: the intangible cultural heritage" and held in June 1993 that among other issues "(s)pecial attention was requested for minority and indigenous heritage" (Smeets, 2021, p. 4). Noriko Aikawa, then Director of Intangible Heritage Unit, has reminded that "(i)n June 1997, the Executive Board again recommended that emphasis be placed on the preservation of oral traditions, endangered languages, and forms of cultural expression, particularly those of minorities and Indigenous peoples" (UNESCO, 1997, cited in Aikawa, 2001, p. 16). Also in 1999, when the efficiency and challenges of the named Recommendation were globally assessed, one of the expert recommendations was to "encourage further collaboration between intergovernmental agencies such as UNESCO, WIPO (World Intellectual Property Organization), and WGIP (UN Working Group on Indigenous Populations)" (Seitel, 2001, p. 301).[8] There is a longer history of connections between UNESCO and WIPO in this field (see Hafstein, 2018; Martinet, 2019), which will remain beyond the scope of this chapter. The global assessment of the UNESCO 1989 Recommendation demonstrated a dedicated attention and extensively explored path to bring forward the defense of the interests of Indigenous peoples with regard to their heritage (Seitel, 2001).[9] A separate attention to Indigenous peoples and their culture was thus expressed at some point by both experts and governmental representatives, without leading to a respective follow-up in the process of drafting the 2003 Convention.

The 2003 Convention is a testimony of an international consensus and readiness to develop policy measures that would support the safeguarding of intangible cultural heritage. However, there are only a few obligations to States Parties stated within the Convention, and none of those provide sufficient grounds for claiming concrete rights of communities, groups, or individuals with regard to their heritage. Instead, the Convention serves as a platform for international cooperation, encouraging national governments to act at the national level and to eventually do more than the Convention stipulates, but this remains up to governmental decisions.

The absence of a focused attention on Indigenous heritage in the Convention and of defining respective rights and obligations may, on one hand, be viewed as "a missed opportunity" for the protection of the intangible cultural heritage of Indigenous peoples. On the other hand, the ongoing intergovernmental debates at WIPO on a possible agreement to protect traditional knowledge, traditional cultural expressions, and genetic resources witness to what extent the task to agree upon the protection and respective rights may become a globally non-consensual undertaking. Meanwhile, the global outreach of the UNESCO 2003 Convention and also of concerns about the safeguarding of intangible cultural heritage may be used as a reference to raise international awareness about Indigenous heritage protection, strengthen the common ethical stance, develop further normative instruments at national and regional levels, and do so in dialogue with broader developments on Indigenous rights within the United Nations system.

8.3. The rights of Indigenous peoples in ethical principles

Ethical Principles for Safeguarding Intangible Cultural Heritage (hereafter: Ethical Principles) were debated and further adopted by the Committee in 2015. Although none of the 12 principles specifically addresses the safeguarding of Indigenous heritage, they do encompass it implicitly. As it is stated in their Preamble:

> The Ethical Principles for Safeguarding Intangible Cultural Heritage have been elaborated in the spirit of the 2003 Convention for the Safeguarding of the Intangible Cultural Heritage and existing international normative instruments protecting human rights and the rights of indigenous peoples. They represent a set of overarching aspirational principles that are widely accepted as constituting good practices for governments, organizations and individuals directly or indirectly affecting intangible cultural heritage in order to ensure its viability, thereby recognizing its contribution to peace and sustainable development.
>
> *(UNESCO, 2015)*

The mention of international normative instruments that protect human rights and the rights of Indigenous peoples[10] is a significant reminder in this Preamble. Furthermore, as highlighted by heritage scholar Marc Jacobs (2016, p. 79), the vocabulary of this Preamble is inspired by the UN 2030 Agenda, as well as by Article 13 of the UNESCO 2005 Convention for the Protection and Promotion of the Diversity of Cultural Expressions. According to the article, "Parties shall endeavour to integrate culture in their development policies at all levels."[11] Overall, the concerns about Indigenous peoples and their culture are much more explicit in the 2005 Convention when compared to the 2003 Convention. Despite the 2003 Convention's silence with regard to rights, beyond the principle of participation stipulated in Articles 11 and 15, Ethical Principles do refer to the rights of communities, groups and, where applicable, individuals. Principle 2 states:

> The right of communities, groups and, where applicable, individuals to continue the practices, representations, expressions, knowledge and skills necessary to

ensure the viability of the intangible cultural heritage should be recognized and respected.

(UNESCO, 2015)

The draft of Ethical Principles raised debates within the Committee with regard to Indigenous peoples, among other issues. However, a debate on a more explicit reflection on social inclusiveness did not prove to be successful. When discussing Principle 2, there was a proposal made by Hungary to insert a specific reference to Indigenous peoples and minorities in this paragraph. While the proposal concerning Indigenous peoples did not raise direct opposition, the mention of minorities did. For example, Turkey reminded the Committee about the obligations of States Parties to the Convention to safeguard intangible cultural heritage present on their territories "be it heritage of communities, groups and, in some cases, minorities or majority groups" (UNESCO, 2016, p. 187). After rather extensive discussions among the delegations within the Committee, this proposal was not adopted, and the Ethical Principles followed the generic wording used within the Convention. While being aware of the relevance of such debates and concerns of social inclusiveness, there was an overall awareness of the tensions that arise when trying to specify legal subjects concerning intangible heritage safeguarding once they go beyond the neutral and undefined concepts of "communities, groups and individuals" (on inclusiveness in UNESCO intergovernmental discourse on intangible heritage, see Kuutma and Vaivade, 2021, p. 525). Thus, social inclusiveness reflected in the UN Agenda 2030, with the proclaimed central and transformative promise "Leave No One Behind", remains mostly implicit within the Ethical Principles.

8.4. The "discursive strength" of the UN Agenda 2030

The adoption of the UN Agenda 2030 has had praise, as well as criticism, including that its "discursive strength" could be undermined by the high number of goals adopted as a tool for a target-driven global policy-making (Langford, 2016, p. 168). This does not seem, however, to be an obstacle to enhancing references to sustainable development with regard to intangible cultural heritage safeguarding in general and the implementation of the 2003 Convention in particular. Besides, it also brings attention to Indigenous peoples.

In the Operational Directives for the Implementation of the Convention, attention to Indigenous peoples became explicit with the introduction of Chapter VI, "Safeguarding intangible cultural heritage and sustainable development at the national level," adopted in 2016, a decade after the Convention entered into force. This chapter explicitly addresses social inclusiveness, cohesion, and equity and also brings attention to Indigenous peoples. Thus, the context of sustainable development, and in particular that of social cohesion, became a significant turn in providing a more nuanced terminology for intangible heritage safeguarding policies, naming "indigenous peoples, migrants, immigrants and refugees, people of different ages and genders, persons with disabilities and members of vulnerable groups" as subjects of intangible cultural heritage safeguarding at the national level (UNESCO, 2022a).

Slightly later, in 2018 the General Assembly of the Convention adopted the Overall Results Framework for the 2003 Convention. It recognizes sustainable development as part of the wished impact of the Convention, formulated as follows: "Intangible cultural heritage is safeguarded by communities, groups and individuals who exercise active and ongoing stewardship over it, thereby contributing to sustainable development for human well-being, dignity, and creativity in peaceful and inclusive societies" (UNESCO, 2018a, p. 1). This Framework thus refers to social inclusivity and contains a note that explains:

> References to 'inclusive', 'inclusively' or 'on an inclusive basis' should be understood to mean 'inclusive of all sectors and strata of society, including indigenous peoples, migrants, immigrants and refugees, people of different ages and genders, persons with disabilities and members of vulnerable groups'.
>
> *(Ibid., p. 2)*

The attention to social inclusiveness has come hand in hand with highlighting linkages between intangible cultural heritage and sustainable development, which, after all, can be seen as a manifestation of the "discursive strength" of the UN Agenda 2030.

8.5. Overcoming a conceptual distance within the UN

The rights of Indigenous peoples over several decades have become a distinct field within the United Nations system and agenda (see Dahl, 2012; Åhren, 2016; see also United Nations, 2022a). A significant and historic step was finally taken by the adoption of the United Nations Declaration on the Rights of Indigenous Peoples (UNDRIP) in 2007, a year after the UNESCO 2003 Convention had entered into force. The UNDRIP stipulates, among other issues addressed, that:

> Indigenous peoples have the right to maintain, control, protect and develop their cultural heritage, traditional knowledge and traditional cultural expressions, as well as the manifestations of their sciences, technologies and cultures, including human and genetic resources, seeds, medicines, knowledge of the properties of fauna and flora, oral traditions, literatures, designs, sports and traditional games and visual and performing arts. They also have the right to maintain, control, protect and develop their intellectual property over such cultural heritage, traditional knowledge, and traditional cultural expressions.
>
> *(United Nations, 2007, Article 31, part 1)*

This Article provides a conceptually encompassing view of the manifestations of the cultures of Indigenous peoples. Although the UNDRIP is a soft-law instrument, it constitutes a turning point in building customary international human rights law. Moreover, it has affected the work of UNESCO, its policies (UNESCO, 2018b), and its actions. Nevertheless, it is an ongoing process to establish meaningful and impactful articulation between these operationally separate paths of international cooperation and decision-making within the UN – ICH safeguarding on one hand and the protection of Indigenous peoples' rights on the other.

Within a broader picture of defending Indigenous rights through the instruments adopted and the mechanisms established at the UN, the 2003 Convention could be a reference at different levels. The Convention could serve, first of all, Indigenous peoples as an additional reference to defend their interests, at international, regional, and national levels. However, it has been recognized in the framework of the UNPFII that there is a lack of knowledge among Indigenous people about the 2003 Convention (UNESCO, 2019). This is also due to the focus of the UNPFII on normative instruments that would be specifically developed with regard to Indigenous peoples and their rights. Lately, the argument for the implementation of the Convention has scarcely been used by Indigenous peoples within the UN, beyond UNESCO, to raise awareness of their rights and interests. This can be observed within the developments at the UNPFII (for instance, United Nations, 2021 and 2022b), and also in the deliberations by the Special Rapporteur of the Human Rights Council on the rights of Indigenous peoples and by the Expert Mechanism on the Rights of Indigenous Peoples, where references to the 2003 Convention have been scarce.

As for UNESCO, the Convention resonates with the organization's work in cultural and other sectors with regard to Indigenous peoples. In 2018, the "UNESCO policy on engaging with indigenous peoples" was adopted in order to implement the UNDRIP "across all relevant programme areas" (UNESCO's Medium-Term Strategy for the period 2014–2021, cited in UNESCO, 2018b, p. 4). Soon after, the International Year of Indigenous Languages 2019 brought particular attention to Indigenous peoples, including in relation to the implementation of the 2003 Convention.[12] That year, a roundtable titled "The Convention for the Safeguarding of the Intangible Cultural Heritage: Opportunities for Indigenous Peoples" was organized as a side event at the 18th session of the United Nations Permanent Forum on Indigenous Issues (UNESCO, 2019). It raised a relevant and needed question on the possible usefulness of the 2003 Convention for defending the rights and interests of Indigenous peoples with regard to their heritage. It also brought attention to the articulation between the Convention and other instruments within the UN system (on such articulation aspects, see Cornu et al., 2020) that address the culture of Indigenous peoples, such as the Convention on Biological Diversity (1992), the Indigenous and Tribal Peoples Convention (No. 169) of the International Labour Organization (1989), and the UN Declaration on the Rights of Indigenous Peoples (2007). At the time of the roundtable, more than a decade had already passed since the Convention entered into force in 2006. In the evaluation of UNESCO's action on the International Year of Indigenous Languages 2019, the need to draw on the organization's intersectoral strengths was highlighted (UNESCO, 2021, p. 39); and attention to Indigenous peoples remains on the agenda of the Secretariat of the 2003 Convention still today (UNESCO, 2022b), namely as part of the capacity-building programme, and in light of the International Decade of Indigenous Languages 2022–2032.

Within the UN, the right to maintain and develop cultural identities of Indigenous peoples within larger national communities has been at the core of debates on the rights of Indigenous peoples (Vaivade, 2018, pp. 171–173). The role of heritage and the relevance of the 2003 Convention in that regard have remained, however, mostly unnoticed. For instance, in the global assessment of the Second International Decade 2005–2015 of the World's Indigenous People, no explicit linkages to the 2003 Convention are made (United Nations, 2014a). The same observation goes to the outcome document of the World Conference on Indigenous Peoples held in 2014, which does not include any reference to heritage and its safeguarding, meanwhile drawing attention to associated concepts such as "traditional knowledge, languages and practices" (United Nations, 2014b). Presumably, the points of articulation between protecting the rights of Indigenous peoples and safeguarding their intangible cultural heritage remain intuitive, indirect, and still need to be conceptualized clearly within policy-making and law at the intergovernmental level. The absence of such a clear articulation also invites one to dwell on the question of whether the concept of heritage is still dominantly associated with the tangibility of past legacies, instead of being understood as culturally shaped, vibrant, and ever-changing tangible and intangible expressions of human creativity in the present and future.

Finally, it remains crucial how the articulation between the 2003 Convention and the rights of Indigenous peoples is developed at the national level, as well as regionally in cross-border formats of cooperation, which are particularly important for Indigenous peoples living across the territorial borders of States.[13] Global normative instruments remain soft in terms of defined legal obligations and rights for the safeguarding (including the protection) of Indigenous intangible cultural heritage. Therefore, those are national legislations and regional normative instruments that matter substantially, and this is relevant also more generally for the implementation of the 2003 Convention (Cornu et al., 2020; Vaivade, 2020).

8.6. Conclusion

This chapter has shown that sustainable development discourse has had a significant impact on addressing internationally, and as part of the implementation of the 2003 Convention, the rights and interests of Indigenous peoples. Meanwhile, the absence of references to intangible cultural heritage in UN discourse on Indigenous peoples beyond UNESCO continues to witness a conceptual distance between distinct fields of intergovernmental standard-setting and policy-making – namely, the safeguarding of intangible cultural heritage on one hand, and the protection of the rights of Indigenous peoples on the other. However, a dialogue has been undertaken at the UN to consolidate intergovernmental efforts for safeguarding the ICH of Indigenous peoples. This still remains at an early stage regarding the establishment of clear connections. On one hand, the conceptual distance between the intergovernmental discourse on ICH (at UNESCO) and the one on the rights of Indigenous peoples (at UN, and UNPFII and WIPO in particular) witnesses a demarcation between the aims for ICH safeguarding more broadly and for legal protection of rights more specifically. On the other hand, this conceptual distance raises uncertainties about a common understanding of the concept of heritage and hinders opportunities to use the 2003 Convention for strengthening the defense of the rights and interests of Indigenous peoples and for developing national legislation and regional treaties with respect to it.

Despite little attention to Indigenous peoples within the text of the Convention, despite Indigenous peoples being mentioned in the Preambles only (both in the Convention and in the Ethical Principles), and despite the Convention establishing only a few generic obligations to its States Parties (such as to "take the necessary measures to ensure the safeguarding of the intangible cultural heritage present in its territory," Article 11, part (a)), the Convention may still serve as an opportunity and as a reference to addresses the safeguarding (including the protection) of the heritage of Indigenous peoples, and as an argument in policy-making, legislative, and judicial processes, most significantly at the national level in countries that are States Parties, and also regionally. The use, or absence, of the argument of the 2003 Convention, for safeguarding the intangible heritage of Indigenous peoples at national and regional levels, depends, among other factors, on histories, present social contexts, level of awareness about the Convention and its purposes, as well as legal and political strategies. Overcoming, in intergovernmental discourses, the conceptual distance addressed in this chapter may advance similar processes at national and regional levels, thus bridging discourses and strengthening a call to safeguard the intangible heritage of Indigenous peoples, and by doing that eventually contributing to socially more inclusive prospects for development.

Notes

1 This chapter is prepared with the financial support of the postdoctoral research project "Intangible Cultural Heritage as Resource for Sustainable Development in Northern Europe: Rights-Based Approach" (No.: 1.1.1.2/VIAA/3/19/476) funded by the European Regional Development Fund, the Government of Latvia, and the Latvian Academy of Culture.

2 As requested by the Committee in its Decision 6.COM 8.3 on the inscription of this element in 2011, the report on the implementation of safeguarding measures was to be submitted two years after the inscription of the element, instead of the ordinary time span of four years. According to the Operational Directives for the Implementation of the Convention for the Safeguarding of the Intangible Cultural Heritage,

"at the time of inscription, the Committee may establish a specific timetable for reporting on a case-by-case basis, which will take precedence over the normal four-year cycle" (UNESCO, 2022a, Paragraph 161). This right of the Committee to establish a specific timetable for reporting has been put into practice relatively seldomly, in ten decisions on the inscriptions on the List of Intangible Cultural Heritage in Need of Urgent Safeguarding, out of 72 elements inscribed on this list (until October 2022). In addition to the named element in Brazil, a specific timetable for reporting was applied also to elements in Belarus (in 2009 and 2019), Mali (in 2011 and 2021), Guatemala and Uganda (in 2013), Mauritius (in 2019), Egypt (in 2020), and lately Ukraine (in 2022). Thus, in this regard the experience of Brazil was neither the first nor the last case of extraordinary reporting. However, the report by Brazil was the only report on the current status of an element inscribed on the named list examined in 2013, and the second report ever examined by the Committee regarding the inscriptions on this list, after the Committee had examined in 2011 an extraordinary report by Belarus on the element "Rite of the Kalyady Tsars (Christmas Tsars)," inscribed in 2009.

3 The term "Indigenous peoples" does not have a global internationally agreed defi nition,which is absent also from the United Nations Declaration on the Rights of Indigenous Peoples, adopted in 2007. Instead, this term continues to be a subject matter of diverging approaches and interpretations. These debates will remain outside this chapter, presuming a broad common understanding of the meaning of the term and its major characteristics (see Cobo, 1983). Attention will be paid instead to the practice of the use of this and related terms in intergovernmental discourses in relation to the UNESCO 2003 Convention. According to a recently established scholarly practice, this term is capitalized in the chapter, while maintaining its use in citations unchanged.

4 More about personal engagement with the 2003 Convention, see Kuutma and Vaivade, 2021.

5 The original spelling of Enawenê Nawê is maintained in the citation while using Enawene Nawe spelling in the rest of the chapter, as it is also used in respective UNESCO documents.

6 About the interpretation of preambles of international treaties, also in judicial practice, see Klabbers, 2018.

7 The importance of land and self-determination for preserving Indigenous cultural identities is explicitly stated also today, for instance, in the speeches of the representatives of Indigenous peoples at the United Nations Permanent Forum on Indigenous Issues (United Nations, 2021 and 2022b).

8 The named Working Group was established back in 1982 "as a subsidiary organ to the Sub-Commission on the Promotion and Protection of Human Rights" of the Commission on Human Rights, and the Expert Mechanism on the Rights of Indigenous Peoples (EMRIP) was adopted instead, in 2007 (United Nations, 2022a).

9 It was advised in the proposed Action Plan, among others, to create task forces to engage in further study of the

> relationship to other instruments and Draft Documents (UN Draft Document, WIPO [World Intellectual Property Organization], TRIPS [the Agreement on Trade-Related Aspects of Intellectual Property Rights, 1994], CBD [Convention on Biological Diversity, 1992], Maatatu [Mataatua Declaration on Cultural and Intellectual Property Rights of Indigenous Peoples, 1993], SUVA [Suva Declaration, resulted from a UN Development Programme Consultation on Indigenous Peoples' Knowledge and Intellectual Property Rights, 1995] and other Indigenous peoples' declarations).
>
> *(Seitel, 2001, p. 305)*

10 As stated by the Special Rapporteur on the situation of human rights and fundamental freedoms of Indigenous people:

> The practice of international bodies and mechanisms in recent decades has significantly contributed to building an understanding of the rights of indigenous peoples on the basis of general human rights norms and a wide array of international instruments. The authoritative interpretation of these norms has contributed to the gradual crystallization of a universal common understanding of the minimum content of the rights of these peoples as a matter of international law and policy.
>
> *(Anaya, 2008, pp. 10–11)*

The UN Declaration on the Rights of Indigenous Peoples adopted in 2007, according to its Article 43, represents such "minimum standards for the survival, dignity and well-being of the indigenous peoples of the world" (see also Martinet, 2019, pp. 262–267).

11 The Preamble of the 2005 Convention recognizes that the knowledge systems of Indigenous peoples contribute to sustainable development and calls for their protection. As for the articles, Article 2 provides guiding principles, among which the "Principle of equal dignity of and respect for all cultures" explicitly includes the cultures of persons belonging to minorities and Indigenous peoples, while Article 7 on the measures to promote cultural expressions states, *among others*, that Parties shall pay "due attention to the special circumstances and needs of various social groups, including persons belonging to minorities and indigenous peoples."

12 Among the events organized was the exhibition "Sounds of living heritage: A journey through indigenous languages" opened on December 10, 2019, during the 14th session of the Committee that took place from December 9 to 14, 2019, in Bogotá, Colombia.

13 A dialogue in Nordic countries in Europe has been undertaken on the possibilities of developing a regional normative instrument to protect the traditional knowledge of Sámi Indigenous people. This initiative is linked to the implementation of the 2003 Convention (see Ministry of Education and Culture, Finland, 2022).

References

Åhren, Mattias (2016) *Indigenous Peoples' Status in the International Legal System*. Oxford: Oxford University Press.

Aikawa, Noriko (2001) 'The UNESCO Recommendation on the Safeguarding of Traditional Culture and Folklore (1989): Actions Undertaken by UNESCO for Its Implementation' in Seitel, Peter (ed.). *Safeguarding Traditional Cultures: A Global Assessment*. Washington, DC: Center for Folklife and Cultural Heritage, Smithsonian Institution, pp. 13–19, accessible at https://unesdoc.unesco.org/ark:/48223/pf0000132327 (Accessed: 2 February 2022).

Anaya, James S. (2008) *Promotion and Protection of all Human Rights, Civil, Political, Economic, Social and Cultural Rights, Including the Right to Development*. Report of the Special Rapporteur on the situation of human rights and fundamental freedoms of indigenous people, S. James Anaya. Human Rights Council, A/HRC/9/9, accessible at www2.ohchr.org/english/bodies/hrcouncil/docs/9session/A-HRC-9-9AEV.doc (Accessed: 9 February 2022).

Blake, Janet (2001) *Developing a New Standard-Setting Instrument for the Safeguarding of Intangible Cultural Heritage: Elements for Consideration*. CLT-2001/WS/8. Paris: UNESCO.

Blake, Janet (2020) 'The Preamble' in Blake, Janet and Lucas Lixinski (eds.). *The 2003 UNESCO Intangible Heritage Convention: A Commentary*. Oxford: Oxford University Press, pp. 19–35.

Brazil (2013) *Report on the Status of an Element Inscribed on the List of Intangible Cultural Heritage in Need of Urgent Safeguarding*. Intergovernmental Committee for the Safeguarding of the Intangible Cultural Heritage, held in Baku, Azerbaijan, from December 2 to 7, 2013. Report no. 00917/Brazil, accessible at https://ich.unesco.org/en/8com (Accessed: 2 February 2022).

Cobo, José Martínez (1983) *Study of the Problem of Discrimination Against Indigenous Populations: Final report submitted by the Special Rapporteur, Mr. José Martínez Cobo*, 1981–1983, accessible at www.un.org/development/desa/indigenouspeoples/publications/2014/09/martinez-cobo-study/ (Accessed: 15 June 2021).

Cornu, Marie, Anita Vaivade, Lily Martinet, and Clea Hance (2020) (eds.) *Intangible Cultural Heritage under National and International Law: Going Beyond the 2003 UNESCO Convention*. Cheltenham: Edward Elgar Publishing.

Daes, Erica-Irene (1997) *Protection of the Heritage of Indigenous People*. Special Rapporteur of the Sub-Commission on Prevention of Discrimination and Protection of Minorities; Chairperson of the Working Group on Indigenous Populations. Human Rights Study Series. New York, Geneva: United Nations.

Dahl, Jens (2012) *The Indigenous Space and Marginalized Peoples in the United Nations*. New York: Palgrave Macmillan.

Hafstein, Valdimar Tr. (2018) *Making Intangible Heritage: El Condor Pasa and Other Stories from UNESCO*. Bloomington: Indiana University Press.

Jacobs, Marc (2016) 'The Spirit of the Convention–Interlocking Principles and Ethics for Safeguarding Intangible Cultural Heritage', *International Journal of Intangible Heritage*, 11: 71–87, accessible at www.ijih.org/volumes/article/608 (Accessed: 12 October 2022).

Klabbers, Johannes Antonius Maria (2018) 'Treaties and Their Preambles' in Bowman, Michael J. and Dino Kritsiotis (eds.), *Conceptual and Contextual Perspectives on the Modern Law of Treaties*. Cambridge: Cambridge University Press, pp. 172–200, https://doi.org/10.1017/9781316179031.009

Kuruk, Paul (2004) 'Cultural Heritage, Traditional Knowledge and Indigenous Rights: An Analysis of the Convention for the Safeguarding of Intangible Cultural Heritage', *Macquarie Journal of International and Comparative Law*, 1(1): 111–134, accessible at www.austlii.edu.au/au/journals/MqJICEL/2004/5.html (Accessed: 9 February 2022).

Kuutma, Kristin and Anita Vaivade (2021) 'Political Imperatives in the Heritage Regime and the Emergent Collaborative Scenarios on the Ground: Case Studies from the Baltics', *Slovenský národopis/Slovak Ethnology*, 69(4): 519–532, https://doi.org/10.2478/se-2021-0031.

Langford, Malcolm (2016) 'Lost in Transformation: The Politics of the Sustainable Development Goals', *Ethics & International Affairs*, 30(2): 167–176.

Lima Rodgers, Ana Paula, Deise Lucy Oliveira Montardo, Izaque João, José Ricardo Jamal Júnior, Leonardo Pires Rosse, Marília Raquel Albornoz Stein, Rosângela Pereira de Tugny, Spensy Kmitta Pimentel, Verônica Aldé, and Vherá Poty Benites da Silva (2016) 'Song Memory as a Territory of Resistance Among South American Indigenous Peoples: A Collective Documentation Project', *The World of Music (new series)*, 5(1) (Ethnomusicology in Brazil): 81–110.

Martinet, Lily (2019) *Les Expressions Culturelles Traditionnelles en Droit International*. Paris: IRJS Éditions.

Ministry of Education and Culture, Finland (2022) *Nordic Co-Operation in Intellectual Property and Traditional Knowledge: Enhanced Co-Operation in the Nordic Countries on the Issues of Intellectual Property and Protection of Indigenous Peoples' Traditional Knowledge*, accessible at: https://okm.fi/en/project?tunnus=OKM057:00/2020 (Accessed: 10 February 2022).

Seitel, Peter (2001) (ed.) *Safeguarding Traditional Cultures: A Global Assessment*. Washington, DC: Center for Folklife and Cultural Heritage, Smithsonian Institution, accessible at https://unesdoc.unesco.org/ark:/48223/pf0000132327 (Accessed: 2 February 2022).

Smeets, Rieks (2021) 'Overview of the development of the listing mechanisms of the UNESCO Convention for the Safeguarding of the Intangible Cultural Heritage up to 2008'. *Expert Meeting in the Framework of the Global Reflection on the Listing Mechanisms Under the 2003 Convention for the Safeguarding of the Intangible Cultural Heritage*, Online, May 7, 26 and 27, 2021, LHE/21/EXP/3 Rev., accessible at https://ich.unesco.org/en/online-meeting-of-experts-category-vi-01165 (Accessed: 2 February 2022).

UNESCO (1997) *Recommendations by the Executive Board on the Draft Programme and Budget for 1998–99*. General Conference, 29 C/6, accessible at https://unesdoc.unesco.org/ark:/48223/pf0000110016 (Accessed: 9 February 2022).

UNESCO (2003a) *Convention for the Safeguarding of the Intangible Cultural Heritage*. General Conference, accessible at https://ich.unesco.org/en/convention (Accessed: 12 October 2022).

UNESCO (2003b) *Compilation of Amendments from Member States concerning the Convention for the Safeguarding of the Intangible Cultural Heritage*. CLT-2002/CONF.203/3 Rev., accessible at https://ich.unesco.org/doc/src/04548-EN.doc (Accessed: 9 February 2022).

UNESCO (2003c) *Compilation of General Comments from Member States Concerning the Preliminary Draft Convention for the Safeguarding of Intangible Cultural Heritage*. CLT2003/CONF.205/5, accessible at https://ich.unesco.org/doc/src/04550-EN.doc (Accessed: 9 February 2022).

UNESCO (2013) *Evaluation of UNESCO's Standard-Setting Work of the Culture Sector Part I–2003 Convention for the Safeguarding of the Intangible Cultural Heritage: Final Report*. Internal Oversight Service, Evaluation Section, IOS/EVS/PI/129 REV., accessible at https://ich.unesco.org/doc/src/IOS-EVS-PI-129_REV.-EN.pdf (Accessed: 10 February 2022).

UNESCO (2014) *Summary Records of the Eight Session of the Committee*. Intergovernmental Committee for the Safeguarding of the Intangible Cultural Heritage, held in Baku, Azerbaijan, from December 2 to 7, 2013. Document ITH/14/9.COM/4 Rev., accessible at https://ich.unesco.org/en/9com (Accessed: 15 June 2021).

UNESCO (2015) *Ethical Principles for Safeguarding Intangible Cultural Heritage*. Intergovernmental Committee for the Safeguarding of the Intangible Cultural Heritage, accessible at https://ich.unesco.org/en/ethics-and-ich-00866 (Accessed: 9 February 2022).

UNESCO (2016) *Summary Records of the Tenth Session of the Committee*. Intergovernmental Committee for the Safeguarding of the Intangible Cultural Heritage, held at Windhoek, Namibia, from November 30 to December 4, 2015. Document ITH/16/11.COM/4, accessible at https://ich.unesco.org/en/11com (Accessed: 15 June 2021).

UNESCO (2018a) *Overall Results Framework for the 2003 Convention*, accessible at https://ich.unesco.org/doc/src/41571-EN.pdf (Accessed: 10 February 2022).

UNESCO (2018b) *UNESCO Policy on Engaging with Indigenous Peoples*, accessible at https://unesdoc.unesco.org/ark:/48223/pf0000262748 (Accessed: 10 February 2022).

UNESCO (2019) *Traditional Knowledge: Generation, Transmission and Protection.* Roundtable, recording, accessible at https://ich.unesco.org/en/indigenous-peoples (Accessed: 15 June 2021).

UNESCO (2021) *Evaluation of UNESCO's Action in the Framework of the 2003 Convention for the Safeguarding of the Intangible Cultural Heritage.* Internal Oversight Service, Evaluation Section, IOS/EVS/PI 100, accessible at https://ich.unesco.org/en/evaluations-audits-and-governance-00717#2013-evaluation-of-unescos-action-in-the-framework-of-the-2003-convention (Accessed: 10 February 2022).

UNESCO (2022a) *Operational Directives for the Implementation of the Convention for the Safeguarding of the Intangible Cultural Heritage.* General Conference of the States Parties to the UNESCO Convention for the Safeguarding of the Intangible Cultural Heritage, accessible at https://ich.unesco.org/en/directives (Accessed: 12 October 2022).

UNESCO (2022b) *Living Heritage and Indigenous Peoples.* Intangible Cultural Heritage, UNESCO, accessible at https://ich.unesco.org/en/indigenous-peoples (Accessed: 1 February 2022).

United Nations (2007) *United Nations Declaration on the Rights of Indigenous Peoples.* General Assembly, accessible at https://social.desa.un.org/issues/indigenous-peoples/united-nations-declaration-on-the-rights-of-indigenous-peoples (Accessed: 12 October 2022).

United Nations (2014a) *Achievement of the Goal and Objectives of the Second International Decade of the World's Indigenous People.* Report of the Secretary-General, accessible at www.un.org/development/desa/indigenouspeoples/about-us.html (Accessed: 15 June 2021).

United Nations (2014b) *Outcome Document of the High-Level Plenary Meeting of the General Assembly Known as the World Conference on Indigenous Peoples.* Resolution adopted by the General Assembly, accessible at www.un.org/en/ga/69/meetings/indigenous/documents.shtml (Accessed: 9 February 2022).

United Nations (2015) *Transforming Our World: 2030 Agenda for Sustainable Development.* Resolution adopted by the General Assembly, accessible at www.un.org/ga/search/view_doc.asp?symbol=A/RES/70/1&Lang=E (Accessed: 10 February 2022).

United Nations (2019) *Resolution 74/135 "Rights of Indigenous Peoples"*, General Assembly, accessible at https://undocs.org/en/A/RES/74/135 (Accessed: 15 June 2021).

United Nations (2021) *United Nations Permanent Forum on Indigenous Issues*, 20th session, working documents accessible at www.un.org/development/desa/indigenouspeoples/unpfii-sessions-2/unpfii-20th-session.html (Accessed: 15 June 2021).

United Nations (2022a) *Indigenous Peoples at the United Nations.* Department of Economic and Social Affairs, accessible at www.un.org/development/desa/indigenouspeoples/about-us.html (Accessed: 2 February 2022).

United Nations (2022b) *United Nations Permanent Forum on Indigenous Issues*, 21st session, working documents accessible at www.un.org/development/desa/indigenouspeoples/unpfii-twenty-first-session-25-april-6-may-2022.html (Accessed: 12 October 2022).

Vaivade, Anita (2018) 'Intangible Heritage as Source of Identity: International Law and Deontology' in Waelde, Charlotte, Catherine Cummings, Mathilde Pavis, and Helena Enright (eds.). *Research Handbook on Contemporary Intangible Cultural Heritage: Law and Heritage.* Cheltenham: Edward Elgar Publishing, pp. 165–193.

Vaivade, Anita (2020) 'Article 13: Other Measures for Safeguarding. Developing Intangible Cultural Heritage Policies and Legislation at the National Level' in Blake, Janet and Lucas Lixinski (eds). *The 2003 UNESCO Intangible Heritage Convention: A Commentary.* Oxford: Oxford University Press, pp. 200–217.

PART IV

Intangible cultural heritage economics

Decontextualization, precarity, and entrepreneurship

9

DECONTEXTUALIZATION FROM UNESCO TO CHINA

The embarrassment and empowerment of economic uses of intangible cultural heritage

Chiara Bortolotto and Philipp Demgenski

9.1. Introduction

"May I say quite emphatically that this park is not Disneyland," declared the Indonesian delegate during the ninth session of the Intergovernmental Committee for the safeguarding of the intangible cultural heritage (hereafter "the Committee").[1] The delegate maintained a diplomatic composure, despite feeling offended by what he defined as an "accusation that this is simply for tourists." "This" refers to the Beautiful Indonesia in Miniature Park that, in 2014, was proposed for inclusion on the Register of Good Safeguarding Practices (hereafter "the Register") as a "cultural space for safeguarding, development and education in intangible cultural heritage." The proposal describes Beautiful Indonesia as an area of 150 hectares in East Jakarta City comprising "a lake with miniature islands of the Indonesian archipelago . . . surrounded by provincial pavilions, museums and recreation units." It highlights that "within the pavilions, there are traditional houses containing ethnographic objects, such as apparel, handcrafts, and musical instruments" and that "each provincial pavilion is a space for activities and education in the culture of its respective province."[2]

The Consultative Body established by the Committee for the examination of proposals to the Register had decided to turn down the submission. In the aforementioned session held in UNESCO's Parisian headquarters, the president of the Consultative Body explained that the main problem was that "the park appears to result in folklorization and museumification of ICH and its activities seem to be divorced from the functions and the meanings of the heritage in question that are important for the practitioners." The program was criticized as being "oriented mainly to tourists and visitors rather than toward strengthening transmission within communities, with ICH used as recreation and entertainment for others at the expense

DOI:10.4324/9781003244158-14

of the meaning to its own practitioners and communities." In conclusion, the project was declared a "clear case" of "decontextualisation."

The Indonesian delegate argued that recreation and entertainment are part of the performing arts, which is one of the domains of ICH, and that the people performing in the park are all "community members that come from different communities in Indonesia," and are "facilitated" by the park. He furthermore contended that their participation in the park activities "gives them respect and encourages them to safeguard their ICH when they go back to their respective places." Lastly, he explained that "this park does not decontextualize ICH but rather it *recreates the context* . . . so that ICH can be practiced and transmitted among communities in an urban context," concluding that "unless we have cultural spaces, how are we going to safeguard ICH in cities?" (our emphasis).

A lengthy debate among Committee members highlighted how the concerns of the Consultative body were widely shared, despite this project also being regarded as an interesting attempt at safeguarding ICH in an urban context. The Brazilian delegate's reflexive assessment of the discussion is illustrative. He observed "a certain *malaise* of the Consultative body with the proposal of Indonesia" (our emphasis) tied to the fact that a park like Beautiful Indonesia "is considered something that is not part of the Convention, that doesn't belong in this framework."

The vignette is illustrative of the issues explored in this chapter; namely, uses of ICH regarded as decontextualizing within the "authorised ICH discourse" (Bortolotto, forthcoming); the uneasiness and discomfort they incite in the social world of the actors who have normative agency over the definition of ICH; and the views of the actors seen to be "at the heart" of the Convention – the so-called Communities, Groups and Individuals (CGIs) – of such uses both at the international level and in China, where parks similar to Beautiful Indonesia exist everywhere to exhibit and showcase ICH.

Decontextualization has been discussed at length by the Committee on various occasions and, together with "misappropriation," has often been associated with over-commercialization. In the language of the Convention, over-commercialization refers to "bad" commercialization as opposed to "good" commercialization. This distinction, reflected in the catchphrase "commercialisation without over-commercialisation," attempts to acknowledge that the market is an intrinsic aspect of "living heritage" while simultaneously regulating commercial uses of ICH (Bortolotto, 2021). The threat of decontextualization associated with tourism-related activities is regularly evoked as one of the "recurrent challenges" in the assessment of nominations for inscriptions on the Lists, leading the Committee to request, in 2019, that the Secretariat prepare a guidance note on commercialization and the prevention of decontextualization. Festivals and parks are largely regarded as examples of over-commercialization resulting in "denaturation"[3] and therefore not contributing to "inclusive economic development," promoted since 2016 as one dimension of sustainable development in the Convention's Operational Directives. References to decontextualization are present both in the official texts and in the more informal discourse of the actors of the Convention, within and outside its governing bodies. In fact, the Operational Directives specifically raise the issue of decontextualization, recommending that States Parties devise ICH development plans and policies in ways that "do not negatively affect the viability of the intangible cultural heritage concerned or decontextualise or denaturalise that heritage" (UNESCO, 2022, p. 81). Similarly, in a publication by representatives of NGOs accredited to the Convention on the role of museums in ICH safeguarding, emphasis is placed on the potential threat of decontextualization (Đerić et al., 2020). The authors (ibid, p. 107) remark that museums "can contribute to economic sustainability of ICH practitioners, especially within the crafts field," though they also caution that in a museum setting, ICH risks "being isolated from its context." They warn against "over-commercialisation," stressing how this is "closely connected with the loss of meaning, especially when its only purpose becomes the generation of economic benefit for a very restricted part of the community." The domestication of the Convention in the Chinese heritage regime offers a particularly interesting case for observing the display of ICH in new contexts. Such issues are much less of a taboo topic within Chinese heritage legislation or among policy-makers and experts. ICH is overtly used as a means for economic development, particularly as a tourism resource (Su, 2019), and a frequently heard motto is: "selling and buying is the best form of safeguarding."

We argue here that heritage is, in fact, an intrinsically decontextualizing apparatus. The social sciences' characterization of the heritagization process makes this clear, highlighting how the latter establishes a new, reflexive relationship between a group and its way of life (Carneiro da Cunha, 2009; Fabre, 2013, p. 22). This self-conscious register, encoding references to cultural expressions previously considered implicitly as part of the everyday, gives them a "second life" as representations of themselves' (Kirshenblatt-Gimblett, 1998, p. 149) or as "authentic illusions" (Skounti, 2008). Previously implicitly experienced cultural practices of everyday life are showcased on an imaginary stage where they are "sustained, re-created, performed and marketed in a theatre of identities" (Clifford, 2013, p. 29). The awareness of having a "culture" is accompanied by a defamiliarization with it (Foster, 2011), and the need to put such "culture" on display promotes condensation, transportability, and spectacularization, precisely what UNESCO qualifies as "decontextualisation" (Hafstein, 2018). In other words, the change in status of particular expressions extracts them from their life as cultural practices where their cultural value is undeclared, and recontextualizes them in the heritage realm where their cultural value is made explicit. The main mechanisms established by the Convention, namely the so-called Urgent Safeguarding and Representative Lists, are decontextualizing tools par excellence: "whatever is selected as heritage is abstracted from its prior social context and positioned in connection to other practices that are additionally singled out and classified within the grouping of intangible heritage" (Hafstein, 2009, p. 104).

9.2. Exhibiting ICH

It was a hot and humid summer afternoon when we arrived at a heritage park called Grand View Garden (*daguanyuan*), located at the edge of a village in a northeastern Chinese province, famous for kite-making and new year's woodblock printing (*muban nianhua*), two national-level ICH elements. The village had been designated as a so-called "National ICH Production-oriented Safeguarding Demonstration Base" (*feiyi shengchanxing baohu shifan jidi*) in 2014. Registered as companies that produce cultural artefacts according to traditional techniques, these entities exist to promote the production, distribution and selling of ICH items and "to transform ICH resources into cultural products as a form of safeguarding" (State Council, 2012).[4] Inside the park, a sign directed us toward a kite-making museum, where we were introduced to the history of kite-making, different types of kites and kite masters. In the mostly written explanations, emphasis was placed on the long history, tradition and value of the displayed objects, with a few videos illustrating the practice of flying a kite. In one of the vitrines, a board with small window-like openings lit from behind displayed photos of cultural "transmitters" or other practitioners alongside an important visitor: the vice-chairman of the National People's Congress (NPC) or the prince and princess of Cambodia. Back outside, we came across many small wooden huts, meant to be stalls at which snacks, drinks and various artefacts could be sold. Most were shut, but we did see an elderly lady sweeping the ground right outside a door, who ushered us into a small shop selling woodblock prints. "I am running the shop here, but I also produce New Year's Woodblock Prints and I have my own workshop outside in the village," she said, while pointing vaguely into the direction of where the village was located. When we asked how her work was going, she replied "It is not so good, but I have a compilation of woodblock prints made by this village's one and only national-level transmitter. He is over 90 years old." She disappeared through a backdoor and returned shortly with a A-3-sized glossy book, wrapped in a cardboard frame. She put it in front of us, saying "180 yuan, you cannot find many of them anymore." When we mentioned being more interested in her own prints, she seemed disappointed and not particularly willing to talk about them, let alone show us.

The above anecdote offers an emblematic example of how ICH exists in China. There are many parks, expositions, or museums that specialize in exhibiting ICH (Zhu, 2018, p. 54; Massing, 2018). In these places, dynamic cultural expressions often become fossilized heritage. The arrangement and presentation of ICH focuses largely on objects or products and the display of commodities in vitrines. The showcasing of artefacts on shelves, and the largely text-based testimonies of the achievements and "long tradition" of the element detach the ICH artefact from the practice that produced it. The visitor sees only the final or "mute" outcome of a process that is, at best, explained in writing or through images and videos. In some cases, ICH exhibitions make an effort to portray the actual cultural practice through videos or the placing of manikins in certain positions, made to look as if they are actually engaging in a cultural practice. This is quite literally like a "freeze-frame" of an otherwise dynamic and evanescent process. It is precisely such displays that the authors of the volume on the relationship between ICH and museums consider problematic when they observe that "museums are wonderful partners for showing and understanding (promotion, sensitising the public) ICH, but not as final resting places" (Đerić et al., 2020, p. 106).

Similarly, in our visits to other ICH exhibitions, we encountered many performances of ICH elements that can only be narrowly defined as out-of-context staging. They were always carefully prepared, timetabled and acted out. At an exposition park in Beijing, for example, people of the *Dai* minority perform a Water Splashing Festival ritual every day at 1 pm. Visitors, mainly school children dressed in specially provided blue raincoats, indulged in an hour of fun, spraying water on each other, while *Dai* performers in ethnic costumes danced around in a square. Similarly, a group of *Miao* people performed their "knife-pole climbing" (*shang dao ti*) several times a day, a ritual usually only conducted during special events. All these enactments can be understood as a form of decontextualization. Exhibition premises meanwhile foster the commercialization of ICH. They are designed as marketplaces (Maags, 2021) where transmitters' workshops double as small boutiques, incorporating shopping shelves, price tags, and little brochures. Often, when engaging in casual conversation or longer interviews with transmitters inside ICH exhibitions, we were offered a business card and a friendly reminder to "visit our company." Many transmitters, especially those working in arts and crafts, are entrepreneurs (Zhu and Maags, 2020, chap. 5), seeking to exchange their products, services, or performances for money or their practice for a regular salary, often taken far out of their original contexts.

Interestingly, we witnessed similar forms of staged cultural performances take place at the moment of their coronation as heritage within the context of the ICH Committee. That is, the regular meetings of diplomats and heritage bureaucrats from 180 States Parties to the Convention as well as observers from other UNESCO Members States or the academic community and representatives of NGOs who gather to oversee and guide the implementation of the Convention. As some actors of the Convention have regretfully underscored (Aikawa-Faure, 2017; Smeets, 2020), the CGIs present at the meetings of the governing bodies do not participate in the debates and decisions underlying ICH policy-making. Rather, their engagement with the international ICH arena mainly takes a somewhat awkward form: they perform "samples" of their culture on the global stage offered by UNESCO's meetings.

Over the years, we have met many groups of performers representing a given "ICH community," travelling sometimes from a different continent, at the invitation of their governments, to offer others a glimpse of their cultural practices following inscription of the latter on the UNESCO lists. Examples include representatives of "congo culture" from Panama, the szopka tradition of constructing cribs in Poland, the ritual dance of the royal drum from Burundi, the Isukuti dance from Kenya, or the celebrations of the Parranda de San Pedro de Guarenas y Guatire from Venezuela.

In these cases, cultural expressions are not staged for tourists but for state delegates and other participants in the Committee sessions. The performances are so integrated into this context that they influence the very organization of the space, which always includes a podium and makes logistics more challenging compared to that of a World Heritage committee. As the chief of logistics from the UNESCO Secretariat put it: "You don't simply have the mayor of a town, you could have a whole troupe of dancers!"

In some cases, staged performances are not intended to celebrate inscriptions on the lists of the Convention but rather organized by the hosting State to showcase national ICH. This can take more or less overtly nationalistic tones and usually happens during the opening ceremony and other smaller side events during the meeting. For instance, on the occasion of the 2017 opening ceremony of the twelfth session of the Committee in Jeju, Korea, a performance of Arirang folk songs, inscribed on the RL by both South and North Korea, respectively in 2012 and 2014, was presented as embodying "The soul of Korea." Flyers distributed over the following days announced more special events during the weeklong session. For example, one read: "Come participate in Gijisi Tugging rituals and games while enjoying Korean folk music (Nong-ak)." These events were organized during lunch breaks in the parking lot of the International Conference Centre (ICC). As Gijisi Tugging rituals and games had been inscribed on the Representative List two years earlier, in 2015, many participants had the chance to experience what they had previously only encountered through administrative documents.

Thus, even though the official discourse cautions the States against de- contextualization of ICH, the very setting where this discourse is produced offers decontextualizing opportunities. In fact, not only is decontextualization present in the very situations where it is identified as a threat, it marks the consecration of heritage itself. Interestingly, and somewhat ironically, decontextualization is the very first thing that occurs when a cultural practice is inscribed on the ICH List: a condensed sample of the practice is presented to the international delegates of the governing bodies of the Convention.

Staged during a meeting of an international organization or in an exhibition park, cultural expressions become representations of themselves. Turned into performances, they are detached from their original socio-cultural environment and lose their social function, often associated with community rituals or local festivals. In a process similar to that underpinning folklore festivals, their temporal condensation allows them to be exported from their original context to a national tourist destination or global stage. Here, they are often not (culturally or socially) meaningful in or of themselves, but only *made* meaningful because of the heritage status that links them to other crafts or performances showcased in the same context.

9.3. Embarrassment and empowerment

Other occasions in which the States hosting the annual Committee meeting commonly offer ICH experiences are optional excursions organized for the delegates. In 2017, for example, the carefully designed brochure containing the meeting programme and logistics included information on Jeju tourist attractions and a cultural tour programme to visit "UNESCO World natural Heritage" or "UNESCO Intangible Cultural Heritage" in Jeju. We registered for the latter, which proposed an encounter with woman divers called *haenyeo*. The "Culture of Jeju Haenyeo" had been inscribed on the Representative List just the previous year. Along with other regular participants in the ICH Committee meetings, we recalled the short description provided in the nomination file of these women divers who gather marine products making "a unique sound called 'sumbi-sori'" when exhaling after each dive and who "practice a shamanistic ritual for the goddess of the sea (jamsugut)." At the end of an afternoon session, together with state delegates and NGOs representatives, we filed onto a bus, excited to visit the volcanic island of Jeju.

After a 30-minute drive, we arrived at the shore to find 30 women divers waiting in their wetsuits and sea masks for the UNESCO bus to arrive. We were welcomed with hot drinks and invited to taste the shellfish they had just collected. Afterwards, we were encouraged to take a group photo in which they held a banner reading "Haenyeo Tour, 9 December 2017, Jeju, Republic of Korea" along with the logos of the Convention and the 12th session of the Committee. The women thus not only offered themselves as a destination for a thematic tour but also displayed the banner as a caption for the event. This cultural display was not exceptional. As Yun (2015, p. 183) recounts, staged performances of Jeju shamanic rituals were offered as early as the 2002 World Cup in front of a global audience and their frequency intensified to promote their new status as heritage.

We, along with some of the excursion participants, felt uncomfortable in this situation. "No, no, I am not taking this photo" whispered some of them and discreetly walked away toward the sightseeing spot on the sea. Little did they know that a similar feeling of distress, the same "*malaise*" described by the Brazilian delegate in our opening vignette, would again be triggered by what was to follow. On that freezing and windy December evening, the *haenyeo*, most of them in their sixties, would dive into the sea while dozens of tourists wrapped up in warm coats, prepared their cameras to capture the moment. As the divers entered the water, the excited crowd stuck out their cameras, leaning over the parapet of the sightseeing structure. Corroborating our own sensation of discomfort, when walking back to the bus, we overheard two delegates of a western European country sarcastically comment on what they had perceived as an awkward contradiction with the ideals of the Convention: "Well, that was a good example of decontextualisation!"

This remark reflects both embarrassment and a certain irony, as these performances are at once indulged in and then qualified as "decontextualisation" once back in the Committee conference room in discussions over nominations for inscriptions on the Lists. Such embarrassing situations and sentiments are of course not specific to the Korean context. Similar feelings were expressed in other venues. For instance, during the opening ceremony of the Committee session held in Addis Ababa the year before, the staging of local ICH spurred puzzled reactions among some delegates. Hundreds of people invited to attend the event took their seats at dozens of large dining tables. Though the loud music playing did not allow for conversation among NGO representatives and state delegates at our table, their feelings were made clear enough during a short interlude: "It looks like a cruise show" someone whispered uncomfortably. We too had the same sensation when approaching the massive fair facility hosting the event, the Addis Park Millennium Hall. A group of bored-looking women in white costumes was sitting on the sidewalk awaiting instructions. Just inside the hall, dozens of people in traditional dress were likewise waiting, taking pictures, or rehearsing.

These groups, invited to perform on the stage in front of international delegates and local authorities, were there to provide evidence that, as the minister of Culture and Tourism put it in his speech, "Ethiopia is home to authentic culture." This message was further emphasized in the greeting offered in both UNESCO working languages: "welcome to the origins of mankind, *bienvenue dans le pays des origines*." These words doubled as an introduction to a piece of contemporary dance in which performers wore monkey-like costumes to stage a different kind of heritage proudly conserved in the Ethiopian National Museum: the skeleton of Lucy, the first human ancestor to walk on two legs. The staged performances were therefore not only examples of what Committee members characterize as forms of decontextualization but also the very concepts used to introduce them evoked taboo ICH language revolving around authenticity and origins (Bortolotto, 2020). Some delegates praise the quality of such performances and, seduced by their exoticism, share pictures of their "amazing" experiences with friends and family. Yet, for others, who believe that ICH should be part and parcel of the cultural and social life of a given community, the discrepancy between the principles defended during the sessions of the Committee and the ways in which ICH is presented and experienced at their margins is disconcerting.

Interestingly, however, as we followed the travel of the Convention into China, among heritage administrators and experts, this embarrassment about staged ICH faded away. This in part is explained by the more explicit acknowledgment of the metacultural nature of heritage as well as the different roles of the market in the Chinese ICH apparatus. In China, using ICH and allowing it to thrive in the market is commonly seen as an important element of safeguarding and, in fact, presented as one way for ICH "to stay alive," as an interlocutor phrased it. This perspective reflects the specificity of the Chinese ICH regime, shaped by national laws and administrations as well as more recent discourses on using ICH as a tool for economic development. China's ICH Law from 2011 (State Council, 2011), for example, refers to the idea of authenticity (ibid., Article 4), thereby introducing what at the international level is regarded as a taboo concept, inconsistent with the dynamic nature of living heritage (Zhu, 2015; Su, 2020). Emphasis is placed on ICH as a market resource, used for poverty alleviation (State Council, 2017), rural revitalization (Wu, 2019), and tourism. China's official ICH logo has also been used for commercial activities with the clear support of the government (Wang, 2021; Maags, 2021). In recent years, ICH transmitters have been strongly encouraged to innovate and tailor their respective products to market demands (Hu, 2017); there now exist a number of mobile apps that sell ICH products as luxury goods. This may be why the Chinese interlocutors that we met at the meetings accompanying the implementation of the Convention at the international level always highlighted the particularity of the Chinese understanding of the Convention. They explained that the alignment of the Chinese ICH apparatus with the international one is "challenging" in that there is a conceptual "gap" between the Convention and Chinese legislation. In another context, a scholar and ICH advisor to the Ministry of Culture and Tourism remarked that "ICH in China is not actually ICH."

This is not to say, however, that there is no embarrassment at all in China vis-à-vis the "over-commercialization" of ICH in out-of-context situations. The former Vice Minister of Culture and Director of the National ICH Safeguarding Centre, Wang Wenzhang (2013), for instance, identified an intrinsic contradiction between keeping the authenticity of ICH and commodifying ICH. Scholars in folklore, ethnology, or anthropology who assume an important role within the governance and management of ICH in China, have often expressed concern over, as one of our interlocutors put it, "a loss of the cultural value of ICH when commercial activities become too prominent." That said, he immediately relativized his worry by also pointing out that "transmitters actually want to market and sell ICH." Many ICH transmitters in China have indeed welcomed the idea of using ICH for commercial ends. Practitioners at the ICH expositions did not seem overly worried about the artificial setting detached from its social context. "I am glad that I have this platform (*pingtai*) that allows me to transmit and propagate my work," one transmitter said at a temporary ICH exhibit. Another commented that representing his home town at an ICH exhibition was a source of pride not only for himself but also for people at home. Most transmitters also stated that they were financially better off since the introduction of the ICH framework. The possibility of making a livelihood by practicing a cultural trade was often implicitly part of our conversations and interviews with transmitters. The ICH system and exhibitions and festivals in particular have, at least for some selected transmitters, created a platform for economic gain.

We observed similar phenomena at the international level, where mere presence at these events was a source of pride and recognition – much as for our interlocutors in the Chinese ICH parks. During a Committee session held in Mauritus, for example, a woman displaying traditional costumes from Uganda handed us a business card identifying herself as a "ritual guide." When we asked how she felt about offering her services at a UNESCO meeting, she replied without hesitation, "Very OK, very proud." Such a sentiment seemed common among the CGIs in attendance. The women divers were no exception. We met them again a few days after the aforementioned excursion, during the farewell dinner closing the Jeju Committee session. This time they were sitting at large tables in front of the stage for the closing ceremony gala, which included a musical intended to honor the Haenyeo Culture. At the end of the performance, the actual divers, visibly proud and excited, were once again photographed, this time with the banner of the 12th session of the Committee behind them.

Arguably then, decontextualized modes of practicing and using ICH, observed both at UNESCO meetings and in China, are in fact forms of agency and participation, just not those expected or authorized. In other words, CGIs engaging with heritage see their traditions as having already gone metacultural. This is particularly evident in China, where the heritage apparatus explicitly promotes processes of "metaculturalization" and where the uses of heritage for the market and tourism are less controversial. However, these are not new nor isolated examples. As Bendix observes in her study of invented tradition in a Swiss village with a 200-year history of tourism development, the emergence of "new, traditionalized displays points instead toward an affirmation of local and national cultural identity in the face of seasonal mass foreign invasion" (Bendix, 1989, p. 132). Bendix's argument relative to invented traditions applies to decontextualization as well: What matters to these "heritage entrepreneurs" (Pfeilstetter, 2015) is "whether the manifestation will accomplish for them what they intend it to accomplish" (Bendix, 1989, p. 132).

Thus, what seems to be a form of decontextualization and therefore an embarrassing contradiction in the normative context of the Convention may be perceived differently by heritage "bearers." Drawing on Nussbaum's (1995) feminist scholarship on sexual objectification, Baron (2010) contends that cultural objectification does not exclude agency. Following this argument, the cultural (like the sexual) "object" "may subvert her or his objectification for the sake of one or another kind of material advantage" (Baron, 2010, p. 65). Decontextualization here takes on a similar function, providing platforms for using culture as a resource (Yúdice, 2003; Comaroff and Comaroff, 2009) In acknowledging this point, the 'Ethical principles" included in the Operational Directives (ODs) of the Convention refer to the need for decontextualization to be defined by the CGIs themselves (UNESCO, 2022, p. 144). In practice however, the unease with decontextualization within the normative ICH discourse reflects the "experts" point of view, nourished by narratives around "authenticity" and a broader embarrassment vis-à-vis commercial uses of ICH (Bortolotto, forthcoming). This is consistent with the fact that heritage is perceived as a symbolic good, not intended for exchange in ordinary economies (Bourdieu, 1985), and heritage apparatuses are devices to protect cultural practices from market forces and priorities driven by the latter.

9.4. Conclusion

According to normative ideals of sustainable economic development based on notions of "good" commercialization, decontextualization is regarded as a threat to cultural and social practices. In reality, however, authorized ideals of "in-context" ICH safeguarding are difficult to apply in an intrinsically decontextualizing process. Decontextualization thus awkwardly lingers in the meetings of the ICH Committee. This contradiction spurs embarrassment within the normative context of the Convention, where ICH is understood first and foremost as an exercise in good governance. Embarrassment, however, fades as heritage is put into practice and becomes a resource. If these uses of heritage as a resource are already visible within the international arena itself, they become evident on the ground. China serves as a good example of how commercial uses and safeguarding are not seen as mutually exclusive and how decontextualization is acknowledged as part of the heritagization process. As much in China as at the international level, CGIs often embrace the opportunities offered by "decontextualization" and regard display, performances, and for-profit uses of their ICH, at a very minimum, as source of pride and, often, a form of (economic) empowerment.

Community members or ICH transmitters might be objectified, but as Baron (2010, p. 84) argues, "at the same time they may exercise agency to provide perspectives about their traditions on their own terms, advance their interests, and enable their traditions to flourish anew as a result of exposure to new audiences."

Concerns over denaturalization and decontextualization imply the existence of an authentic nature and context for cultural expressions recognized as ICH. Hence, though authenticity is not an admissible concept in the field of ICH and has deliberately been excluded from the Convention, it tacitly underpins its implementation. The notion of "in context" is, meanwhile, an old concept in folklore (Bendix, 1997) and anthropology (Lindholm, 2002). Yet, these disciplines have reinvented themselves several times since their beginnings and have fundamentally overhauled now largely obsolete understandings of culture as bounded, in situ or "in context." So, if we apply a revamped notion of culture understood as a dynamic process, as always adapting to different situations, then its expressions are always – by definition – "in context." The very act of designating cultural practices and expressions as heritage lifts them out of one context and provides them with a new one. If the community is the context for culture as habitus, the stage, whether in an exhibition space in China or the conference room of a Committee Meeting, forms the new and, we argue, the inevitable context of ICH. Hafstein (2018, p. 128) states that ICH and safeguarding belong together like tea and biscuits and observes that "as one part of their safeguarding, the practices and expressions that have been reframed as intangible heritage are festivalised" (ibid., p. 136). In other words, we contend that there is really nothing "unnatural" or "decontextualised" about ICH being performed or staged. On the contrary, the stage is the natural context for ICH.

While we maintain that decontextualization represents an integral part of ICH, this does not mean that we see all forms of staging or the performance and metaculturalization of cultural practices and expressions for political-economic ends as unproblematic. There exist many scenarios, especially in authoritarian regimes, where ICH is instrumentalized for political purposes and where people are exploited and objectified within a context of oppression or discrimination due to race, social class, gender, or religion (Harris, 2020a, 2020b). Similarly, cultural practices and expressions that only thrive because of short-term economic goals within a precarious and high-risk environment structured on exclusion defy the idea of sustainability. Some of the sorts of economic empowerment that we have observed among our interlocutors risk, in fact, eventually rendering communities more vulnerable. Embraced by people who may have little more to sell than their cultural identity (Kirshenblatt-Gimblett, 2006), ICH offers opportunities for improved life conditions yet also bears risks, in that it may exacerbate inequalities and dispossession (Hafstein, 2014), where the "survival practices of the poor" are turned into a "new emerging market" (Elyachar, 2002, p. 510).

These dynamics form, however, part of a larger structural problem, of which ICH is inevitably a part. The embarrassment we observed among actors of the Convention certainly reflects a feeling of impotence vis-á-vis the structural forces that shape this world. Nonetheless, the framework of ICH – and thereby the Convention itself – could greatly benefit from greater acknowledgment on the part of the actors shaping the normative ICH discourse that we live in a world dominated by market principles and entrepreneurialism where all human action is potentially marketable (Harvey, 2005, p. 3) and that decontextualization is, in fact, intrinsic to heritage projects. Clinging on to ideals of "in context" and authentic culture that ought to be safeguarded and protected from the onslaught of the market or other external forces is a well-intentioned yet misguided effort. We contend that the detrimental side of commercial uses of ICH within a neoliberal political economy can only be more fully addressed by embracing and acknowledging the fact that ICH becomes a resource within the new context that the very designation as ICH brings about.

Notes

1 Research for this chapter was funded by the Agence Nationale de la Recherche through the project UNESCO frictions: heritage making across global governance ANR-14-ACHN-0006–01. We are grateful to Christina Maags for her comments on the first draft and to Maya Judd for her proofreading.
2 https://ich.unesco.org/en/9b-best-safeguarding-practices-00746
3 A term used, for instance, in the evaluation of the 'Ceremony of Mehrgan' (Decision 15.COM 8.b.33).
4 Similar to ICH elements and ICH transmitters, there is a national-level inventory, currently comprising around 100 such bases.

References

Aikawa-Faure, N. (2017) 'Introductory remarks', in Uesugi, T. and Mari, S. (eds.) *Global Perspectives on Intangible Cultural Heritage: Local Communities, Researchers, States and UNESCO, with the Special Focus on Global and National Perspectives*. Tokyo: Center for Glocal Studies Seijo University, pp. 7–18.

Baron, R. (2010) 'Sins of objectification? Agency, mediation, and community cultural self-determination in public folklore and cultural tourism programming', *Journal of American Folklore*, 122(487), pp. 63–91. Doi: 10.5406/jamerfolk.123.487.0063.

Bendix, R. F. (1989) 'Tourism and cultural displays: Inventing traditions for whom?', *The Journal of American Folklore*, 102(404), pp. 131–146.

Bendix, R. F. (1997) *In Search of Authenticity: The Formation of Folklore Studies*. Madison: The University of Wisconsin Press.

Bortolotto, C. (2020) 'Le patrimoine immatériel et le tabou de l'authenticité : de la pérennisation à la durabilité', in Csergo, J., Hottin, C., and Schmit, P. (eds.) *Le patrimoine culturel immatériel au seuil des sciences sociales*. Paris: Éditions de la Maison des sciences de l'homme. Available at: https://books.openedition.org/editionsmsh/pdf/16377 (Accessed: 7 December 2022). Doi: 10.4000/books.editionsmsh.16377.

Bortolotto, C. (2021) 'Commercialization without over-commercialization: Normative conundrums across heritage rationalities', *International Journal of Heritage Studies*, 27(9), pp. 857–868. Doi: 10.1080/13527258.2020.1858441.

Bortolotto, C. (Forthcoming) 'The embarrassment of heritage alienability: Affective choices and cultural intimacy in the UNESCO lifeworld', *Current Anthropology*.

Bourdieu, P. (1985) 'The Market of Symbolic Goods', *Poetics*, 14, pp. 13–14.

Carneiro da Cunha, M. (2009) *Cultura com aspas e outros ensaios*. São Paulo: Cosac Naify.

Clifford, J. (2013) *Returns: Becoming Indigenous in the Twenty-First Century*. Cambridge, MA: Harvard University Press.

Comaroff, J. L. and Comaroff, J. (2009) *Ethnicity, Inc*. Chicago: University of Chicago Press.

Đerić, T. N., Neyrinck, J., Seghers, E. and Tsakiridis, E. (eds.) (2020) *Museums and Intangible Cultural Heritage: Towards a Third Space in The Heritage Sector*. Bruges: Werkplaats immaterieel erfgoed.

Elyachar, J. (2002) 'Empowerment money: The culture in Egypt', *Public Culture*, 14(3), pp. 493–513.

Fabre, D. (2013) 'Le patrimoine porté par l'émotion', in Fabre, D. (ed.) *Émotions patrimoniales*. Paris: Éditions de la Maison des sciences de l'homme, pp. 13–98.

Foster, M. D. (2011) 'The UNESCO effect: Confidence, defamiliarization, and a new element in the discourse on a Japanese island', *Journal of Folklore Research*, 48(1), pp. 63–107. Doi: 10.2979/jfolkrese.48.1.63.

Hafstein, V. T. (2009) 'Intangible heritage as a list: From masterpieces to representation', in Smith, L. and Akagawa, N. (eds.) *Intangible Heritage*. London: Routledge, pp. 93–111.

Hafstein, V. T. (2014) 'Protection as dispossession: Government in the vernacular', in Kapchan, D. (ed.) *Cultural Heritage in Transit: Intangible Rights as Human Rights*. Philadelphia: University of Pennsylvania Press, pp. 25–57.

Hafstein, V. T. (2018) 'Intangible heritage as a festival; Or, folklorization revisited', *Journal of American Folklore*, 131(520), pp. 127–149. Doi: 10.5406/jamerfolk.131.520.0127.

Harris, R. (2020a) '"A weekly Mäshräp to tackle extremism": Music-making in Uyghur communities and intangible cultural heritage in China', *Ethnomusicology*, 64(1), pp. 23–55. Doi: 10.5406/ETHNOMUSICOLOGY.64.1.0023.

Harris, R. (2020b) *Uyghur Heritage and the Charge of Cultural Genocide in Xinjiang, Center for Global Policy*. Available at: https://cgpolicy.org/articles/uyghur-heritage-and-the-charge-of-cultural-genocide-in-xinjiang/ (Accessed: 26 September 2020).

Harvey, D. (2005) *A Brief History of Neoliberalism*. Oxford: Oxford University Press.

Hu, Y. (2017) *Plan to Revitalize Traditional Crafts, China Daily*. Available at: https://global.chinadaily.com.cn/a/201704/05/WS59bb4568a310d4d9ab7e20a2.html (Accessed: 13 October 2021).

Kirshenblatt-Gimblett, B. (1998) *Destination Culture: Tourism, Museums, and Heritage*. Berkeley: University of California Press.

Kirshenblatt-Gimblett, B. (2006) 'World heritage and cultural economics', in Karp, I. et al. (eds.) *Museum Frictions: Public Cultures/Global Transformations*. Durham: Duke University Press, pp. 161–202.

Lindholm, C. (2002) 'Authenticity, anthropology, and the sacred', *Anthropological Quarterly*, 75(2), pp. 331–338. Doi: 10.1353/ANQ.2002.0035.

Maags, C. (2021) 'Common, luxury, and fake commodities: Intangible cultural heritage markets in China', *China Perspectives*, 2021/03(September): 7–17. https://doi.org/10.4000/chinaperspectives.12184.

Massing, K. (2018) 'Safeguarding intangible cultural heritage in an ethnic theme park setting: The case of Binglanggu in Hainan Province, China', *International Journal of Heritage Studies*, 24(1), pp. 66–82. Doi: 10.1080/13527258.2017.1362571.

Nussbaum, M. (1995) 'Objectification', *Philosophy and Public Affairs*, 24(4), pp. 249–291.

Pfeilstetter, R. (2015) 'Heritage entrepreneurship: Agency-driven promotion of the Mediterranean diet in Spain', *International Journal of Heritage Studies*, 21(3), pp. 215–231. Doi: 10.1080/13527258.2014.930502.

Skounti, A. (2008) 'The authentic illusion: Humanity's intangible cultural heritage, the Moroccan experience', in Smith, L. (ed.) *Intangible Heritage*. London: Routledge, pp. 74–92. Doi: 10.4324/9780203884973.

Smeets, R. (2020) 'Définitions, rôles et territoires des communautés, groupes et individus dans la Convention pour la sauvegarde du patrimoine culturel immatériel et dans sa mise en œuvre', *Les Cahiers du CFPCI*, 7, pp. 23–55. Doi: 10.3917/esp.1994.78.0015.

State Council (2011) *Intangible Cultural Heritage Law of China*. Available at: www.ihchina.cn/3/10377.html (Accessed: 8 December 2017).

State Council (2012) *Opinions of the General Office of the State Council on Strengthening the Protection of Intangible Cultural Heritage of Our Country*. Available at: www.ihchina.cn/Article/Index/detail?id=11577 (Accessed: 13 October 2021).

State Council (2017) *Opinions of the General Office of the State Council on the Ministry of Culture's Notice on the Revitalization of China's Traditional Arts and Crafts*. Available at: www.ihchina.cn/zhengce_details/11566 (Accessed: 13 October 2021).

Su, J. (2019) 'Understanding the changing intangible cultural heritage in tourism commodification: The music players' perspective from Lijiang, China', *Journal of Tourism and Cultural Change*, 17(3), pp. 247–268. Doi: 10.1080/14766825.2018.1427102.

Su, J. (2020) 'Managing intangible cultural heritage in the context of tourism: Chinese officials' perspectives', *Journal of Tourism and Cultural Change*, 18(2), pp. 164-186. Doi: 10.1080/14766825.2019.1604720.

UNESCO (2022) *Basic Texts of the 2003 Convention for the Safeguarding of the Intangible Cultural Heritage*. Available at: https://ich.unesco.org/en/directives (Accessed: 7 December 2022).

Wang, Li 王历 (2021) '非遗实践、传承者在非遗商业化活动中的权利和义务 (The power and obligations of ICH practitioners and transmitters in the marketization of ICH)', 文化遗产 *(Cultural Heritage)*, 5, pp. 24–31.

Wang, Wenzhang (王文章). 2013. 非物质文化遗产概论 *(Introduction to Intangible Cultural Heritage)*. Beijing: Jiaoyu Kexue Chubanshe.

Wu, Y. (2019) *Intangible Cultural Heritage Brings Life to Rural Revitalization, China Global Television Network*. Available at: https://news.cgtn.com/news/3d3d414f3355444e33457a6333566d54/index.html (Accessed: 13 October 2021).

Yúdice, G. (2003) *The Expediency of Culture: Uses of Culture in the Global Era*. Durham and London: Duke University Press.

Yun, K. (2015) 'The economic imperative of UNESCO recognition: A South Korean Shamanic ritual', *Journal of Folklore Research*, 52(2–3), pp. 181–198. Doi: 10.2979/jfolkrese.52.2–3.181.

Zhu, Y. (2015) 'Cultural effects of authenticity: Contested heritage practices in China', *International Journal of Heritage Studies*, 21(6), pp. 1–15. Doi: 10.1080/13527258.2014.991935.

Zhu, Y. (2018) *Heritage and Romantic Consumption in China*. Amsterdam: Amsterdam University Press. Doi: 10.1080/14442213.2020.1757192.

Zhu, Y. and Maags, C. (2020) *Heritage Politics in China: The Power of the Past*. Abingdon: Routledge. Doi: 10.4324/9780429446429.

10

INTANGIBLE CULTURAL HERITAGE, SUSTAINABILITY, AND THE COVID-19 IN MARRAKECH

Ahmed Skounti and Aba Sadki

10.1. Introduction

In this chapter, we argue that development programs and projects in Marrakech, Morocco, seldom focus on intangible cultural heritage (ICH). Sustainable development activities tend to ignore ICH bearers, such that any marriage between intangible cultural heritage and sustainable development is more a "wishful thinking" than a "realistic outcome," to paraphrase Sophia Labadi (2011). Here, we focus on the cultural space of the Jemaa el-Fnaa square in Morocco, which serves as a window onto the pitfalls of the relationship between intangible cultural heritage and sustainable development. We furthermore address the COVID-19 pandemic, which added a layer of complexity to our analysis.

In 2001, UNESCO proclaimed the cultural space of the Jemaa el-Fna square a Masterpiece of Oral and Intangible Cultural Heritage of Humanity and it was later included on the UNESCO Representative List of the Intangible Cultural Heritage of Humanity in 2008. The square is located inside the walled medina of Marrakech, a world heritage site (Skounti, 2012). This international recognition was viewed by local actors, including ICH bearers in the square, as an opportunity to enhance their living and social conditions, as many rely on the generosity of visitors and tourists. It nourished hopes for a better future, despite somewhat less enthusiasm on the part of institutional public actors. Years later, these ICH bearers – mainly comprising performers such as storytellers, animal trainers, acrobats, dancers, singers, and fortune tellers – still struggle to survive. With the COVID-19 pandemic, the authorities decided to prohibit all activity in the square. The ban, put in place in March 2020, was not lifted for more than a year and indubitably weakened the entire community of the square, particularly affecting the ICH bearers who had no alternative safety net.

DOI: 10.4324/9781003244158-15

In what follows, we describe and analyze the entanglements between intangible cultural heritage and sustainable development in the Jemaa el-Fna square. This setting is particularly interesting in that the square hosts performances straddling two worlds: commerce and culture (Adjaye, 2016). Interviews conducted with ICH bearers and institutional and NGO actors during the first half of 2021 allow us to capture the sometimes challenging intersection between intangible cultural heritage and sustainable development in a fragile social context exacerbated by uncertain pandemic times. We also draw on our own experience as cultural heritage specialists, having worked for years in the Moroccan Ministry of Culture, respectively, in an academic institution as a professor (INSAP) and in a local government agency as a heritage professional (Regional Cultural Directorate, Marrakech). As Moroccans belonging to the same broad sociocultural context as the ICH bearers, we necessarily adopted a critical and self-reflexive approach. We were particularly attentive to any friction between our professional commitment to the medina's heritage preservation and the expected objectivity of our academic work. Bourdieu's thoughts on reflexivity, as well as the work of other prominent scholars (Bourdieu, 2022; Morange and Schmoll, 2016; De Lavergne, 2007), was inspiring in this regard. Our qualitative approach (Diaz, 2005) and carefully considered strategies of data extraction, processing, and communication (Fassin, 2008; Valentine, 2005) furthermore helped to incorporate important ethical considerations. For example, we were constantly aware of the risks of involuntarily pressuring interviewees given our professional positions, the need to respect their freedom of participation and expression, the potential sensitivity and confidentiality of the collected data, and the additional political and economic complexity due to the COVID-19 pandemic.

10.2. Oscillating between recognition and disappointment

The UNESCO Convention for the safeguarding of the intangible cultural heritage (henceforth Convention) links intangible cultural heritage safeguarding (ICH) with sustainable development (SD). The "whole text of the Convention reflects implicitly principles of sustainable development," including the definition of safeguarding or "insuring viability" of ICH elements (Labadi, 2011, p. 115). The implementation of this normative instrument at the international level has revealed both the potential of ICH in terms of SD and the tensions underlying the economic uses of ICH, including the practices and traditional knowledge inscribed on the UNESCO lists. Heated debate has, for example, emerged over the issue of commercialization and over-commercialization (Bortolotto, 2021) of heritage. A growing need to explicitly link ICH and SD manifested in the 2016 addition of the sixth chapter to the Convention's Operational Directives (UNESCO, 2020), specifically on this topic. Nevertheless, it remains unclear "how exactly the connection between ICH and development should be conceptualized and how local or national governments could put it into practice" (Meissner, 2017, p. 295). For the Jemaa el-Fna square specifically, another layer of complexity is added by the site's World Heritage status and gentrification of the medina during the first decade of the twenty-first century, amplified by UNESCO's proclamation in 2001, which raised demand for real estate around the square (Coslado et al., 2013).

The square is located inside the walled city of Marrakech, between the Koutoubia Mosque and the bazaars. Since its inception centuries ago,[1] the square has offered a physically empty yet culturally full space inside the historic city. Though located at the spatial heart of the medina, its activities are socially more marginal, the performers granted a tolerated freedom. The square has three intricated functions common to the area as a whole: commerce, spirituality, and recreation. It is at once a space of urban transition and integration. It is also a place of "spontaneous" creativity, offering various performing arts, such as music, dance, storytelling, snake charmers, minstrels, acrobats, street preaching, fortune telling, and henna tattooing (Skounti, 2009, p. 85). Likewise, it is a refreshment area and an outdoor dining venue, where one can purchase a variety of drinks, fruits, and dishes. The square is surrounded by commercial, craft, and residential neighborhoods and is bordered by height-limited shops, cafes, restaurants, hotels, banks, and offices.

The square has always attracted political power. Before coming under the French Protectorate in 1912, it was used for parades and other manifestations of authority. In 1922, it was classified as a historic area, a decision that has indubitably shaped its present urban form. The royal decree (*Dahir*) was accompanied by a plan delineating the limits of the empty space with capital letters from A to O.[2] Since then, any construction on the square has been forbidden, and the height of the surrounding buildings is limited to 8.5 meters. The post office and central bank buildings added during the colonial period aligned with these requirements. Later, administrative buildings, restaurants, and coffee shops were added. These developments replaced old buildings or were located on empty lands around the square. Legal and administrative measures were simultaneously taken to protect the square and, by the same token, allowed cultural expressions and performances to be transmitted from generation to generation. A source of income for its custodians, these cultural activities gradually became a cultural product oriented toward national and international tourism.

These functions of the square have been maintained over the last century, with a continued coexistence of commercial and cultural activities. Actors and visitors have, however, observed an imbalance in favor of the commercial. Concerns about the disappearance of cultural expressions and performances emerged starting in the late 20th century. The late Spanish writer Juan Goytisolo, who lived for more than 30 years in Marrakech beginning in the 1970s (Schmitt, 2005, pp. 178–179), voiced this worry, in addition to diverse local and national intellectuals. The movement culminated in a meeting in Marrakech in 1997 organized with the participation of UNESCO, international experts, and the Moroccan authorities (Skounti, 2009, p. 80). The concept of "oral heritage" was proposed as an umbrella term to capture what had until then been called "folklore" or "traditional culture." The meeting was followed by the establishment of the Proclamation of Masterpieces of Oral and Intangible Cultural Heritage program in 1999 (Aikawa-Faure, 2009, pp. 14–20). The Jemaa el-Fnaa square was a constant backdrop to these discussions and indeed provided the "foundation" for the concept of "intangible cultural heritage" (Schmitt, 2008).

During the preparation of the nomination that led to the proclamation of the Jemaa el-Fna square as a Masterpiece of the Oral and Intangible Cultural Heritage of Humanity in 2000–2001, "the performers in Jemaa el-Fna square who were directly affected, the 'bearers' of the intangible traditions, were not involved; in the Proclamation process they were objects of reflection rather than acting subjects" (Schmitt, 2008, p. 101). They were only informed during interviews conducted by civil servants in the Culture Department. One of the authors of this chapter was among the officials responsible for the preparation of the nomination.[3] The tight agenda did not allow for extensive consultations with the performers in the square. Interviews were conducted with the heads of troupes. At the time, there was little awareness among civil servants, at least at the local level, about the importance of community participation. The bearers were thus viewed more as primary sources of information than as active actors in the nomination process. Their expectations were, however, high, as this was the first time they had become the object of public interest. Torn between doubt and hope, there was a sense that something was being prepared with the potential to improve their status. The promised international recognition that would result at the end of the process was interpreted as having the power to enhance their social and economic conditions. Specifically, they expected to be lifted from their state of precariousness (Schmidt, 2005, p. 190).

In emphasizing the concept of "cultural space" (included in the title of the nomination itself), the aim was to stress the square's "cultural" dimension relative to its competing "commercial" dimension. Moreover, discussions focused more on the storytellers than the other activities performed in the square. Indeed, still today there seems to be an implicit hierarchy, with oral expressions at the top while street food occupies the bottom rung. The other activities range in between, from the lesser to the most commercial. Conversely, in terms of revenue, those garnering the highest income are street food stall owners and orange juice and dry fruit sellers, while those earning the least are the storytellers and other performing artists.[4] Though storytellers occupy the top of the performance pyramid, the viability of this category has suffered. In fact, only seven out of nine storytellers were performing in the square at the time of the proclamation. Surveys undertaken in 2006 and 2012 showed a steady decline in this category of artists. The end of storytelling in the square coincided with international recognition. The storytellers' average age was on the high side, and no transmission was ensured to younger generations, with the exception of a single case. The storyteller Abderrahim El Maqouri, alias El Azaliya, took it upon himself to teach his skills first to his son and then to his daughter (Ladenburger, 2015).

Meanwhile, through the "alien gaze" of international recognition, as V. Hafstein puts it, the "Jemaa el-Fna [was] symbolically reformed from a rogue element to a public theatre of power and Marrakesh-ness" (2015, p. 155). For decades and even centuries, the square was not held in high esteem by the local population, particularly the more virtuous families. The square's actors were at the margins of the cultural mainstream. They were arguably a magnifying mirror of society, while simultaneously standing outside of conventional socioeconomic activities and standard behavioral habits. Moreover, the shadow of the Koutoubia Mosque hovers over Jemaa el-Fna Square, literally, and figuratively. The sacred goes hand in hand with the profane in licentious proximity. Orthodox and heterodox discourses and performances brush up against one another. Moralizing discourse crosses the salacious anecdote. It is not uncommon to hear remarks that are hardly gentle to the sensitive ear while the sound of the muezzin's voice calling to prayer simultaneously fills the air (Skounti, 2017a, pp. 171–172).

One of the first actions of the Association of Friends of Jemaa el-Fna Square Oral Heritage of Humanity (*Association des Amis de la Place Jemaa el-Fnaa Patrimoine oral de l'humanité*) was the fashioning of a T-shirt bearing the expression: *Ould Jemaa el-Fnaa wa biftikhar* (Child of Jemaa el-Fnaa and Proud). This was intended to help instill a positive view of the square, furthered by the implementation of the Preservation, Revitalization, and Promotion of Jemaa el-Fnaa Square project, designed by the association with the support of the UNESCO field office in Rabat and the Ministry of Culture, and implemented with financial assistance from the Japanese Fund-in-Trust.[5] The project, carried out between 2004 and 2008, addressed issues such as awareness-raising, documentation, and one-off financial support granted to storytellers. Specifically, a database of documents pertaining to the square was created. The project furthermore enabled nine storytellers of the square to perform in schools before young students. Artistic workshops were organized, and young students painted in the open air their personal representations of the square. A booklet on the square's history and intangible cultural heritage was also prepared by two scholars and printed by the UNESCO office, and 1000 copies were distributed in the schools of Marrakech and its surroundings.[6] However, as the project was not discussed with the performers in the square, there was a gap between their expectations and the funded activities. Moreover, only storytellers benefited from a single, symbolic financial contribution. This fueled animosity between some categories of performers, who misunderstood the reasons why they had not been granted monetary support. A situation emerged where the empowered were seemingly on the side of experts and heritage professionals, rather than on the performers' side (Beardslee, 2015). The sustainability of the square as a cultural arena was (and remains) at stake.

10.3. ICH as a blind spot for development projects

The double international recognition of the square as World Heritage (Skounti, 2012) and as an intangible cultural heritage has posed a challenge in terms of its management on the part of local actors. The requirements of both UNESCO conventions do not always align with the available expertise within local institutional entities, and a gap has emerged between, on the one hand, international conservation, and safeguarding discourse, and on the other, local action frameworks. Government officials often consider the obligations under these UNESCO conventions as impediments to projects designed for the development of the square and the larger medina. In what follows, we focus on the most recent project concerning Jemaa el-Fna square, highlighting the difficulties that arise when simultaneously seeking to enhance the urban fabric around the square and protect its cultural heritage.

In 2020–2021, an urban requalification project was implemented by Al Omrane Marrakech-Safi, the local branch of a government housing agency. At the time, Morocco, like the rest of the world, was heavily impacted by the COVID-19 pandemic. Beginning in March 2020 and for more than a year, all activities in the square were prohibited. This meant that the modest revenues of the Jemaa el-Fna performers were suddenly and entirely interrupted. The project team, mainly composed of young architects, sought the support not only of designers and landscape architects but also of a historian and an anthropologist specialized in cultural heritage. A multidisciplinary group was thus formed. One of the co-authors (Ahmed Skounti) filled the position of anthropologist, while the other (Aba Sadki) acted as a cultural heritage specialist, reviewing and commenting on the deliverables proposed by the Al Omrane team. Notwithstanding the recommendations expressed by both authors, neither the square's cultural performers nor commercial activity owners were formally involved in the process.

During several face-to-face and remote meetings during late 2020 and early 2021 as well as field visits and consultations, the team designed a project to enhance the urban setting of the square. To this end, a history of the square was first drawn up to better understand the development that had led to the present situation. Then, a legal framework for the intervention was prepared aimed at meeting the requirements of the World Heritage Convention (1972) and the 2003 ICH Convention. Both the square's tangible and intangible dimensions needed to be considered as well as how best to bring the two convention frameworks together at the local level in a coordinated manner. This raised several questions on the ground, such as what should be protected under the 1972 Convention? And what should be safeguarded under the 2003 Convention? From a world heritage perspective, the square is to be protected as part of the physical fabric of the town, with height-limited buildings surrounding its free-plan together with other delimited landscape characteristics. From an intangible cultural heritage perspective, the communities, groups, and individuals performing on the square hold the right to use the space for their daily activities, as they have done for years. Yet, from a broader heritagization process perspective, establishing common ground among diverse stakeholder views was not always easy. Implementing a participatory approach was complicated by the dual need for institutional actors to discuss the urban requalification proposal with both the owners of restaurants, cafes, and shops surrounding the square and the square's cultural performers and commercial activity owners.[7]

The team presented its study – framed by the binding requirements of the World Heritage Convention and the Intangible Cultural Heritage Convention[8] – in March 2021 to national and local commissions in charge of the overall supervision and follow-up. An urban and architectural analysis made it possible to contextualize the Jemaa el-Fna Square within the wider urban fabric of the medina, with its compact density, road networks, and diverse economic functions. The analysis identified modifications to the built environment around the square over the last century, with a focus on the last three decades. Upon the suggestion of Ahmed Skounti, they were classified according to three categorical scales represented by different colors: acceptable (green), moderately acceptable (orange), and in violation of regulations (red), for example, infringement of heritage legislation regarding height and/or encroachment on public space. Removal, with the owners' consent, of modifications in this latter category was recommended. A study of the landscape of the square furthermore showed several anomalies affecting the free plan and the alignment of the Arset El Bilk Garden, as well as supported a widely agreed upon need to differently distribute the open-air restaurants and trade activities in the square to free up more space for cultural performances. Meanwhile, an examination of the illumination of the square revealed a heterogeneous spectrum of lighting sources, leading to a recommendation to harmonize the latter as well as the color. While the design team applauded the diversity and ingenuity of the fixtures used by the traders (herbalists, orange juice stands, and dried fruits) and the cultural performers, it also pointed out the lack of ergonomics and adaptability of the existing furniture. Alternative solutions were proposed, meant to be discussed with the traders and performers.

The safeguarding of the intangible cultural heritage in the square was a major concern, even if not clearly identified as such in the initial project. The study recommended that multiple consultations be done with all stakeholders, particularly the cultural performers, the aim being to consider the views of the ICH bearers in an approach that broadly included the entire medina as a world heritage site. The project team proposed the creation of a House of Living Human Treasures (LHT) in the villa adjoining the Al-Maghrib Bank, so as to provide cultural performers with the dedicated center, beyond the planned museum in the bank's empty headquarters.[9] The House of LHT would respond to the stakeholders' grievances as well as provide health care and social assistance while also offering the performers a venue for meetings, trainings, and transmission.

Some of the recommendations submitted to the local public actors were implemented, especially efforts to stop urban and architectural infringements around the square. However, the project was not problem-free. The café, restaurant, and shop owners only heard about the study in early 2021, and little information was provided as to how the proposed recommendations were to be implemented, including who was to bear the costs. Those whose businesses were in the red zone were informed during consultation meetings organized by the local authorities. Some tried to defend their building, arguing that the modifications had been made prior to the proclamation of the square in 2001. They were nonetheless encouraged to allow demolition of the parts of their properties that were higher than the regulatory 8.5 meters or that encroached on public space. Some attempted to informally argue their case with the authorities and certain project team members. For example, Ahmed Skounti was approached in February 2021 by a restaurant owner, worried that his property was in the red category as he had added a rooftop dining room with the verbal approval of the national higher authorities in the mid-1990s. He claimed that this addition was documented in a photo exhibition that had been displayed in the municipal hall prior to the preparation of the nomination for the Jemaa el-Fna square. The owner was in search of the exhibition photographs to support his case and avoid the recommended removal of the rooftop room that had been in use for more than two decades. He furthermore underlined the detrimental impact of the COVID-19 pandemic as yet another reason for not imposing a sanction on his business.

Another weakness of the project was that a participatory approach was not adopted from the beginning, mainly with the ICH bearers. Those primarily concerned with the urban requalification project were not consulted prior to the study's launch. In fact, community participation has generally not been incorporated into the procedures and regulations of such projects. This issue has been extensively discussed in the literature (Smith and Akagawa, 2008; Adell et al., 2015; Labadi, 2013; Bortolotto, 2011), and both Ahmed Skounti and Aba Sadki drew attention to this matter during the meetings held in late 2020 and early 2021. The aforementioned requirements of both the 1972 and 2003 Conventions were intended to provide guidance in the decision-making process. Once the study had been completed, the authorities accepted the need, following Article 15 of the 2003 Convention, to enter into discussions with the square's stakeholders. The cultural performers were encouraged to organize into associations, activate existing groups, and appoint representatives to speak on their behalf. However, the lack of a formal procedure for community participation and the challenges of the COVID-19 pandemic hindered these efforts. We observed what Crozier and Friedberg (1977) have described as the relationship between the actor and the system, and the control the system exerts over the actor. In the meetings we attended, the public official representing the region's Department of the Interior was clear about who leads the process and how things should be managed. He discussed disagreement between the local authorities and the municipality over the uses of buildings around the square, reiterating that it was the municipality that was empowered with delivering authorizations in a UNESCO double-recognized heritage area. At the same time, he seemed to be more concerned about commerce owners than about the ICH performers. The latter category had clearly become the weakest rung on the ladder of actors concerned by the project.

10.4. ICH and precariousness in times of the COVID-19 pandemic

Tourism is a very significant part of the economy of Jemaa el-Fna Square and the city of Marrakech as a whole. The ban on artistic performances and commercial activities in the square between mid-March 2020 and mid-May 2021 deeply affected the lives of the ICH bearers and the entire community working in the square. This unprecedented situation revealed the lack of a rescue net for ICH bearers in Marrakech, or in fact, nationwide. Most had no access to health care, medical coverage, or social insurance. When the crisis hit, they had no alternative income, and few had any savings. Their way of life came to an abrupt halt. With no public or private support, they posted several videos on social media to share their situation and make their voices heard.

There is no systematic census of traditional artists and ICH bearers working in the square, and they thus did not benefit from the government's financial support ($80 per person) to low-income families in the first stage of the pandemic. Nor did they receive any funding from the Ministry of Culture, as there was no support framework in place for street artists. However, most ICH bearers of the Jemaa el-Fna Square did not fall into the official category of "artists" anyway. A few did hold an artist's card granted by the Ministry of Culture, but this does not provide access to any social or medical services in case of illness, disability, or aging. Moreover, the ICH bearers were not able to reach out to local government authorities to discuss their living conditions during the Covid crisis, nor could they demonstrate due to sanitary restrictions. The most significant support they received during the pandemic came from private donors and local NGOs. For example, the tour guide association and some local tour operators offered $6,000 in support of six different artists and ICH bearer associations ($1,000 per association) in 2021. A local NGO collected food donations for 40 artists and ICH bearers during the month of Ramadan that same year. As one of our interviewees said, "No one bothered to worry about our situation and our living conditions except a few goodwill benefactors who slightly supported us for humanitarian reasons." As most were illiterate or had only limited schooling, their voices were largely not heard or even ignored, mainly by the local government authorities. They have, as highlighted earlier, thus often been excluded from public projects linked to their social and economic well-being.[10]

To bring the square back to life after more than a year of total shutdown, the authorities developed different recovery measures during the second half of 2021. These included lifting travel restrictions, raising traveler confidence, and a limited reopening of the square for restaurants and trade activities from May 2021 on. As cultural activities and tourism services are very interdependent in Marrakech, the aim was to get all these related trades up and running in a coordinated way to successfully reanimate the square's economy. The ups and downs of the pandemic during the second half of 2021 led public officials to implement a careful combination of openings and limited shutdowns. While commercial services were slowly reactivated, cultural activities were not able to completely recover from the ongoing pandemic. The ICH bearers experienced difficult times. Interviews reflect the disappointment they felt, toward both the Moroccan government and UNESCO. They were unanimous in their disillusion years after the international recognition of the square, deemed to have primarily benefitted the trade and restaurant activities. This perhaps also explains the expansion of commercial activities at the expense of cultural ones. Indeed, the social and economic conditions of the ICH bearers are believed to have remained the same following the Proclamation of the square as a Masterpiece of the Oral and Intangible Cultural Heritage in 2001. Likewise, little changed after the inclusion of the cultural space of Jemaa el-Fna on the Representative List of the Intangible Cultural Heritage in 2008. Many ICH bearers consider their work to be "futureless," discourage their children from following in their footsteps and, with very few exceptions, refrain from transmitting their knowledge and know-how to younger apprentices. In short, they have come to consider their lives as a failure. A number of the ICH bearers with whom we spoke recounted their conditions with a marked degree of cynicism. They saw themselves as forming the local pillar of international recognition, from which the whole square, city and country had profited, yet they remained the poor relation in the square. From their perspective, UNESCO had not recognized the buildings' facades surrounding the square as an intangible cultural heritage – *they* were the focus of the UNESCO inscription; nevertheless, they had been deprived of its benefits, which have instead gone to other parties. As one of the interviewees sarcastically put it, "In fact, since the inscription, we got the message: our heritage is *intangible*. How can you hold something that is insubstantial?"

Surveys implemented in the square reveal that the cultural activities practiced there are far from equal – a hierarchy exists in terms of both attractiveness and viability.[11] Here, we focus on storytelling, unanimously considered the most endangered ICH element in the Jemaa el-Fna square. When the square was proclaimed a masterpiece in 2001, there were nine storytellers, all of them over the age of 50. Over the last 20 years, they have progressively left the square, one after the other, largely driven by the intolerable discrepancy between their status as bearers of an internationally renowned cultural tradition and their unchanged socioeconomic conditions. The expansion of commercial activities, fierce competition with the other cultural performances, and the lower potential for adaptation have also pushed storytellers to resign. Indeed, the square has progressively become noisy, making it a less suitable context for this activity. Some of the storytellers continued to perform outside the square, mainly in festivals both nationally and internationally. For instance, Abderrahim El Makouri, known as Al Azaliyya, trained one of his sons and is now transmitting his craft to his younger daughter. With the pandemic and ban on performances in the square, he began teaching storytelling in an informal school established in September 2021 by the NGO Al-Munya in its headquarters, in the medina of Marrakech. The objective is to transmit this art to younger people through storytelling courses. Other initiatives to expand performances beyond the square were put in motion before the pandemic and continued to support storytelling during the shutdown. The Café Clock in Marrakech, a cross-cultural space, is illustrative of this regard. One of our interviewees, Bochra Laghssais, performed there twice a week between 2015 and 2018. At the time, Bochra was continuing her university studies, having moved for this purpose from Tinghir province to Marrakech. She had learned storytelling from her grandmother. In Marrakech, she met master storyteller Ahmed Ezzarghani, who had been performing in the Jemaa el-Fna square for decades. Bochra and other apprentices listened and recorded his stories in Moroccan Arabic (Darija). Every Sunday, she practiced before him in the Café Clock, and he gave her advice and comments on her voice, intonation, and body language. She eventually became a professional storyteller in this same café before moving to Spain to pursue her doctoral studies. As observed earlier, Bochra pointed out that the Jemaa el-Fna Square has "become loud due to a lot of other activities happening near the storytellers, such as snake charmers, music and dances, acrobats, etc." She noted the faster pace of today's living, commenting that "people want fast performances. Staying for an hour or two hours to take in the wisdom of a story is difficult. . . . People are in a rush, not like before." In her opinion, for storytelling to continue in the square, modern devices are needed "such as microphones and speakers so it would be possible to listen while other activities are also happening." She further reflected that the critical situation of ICH safeguarding in the square is linked with technology and social media expansion, underlining that "the internet as an alternative means of entertainment threatens traditional performances such as storytelling." These challenges highlight the importance of creative projects that allow to keep ICH alive in a changing world. Her experience at Café Clock "is a good example of modern transmission methods enhancing experiential learning of ICH practices like storytelling." As to new young practitioners and their living conditions, Bochra remarked that in the Jemaa el-Fna Square "storytellers earn only from the tips they collect while telling a story inside an audience circle." At Café Clock, Boucha adds that the young storytellers 'have a fixed payment after each performance in addition to any tips from guests. Sometimes invited by traditional houses or riads in the medina to perform at events and parties.'

In addition, using international languages such as English and French makes their storytelling more accessible. These opportunities offer young ICH practitioners the possibility of earning a decent living, unlike the artists of the old tradition in the square. Bochra was optimistic about the future of storytelling despite concerns of a technology and social media revolution "taking over traditional means of entertainment." She was hopeful that storytelling would remain in the square.

10.5. Conclusion

This chapter discusses the complex interactions between ICH and SD in the Jemaa el-Fna square, as well as considers the impact of the COVID-19 pandemic. Indubitably, the latter introduced new challenges in terms of the potential contribution of ICH to SD, in an already fragile and uncertain setting. In Marrakech, the pandemic gave rise to unexpected claims in ICH safeguarding, which public policy was not prepared to address. It also unveiled the shortcomings of public development programs and projects relative to both implementing SD principles and the safeguarding of ICH as defined in the 2003 Convention. A clear gap was apparent between the discourse on sustainable development and reality, where ICH bearers were marginalized in public development programs. Their status has not changed since the Proclamation program, and they continue to be treated as "reflection objects" rather than "acting subjects." In particular, the square's last urban requalification project (2020–2021) did not adopt a participatory approach to involve the ICH bearers.

The pandemic also made evident an imbalance in the functions of the square's cultural space – namely a predominance of commercial activities over cultural performances – and heightened concerns raised since the end of the twentieth century over the disappearance of cultural expressions. Nonetheless, awareness-raising, consultation, and community participation remain as low as during the nomination process, and this has hindered the transmission process of cultural and artistic practices to future generations.

With regard to the links between ICH and international tourism (a major economic sector in Marrakech), the pandemic underscored the interdependence of culture and tourist services in the square and the larger city. The well-being of many ICH bearers and the sustainability of their cultural practices and artistic expressions depend largely on tourism. The sudden halt of the latter due to COVID-19 negatively affected them, as they necessarily had to suspend their primary means of subsistence. In the absence of official support for street artists, these performers' lives depend more on international tourism than on local development programs and projects. Moreover, despite ICH bearers being a critical component in the tourist marketing of the square and the city, with the COVID-19 crisis many realized that being an ICH bearer in Jemaa el-Fnaa is, in their words, a "futureless" career. The pandemic furthermore brought to the fore the dangers of "monoculture" tourism and the importance of diversifying economic activities.

Recent new initiatives to improve transmission and teaching methods have included extending certain cultural and artistic practices to intercultural spaces, as well as the use of modern technological means to adapt to tourist demand and young people's needs. For instance, Artists like comedian Abdelilah Lemseyyeh broadcast his shows on Facebook and YouTube. The Café Clock provides a space for performances outside the square. Meanwhile, instances of storytellers of different generations working together provide crucial examples of opportunities for ICH transmission and reflect a potential shift to making the latter more sustainable.

Greater insight in terms of ICH bearers' socioeconomic conditions as well as the particularity of the larger context in which they are embedded helps to gain a deeper understanding of the complex interactions between ICH and SD. For instance, neglecting ICH bearers in urban requalification projects leads to negative consequences regarding ICH safeguarding, underlining the importance of enhancing community participation. ICH and SD must positively correlate to improve ICH bearers' viability and sustainability.

Notes

1 The square is believed to have existed since the foundation of the city of Marrakech by the Almoravids Dynasty in 1070 A.D.

2 Royal Decree (*Dahir*) of July 20, 1922 (*Bulletin Officiel* n° 509, 25 Juillet, 1922, p. 1188).

3 Ahmed Skounti along with Azzouz Boujamid, heritage professional in the Department of Culture, and Abdellah Alaoui, professor at the National Institute of Archaeology and Heritage (*Institut national des sciences de l'archéologie et du patrimoine*), worked closely with the members of the Association of Friends of Jemaa El Fna Square Oral Heritage of Humanity (*Association des Amis de la Place Jemaa El Fna Patrimoine Oral de l'humanité*).
4 On the competing values of intangible heritage when it comes to safeguarding, see Skounti (2017b, pp. 72–74).
5 See the UNESCO website: Preservation, Revitalization and Promotion of Jemaa el-Fna Square, Marrakech – intangible heritage – Culture Sector – UNESCO. Accessed on June 7, 2021.
6 One of the authors contributed to this booklet (Skounti and Tebbaa, 2006).
7 This paragraph draws on the UNESCO MOOC on living heritage and sustainable development, in which one of the co-authors acted as an instructor. See: https://ich.unesco.org/fr/massive-online-open-course-mooc-01228
8 Paragraph 172 of the Operational Guidelines of the World Heritage Convention

> invites the States Parties to the Convention to inform the Committee, through the Secretariat, of their intention to undertake or to authorize in an area protected under the Convention major restorations or new constructions which may affect the Outstanding Universal Value of the property.

Article 15 of the 2003 Convention provides that "each State Party shall endeavour to ensure the widest possible participation of communities, groups and, where appropriate, individuals that create, maintain and transmit such heritage, and to involve them actively in its management."
9 The restoration and rehabilitation of the old building of the regional central bank into a museum of intangible cultural heritage has been managed by the National Museum Foundation, a public agency created in 2011.
10 Two projects should be mentioned in this regard: the requalification of the square analyzed above and the creation of the ICH museum, both within the framework of the last two programs *Marrakech, Cité de Renouveau Permanent (2014–2017)* and *Mise en Valeur de la Medina (2018–2022).*
11 Skounti and Tebbaa (2012). *La Place Jemaâ El Fna: Situation Actuelle et Devenir*. Unpublished study for the MONTADA project carried out by the Development Centre of the Tensift Region (CDRT-Marrakech).

References

Adell, N., R. F. Bendix, C. Bortolotto, and M. Tauschek. (eds.) (2015) *Between Imagined Communities of Practice: Participation, Territory and the Making of Heritage*. Göttingen: Göttingen University Press.

Adjaye, D. (2016) 'Djemaa el-Fna, Marrakech: Engaging with Complexity and Diversity', in Marron, C. (ed.) *City Squares: Eighteen Writers on the Spirit and Significance of Squares Around the World*. New York: Harper Collins, pp. 83–92.

Aikawa-Faure, N. (2009) 'From the Proclamation of Masterpieces to the Convention for the Safeguarding of Intangible Cultural Heritage', in Smith, L. and N. Akagawa (eds.) *Intangible Heritage*. London: Routledge, pp. 13–44.

Beardslee, T. (2015) 'Whom Does Heritage Empower, and Whom Does It Silence? Intangible Cultural Heritage at the Jemaa el Fna, Marrakech', *International Journal of Heritage Studies*, 22(2), pp. 89–101.

Bortolotto, C. (ed.) (2011) *Le patrimoine culturel immatériel. Enjeux d'une nouvelle catégorie*. Paris: éditions de la Maison des sciences de l'homme.

Bortolotto, C. (2021) 'Commercialization without Over-Commercialization: Normative Conundrums across Heritage Rationalities', *International Journal of Heritage Studies*, 27(9), pp. 857–868.

Bourdieu, P. (2022) *Retour sur la réflexivité*. Paris: éditions de l'Ecole des hautes études en sciences sociales.

Coslado, E., McGuinness, J., & Miller, C. (Eds.) 2013. Médinas immuables? *Gentrification et changement dans les villes historiques marocaines (1996–2010)*. Rabat: Centre Jacques-Berque. doi :10.4000/books.cjb.275.

Crozier, M. and E. Friedberg (1977) *L'acteur et le système. Les contraintes de l'action collective*. Paris: Editions du Seuil.

De Lavergne, C. (2007) 'La posture du praticien-chercheur: un analyseur de l'évolution de la recherche qualitative', in *Recherches qualitatives – Hors-Série – numéro 3, Actes du colloque Bilan et prospectives de la recherche qualitative*. Association pour la recherche qualitative, pp. 28–43.

Diaz, F. (2005) 'L'observation participante comme outil de compréhension du champ de la sécurité', *Champ pénal/Penal field*, 2, n.p [online]. Available at: http://journals.openedition.org/champpenal/79

Fassin, D. (2008) 'L'éthique, au-delà de la règle', *Sociétés contemporaines*, 71(3), pp. 117-135.

Hafstein, V. (tr.) (2015) 'Learning to Live With ICH: Diagnosis and Treatment', in Foster, M. D. and L. Gilman (eds.) *UNESCO on the Ground: Local Perspectives on Intangible Cultural Heritage*. Bloomington: Indiana University Press, pp. 143–160.

Labadi, S. (2011) 'Intangible Heritage and Sustainable Development: Realistic Outcome or Wishful Thinking?', *Heritage & Society*, 4(1), pp. 115–118.

Labadi, S. (2013) *UNESCO, Cultural Heritage, and Outstanding Universal Value: Value-Based Analyses of the World Heritage and Intangible Cultural Heritage Conventions*. Plymouth: AltaMira Press.

Ladenburger, T. (2015) *Al-Halqa*. Berlin: Auflage 1001.

Meissner, M. (2017) 'The Valorisation of Intangible Cultural Heritage: Intangible Cultural Heritage as Cultural Capital in Sustainable Development', in Lira, S., R. Amoêda, and C. Pinheiro (eds.) *Sharing Cultures: Proceedings of the 5th International Conference on Intangible Heritage*. Barcelos: Green Lines Institute for Sustainable Development, pp. 295–304.

Morange, M. and C. Schmoll (2016) *Les outils qualitatifs en géographie: Méthodes et applications*. Paris: Armand Colin.

Schmidt, T. (2005) 'Jemaa El Fna Square in Marrakech: Changes to a Social Space and to a UNESCO Masterpiece of the Oral and Intangible Heritage of Humanity as a Result of Global Influences', *The Arab World Geographer*, 8(4), pp. 173–195.

Schmitt, T.M. (2008) 'The UNESCO Concept of Safeguarding Intangible Cultural Heritage: Its Background and Marrakchi Roots', *International Journal of Heritage Studies*, 14(2), pp. 95–111.

Skounti, A. (2009) 'The Authentic Illusion: Humanity's Intangible Cultural Heritage: The Moroccan Experience', in Smith, L. and N. Akagawa (eds.) *Intangible Heritage*. London and New York: Routledge, pp. 74–92.

Skounti, A. (2012) 'The Red City: Medina of Marrakesh', in Galla, A. (ed.) *World Heritage: Benefits beyond Borders*. Cambridge: Cambridge University Press and Paris: UNESCO Publications, pp. 82–93.

Skounti, A. (2017a) 'L'espace culturel de la Place Jemaa El Fna', in Skounti, A. and S. Hossini (eds.) *Patrimoine vivant du Maroc. Eléments de la Liste représentative du patrimoine immatériel de l'UNESCO*. Rabat: Ministère de la Culture et Axions Communications, pp. 56–99.

Skounti, A. (2017b) 'The Intangible Cultural Heritage System: Many Challenges, Few Proposals', *Santander Art and Culture Law Review*, 2(3), pp. 61–76.

Skounti, A. and O. Tebbaa (2006) *La Place Jemaa El Fna, patrimoine de Marrakech, du Maroc et de l'humanité*. Rabat: Publications du Bureau de l'UNESCO.

Smith, L. and N. Akagawa (2008) *Intangible Heritage*. New York and London: Routledge.

Valentine, G. (2005) 'Geography and Ethics: Moral Geographies? Ethical Commitment in Research and Teaching', *Progress in Human Geography*, 29(4), pp. 483-487.

UNESCO (2020) *Operational Directives for the Implementation of the Convention for the Safeguarding of the Intangible Cultural Heritage*.

11

POPULAR MUSIC AND HERITAGE EMBARRASSMENT IN BRAZIL[1]

Carlos Sandroni

11.1. Introduction

The Institute of Brazilian Historical and Artistic Heritage (IPHAN) was created in 1936, but it was only in 2000 that Decree-law 3.551 instituted the federal protection of intangible cultural heritage (ICH). According to Article 2 of this decree-law, the only assets considered eligible for ICH recognition are those for which "historical continuity" and relevance to the "memory, identity, and formation of Brazilian society" can be claimed (IPHAN, 2000).

A concern for the "national relevance" of popular music has figured in Western thought, as is well known, at least since the late eighteenth century (Herder and Bohlman, 2017). Historical relevance to Brazil's cultural identity has often been ascribed to musical traditions. Indeed, this has been the case at least since novelist José de Alencar's 1874 *O nosso cancioneiro* (Alencar, 1993), though we might also point to literary critic Sílvio Romero's 1883 collection of songs in *Cantos populares do Brasil* (Romero, 1954), or author and musicologist Mário de Andrade's *Ensaio sobre a música brasileira*, from 1928 (Andrade, 1972).

The heritagization of samba in 2007 is a case in point. Treated as a musical emblem of Brazil since the 1930s, samba has also been a topic of heavy academic scrutiny since the 1970s, especially at the turn of the twenty-first century. Most of this scholarship indeed looks at the genre as an icon of "national identity" (Augras, 1998; Vianna, 1999; Frota, 2003; Cunha, 2004; Hertzman, 2013; Sandroni, 2021).

We see something similar in the case of *forró*, a genre of music and dance less well-known outside Brazil, but which was inscribed in the Brazilian ICH list in 2021. In certain contexts, we can surely claim that *forró* "represents Brazil" musically, just as it is possible to say the same thing regarding other music and dance forms that are also recognized by IPHAN as national heritage: *frevo*, *jongo* and

DOI:10.4324/9781003244158-16

maracatu, for example. It is more common, however, to say that *forró* "represents the Northeast," the region of origin of its most important composers and performers. As Michael Silvers (2018, pp. 22–23) puts it, "*Forró* can be a musical shorthand for the Northeast . . . [*forró*] is a historically and musically significant element of the northeastern soundscape." Its unquestionable national reach is a result of the dissemination of northeastern culture in Brazil, due to the significant migratory flows of northeasterners to the country's Southeast over the course of the twentieth century, but also to the fact that even before that the region had come to be regarded as the very origin of Brazil: the location of the first capital, of the first economic cycles of the Colony, etc. It is not by chance that in their discussions of "Brazilian music," the three literary-musical references I cited earlier – Alencar, Romero, and Andrade – focused their attention entirely on the music of the Northeast. The "mysticism" of the Northeast (Bastide, 1945) as a place of purity, of an authentic Brazil, is alive and well in the twenty-first century, despite the efforts of Durval Muniz de Albuquerque Júnior (2014) and other "social constructionists" (Hacking, 1999) to eliminate it.

"Samba" and "forró" are both terms that designate, in their own ways, genres of music and dance that can satisfy the criteria of historical continuity and national relevance stipulated in Decree-law 3.551 and IPHAN's policies generally. As such, they qualify for recognition as intangible cultural heritage (ICH) and indeed have been so recognized. The topic becomes more interesting, however, when we learn that the same terms *also* designate musical practices that, having gained widespread attention in the Brazilian media and commercial spheres, do *not* appear, at first glance, to be relevant to the nation's history or identity.[2]

The unquestionable commercial success of samba and *forró* as popular music evinces, indeed, that this kind of success is not incompatible with the value of cultural heritage; yet, by the same token, it makes clear that there are distinct perspectives concerning the value of music. The heritage approach (both in the Brazilian context and on a global scale) favors the perspective of history, culture, and identity, but this plays out amid frequent tensions with other perspectives of valuing the same music genres which, via a different angle, can be seen as "commercial products."

When the effort to keep these perspectives separate is unsuccessful, it can lead to what anthropologist Chiara Bortolotto (2021), taking inspiration from Michael Herzfeld (2014), has called "heritage embarrassment." This "embarrassment" refers particularly to heritage items that are themselves successful commercial products (Robinson and Silverman, 2015). This is the case with sites of tourism, certain types of handicrafts, and especially foodstuffs. At the international level, cases such as that of "French cuisine" or "Neapolitan pizza" are emblematic (Bortolotto, 2017). The efforts to recognize these items as ICH involve strong commercial and touristic interests, which may seem a far cry from the spirit and letter of the 2003 Convention, but which are nonetheless unavoidable when going through the process. Recognition can only be obtained at the cost of assembling the candidacy dossiers according to a "heritage perspective." This implies, in this case, a foregrounding of the historical, ethnographic, and identity-related aspects of the, say, foodstuffs – and chiefly, in fact, of the processes by which they are produced – leaving in the background, or even obscuring entirely, their value as objects of consumption and as generators of income and employment. But it would be difficult to deny that commercial value is intrinsic to many of the things recognized, nominated, or eligible for nomination/recognition as heritage. In these cases, "heritage entrepreneurs"[3] can try to convert this value into part of what they can offer, but in doing so, they cannot allow the commercial considerations to exceed certain boundaries, which would lead to the aforementioned "embarrassment," placing the whole undertaking at risk. (Bortolotto, 2021).

Taking these problems into account, in this chapter I will discuss the recognition of samba and *forró* as Brazilian ICH. These musical genres have been performed for decades by professional musicians with tremendous commercial success; this distinguishes them from other music and dance traditions that have also been recognized as Brazilian cultural heritage but are much less commercially successful – in some cases, not even trying to have *this kind* of success. My aim here is to comment on how this duplicity of perspectives was dealt with by samba and *forró* musicians and dancers, in dialogue with IPHAN, as they avoided or evaded the "embarrassment" of being seen (and being listened to and danced to) as both commercial products and cultural heritage.

11.2. Brazilian sambas between representativity and risk

In April 2023, songwriter and singer Gilberto Gil, who was then the Brazilian Minister of Culture, announced that "samba" would be the country's candidate for the UNESCO "Proclamation of Masterpieces of the Intangible Heritage of Humanity." This was "samba" without any specifications: "Brazilian samba" in general. When the word "samba" is used in this way, especially considering how the whole world would understand it, people immediately think of Rio de Janeiro's samba: the samba of samba schools, Carnival, percussion ensembles, and professional composers and performers with widespread fame in Brazil (such as Cartola, Paulinho da Viola, Zeca Pagodinho). And this generic usage of the word "samba" has, since the end of the 1930s, referred to a musical genre of tremendous commercial success, reaffirmed decade after decade on 78rpm discs, LPs, cassette tapes, CDs, and streaming platforms.

The first initiative undertaken by UNESCO to stimulate support for ICH, the "Proclamation of Masterpieces of ICH," was introduced in 1997/1998 and was in effect from 2001 to 2005. It led to the creation of an international convention on the topic, accepted by the UNESCO General Conference in 2003 and ratified by Brazil in 2006. The 2003 Convention established a "Representative List" and an "Urgent Safeguarding List" of ICH, but the "Proclamation" of 2001–2005 did not make this distinction, thus requiring that *all* candidates demonstrate the need for "urgent safeguarding." In other words, at that moment, to enter the running (and above all, to win!) the candidate had to demonstrate not just that it had the qualities of a "masterpiece," but also that it *ran the risk* of dying out, and that UNESCO's recognition would be a suitable means of combating this risk.

In this context, "Brazilian samba" was not a viable candidate (Sandroni, 2005): It was too commercial, too successful, too well known – no risk at sight. Accordingly, UNESCO sent word to the institution's Permanent Delegation from Brazil that, while they looked favorably upon the idea of Brazil presenting a candidate, the object put forth would have to be reconsidered, "to avoid what happened with Argentina's proposal of tango" (Asfora, 2004).[4] At the same time, IPHAN professionals and external consultants,[5] reading the regulations of the "Proclamation" (UNESCO, 2001) closely, realized that it would be imperative that the candidate be replaced by another.

Between April and June 2004, thus, "Brazilian samba" was ruled out as a candidate for UNESCO's "Proclamation of Masterpieces of Intangible Heritage"; *samba de roda* from the region known as "Recôncavo" in the state of Bahia was proposed as its replacement. A local, traditional dance with virtually no exposure to the pop music scene, *samba de roda* was at the time far less well-known within Brazil or internationally; it was much easier to argue that it was in need of urgent safeguarding. This substitution met the recommendations of Director-General of UNESCO, Koichiro Matsuura, who, in an official meeting with minister Gilberto Gil, "actively encouraged him to construct the Brazilian proposal in order to emphasize the various cultural aspects found at the roots of samba, and the diverse types of samba expressions that are at risk of disappearing" (Asfora, 2004). "Samba" was thus replaced by "roots of samba," an idea to which we will later return. The new candidature was successful, and *samba de roda* was inscribed, together with 26 other cultural assets from all over the world, in the "Proclamation of Masterpieces of ICH" announced by the institution in November 2005.

11.3. The origins of samba, the origins of forró

The success of *samba de roda* at UNESCO engendered conversations, in the media, about the possibility of heritagizing other traditions linked to popular music. As could be expected, Rio de Janeiro's samba musicians took it as a blow to their pride, as they were disappointed with not being chosen as the 2004 candidate. Nevertheless, it did not take them long to mobilize around the new possibilities.

In contrast with what happened in the case of Bahian samba, however, it was not "samba from Rio de Janeiro" that became the candidate. In conversation with IPHAN, the Centro Cultural Cartola (Cartola Cultural Center), an institute largely viewed as representative of the "community tradition bearers" of the city's samba, chose instead to define the cultural asset as the "*Matrizes* do samba no Rio de Janeiro" (*Origins* of samba in Rio de Janeiro). How to understand this notion of "origins" (which, as we will see, will reappear years later in the case of *forró*)?

In the "Introduction" to the dossier on the *Matrizes do samba no Rio de Janeiro*, we read that the research supporting its recognition as ICH sought

> to situate the value of samba in Rio de Janeiro as a form of heritage, showing its fundamental role in the cultural tradition of this city and as a national cultural reference, given that it is an important factor in the affirmation of Brazilian identity.
>
> *(Nogueira, 2014, p. 14)*

The idea of establishing "the value of samba in Rio de Janeiro *as a form of heritage*" illustrates what I stated earlier regarding the possibility of viewing a musical genre from different perspectives. The perspective of heritage, while not precluding other possible perspectives, emphasizes attributes linked to "tradition," "cultural reference," "Brazilian identity." However, the attributes that support this treatment are framed here as marking samba's "origins" (*matrizes*).

In the dossier, we also read that it was guided by the "respect, recognition, and transmission of its [samba's] tradition, in the characteristics that identify it and differentiate it from other versions that, today, have become a form of spectacle" (Nogueira, 2014, p. 15). Here, we see the emergence of a decisive contrast: the "samba tradition" is opposed to the "spectacle," one of the dimensions the genre takes on. There are some well-known criticisms leveled by certain samba musicians and researchers who support a pro-traditionality position and are against the "spectacularizing" ("espetacularização," a very pejorative verbal form) of Carnival and carnival parades (Cavalcanti, 1994, p. 51; Lima, 2018). Similar criticisms are generally heard in Brazil whenever media or touristic adaptations are made of music and dance genres previously limited to more "community" settings.

Pitted against such spectacularizing, therefore, the heritage view of Rio de Janeiro's samba favored three types of samba "origins": "samba de terreiro" (insider's, community samba), "partido-alto" (improvised samba), and "samba-enredo" (the samba style presented at samba schools parades). These three forms of samba were judged to be "those that imply relations of sociability. Their practice is rooted in the daily life of samba performers, in the life of the people, having, thus, historical continuity" (Nogueira, 2014, p. 16). "Sociability," "daily life," "life of the people": The vocabulary emphasizes direct contact, without a stage, without tourists, perhaps without superstars; performed and enjoyed within the "samba school," in a bar or pub around a table, or the backyard. Although one can *also* hear samba *de terreiro, partido alto*, and samba-*enredo* on the radio, DVDs, or one's favorite streaming service, what really matters for the enjoyment and existence of these genres – from the heritage perspective – is the bodily contact, so to speak, the possibility of participating in them directly.

In the case of *forró*, we also find the idea of origins as an important argument in the defense of its heritagization. Going even further, however, is the terminology used to label the "cultural asset," which, although perhaps redundant, ends up being an effective form of emphasis: "matrizes *tradicionais* do forró" (*traditional* origins of forró). This turn of phrase makes it quite clear, once again, that we are witnessing a specific perspective in dealing with a given type of *forró*. As in the case of samba, to understand why it is necessary to be so specific about the type of *forró* at stake requires a general knowledge about the history of the genre.

Forró is a genre of music, dance, and collective performance strongly associated with northeastern identity. The "heritage community," in the case of *forró*, includes musicians, dancers, and fans of the genre who are somehow related to the Northeast. *Forró* is also associated with the festive period of the June and July Catholic saints, beginning with the vespers of Saint Anthony's day (from June 12 to June 13) all the way through to the feast day of Saint Anne (commemorated on the final Saturday of July). These are the "June festivities," or simply "São João" (St. John, June 24), an all-encompassing term that refers to the whole period. "São João" is a popular festive tradition that, especially in the northeast of Brazil, has become notable for its association with traditional countryside or "hillbilly" (*matuto*) culture.

But if *forró* is associated with northeastern traditionalism, it also belongs, like Rio's samba, to a long history of commercial success. The word "*forró*" is found in Portuguese dictionaries starting in the early twentieth century as a term synonymous with a party at which people drank alcoholic beverages, made music, and danced. But the history of *forró's* success begins in earnest with the career of Luiz Gonzaga (1912–1989), a man from the countryside (*sertão*) of the state of Pernambuco (in the Northeast) who moved to Rio de Janeiro to make his living as a professional musician. At the turn of the 1950s, Gonzaga recorded "Forró de Mané Vito" (Mané Vito's Forró, Gonzaga-Zé Dantas, 1949), and a few years later, Jackson do Pandeiro (1919–1982), who was from the state of Paraíba (in the Northeast), made his first recording, "Forró em Limoeiro" (Forró in Limoeiro, Edgar Ferreira, 1953).

By the 1980s, the word "forró" was used to designate a number of different things. First, it is the typical name for the commercial establishments at which northeastern music is performed, sung, and danced, whether in the Northeast or cities with large populations of immigrants from the Northeast (São Paulo, Rio de Janeiro, Brasília). It also becomes a common umbrella term for "suites" of dance music that include different rhythms: *xote, baião, xaxado, quadrilha*, and even a specific rhythm called "forró," a type of sped-up *baião* that is also influenced by the northeastern *embolada* genre (Santos, 2013). Examples from the last phase of Gonzaga's career include hits such as "Forró número um" (Number One Forró, Cecéu, 1985) and "Forró de cabo a rabo" (Forró from Front to Back, Gonzaga e João Silva, 1986).

Gonzaga died in 1989, leaving *forró* well established as a multifaceted performance, music, and dance that was widespread all over Brazil but especially popular in his native region of the Northeast – for a reliable panorama, see *O fole roncou: uma história do forró* (Marcelo and Rodrigues, 2012). In the 1990s, the dynamism of the *forró* scene would end up producing new versions of the genre;

these innovations, which continue well into the twenty-first century, find their most popular and controversial example in Emanoel Gugel, a businessman from Ceará, and in the band he created, Mastruz com Leite (whose first disc, *Arroxa o nó*, dates from 1992). In the words of Felipe Trotta,

> The result of his observations on the music industry in Fortaleza, . . . Gurgel 'put together' the forró band Mastruz com Leite. With no experience or musical qualifications, Gurgel invests capital and has the idea of an aesthetic character for this forró that was to be 'progressive and stylized' [according to the text of the band's website, cited by the author] and crowd the dancefloor. As such, he chooses musicians, singers, dancers, and songs to produce an aural and visual spectacle that has a big impact. To get the word out about the band, Gurgel structures a broad promotional strategy. . . . In the wake of Mastruz, a number of other bands emerge, also put together in a similar way by producers-businessmen in the entertainment business.
>
> *(Trotta, 2010, p. 29)*

The *forró* bands that followed in the wake of Mastruz com Leite's success have been called, very pejoratively, "*forró eletrônico*" (electronic forró), "*forró de plástico*" (plastic forró), and more recently, given its fusions with so-called contemporary *sertanejo* (Brazilian country music), "*forronejo*." Here, I will call their music "stylized forró," which is, as we have just seen, a self-assigned definition; for its practitioners and fans, however, it is simply "*forró*." The "pejorative" here emanates from the adepts of types of *forró* perceived by them as "more traditional" or "more authentic." There has been no lack of critical reaction to the music and the success of Mastruz com Leite; later, of Aviões do Forró (first CD, 2002); and even later still, of Wesley Safadão (the first CD with his name featured released in 2012). The successes and the criticisms, it seems, are likely to continue. . . . But one of these critical reactions in particular is especially interesting for us here. For, paraphrasing Marx, we can say that some critics of stylized *forró* proposed replacing "the weapon of criticism" not with "criticism by weapons," but rather with the "weapons of heritage."

11.4. *The mobilization in defense of "roots"* forró

Around 2010, an NGO whose headquarters are in João Pessoa (the capital of the state of Paraíba), the Associação Balaio Nordeste,[6] began to mobilize traditionalist *forró* musicians. The association was headed by Joana Alves, an enthusiast of traditional *forró* who would become a national leader in encouraging people to get behind this issue. The first time the Associação Balaio Nordeste partnered with IPHAN was in late 2010.[7] At the time, a video titled *Por amor ao forró* (For the Love of *Forró*) was being made about an important name in Paraíba's *forró* scene,[8] the musician Pinto do Acordeon (Associação, no date). A year after TV-Cidade (from

João Pessoa, capital of the Paraíba state) began production of the video with the support of Associação Balaio Nordeste, IPHAN agreed to support the final phase in the production of the video. Written by the local bureau of IPHAN in Paraíba team, the document "Termo de Referência" (Term of Reference, 10/11/2010), which justifies the concession of support, reads:

> *Forró* is one of the great contributions of Brazil to the musical diversity of our planet, and IPHAN's partnership becomes fundamental at a moment when the paths to the recognition of *forró* as cultural heritage of Brazil are being discussed.
>
> *(IPHAN, 2010–2015)*

The production of the video was concluded and can today be found online, with IPHAN listed as a sponsor (Associação, no date).

A few months later, on April 27, 2011, a meeting took place at the headquarters of the local bureau of IPHAN in Recife (the capital of the state of Pernambuco). Among the participants were professional experts from the institution as well as well-known *forró* performers (including the singers Santana and Cristina Amaral) and representatives of local cultural associations linked to the issue. The objective of the meeting, as explained in its minutes, was "to initiate the discussion about the process of Inscribing Forró in the Brazilian intangible heritage list." There is not yet any mention of "traditional origins."

Not even two months later, however, a new organization created in João Pessoa, the Fórum Forró de Raiz (Roots *Forró* Forum), which brought together the Associação Balaio Nordeste and many *forró* musicians, submitted a request for the "traditional origins of *forró*" to be recognized as Brazilian ICH, via the local bureau of IPHAN in João Pessoa. The application was submitted solemnly, on June 16 that same year, in a public performance involving more than 20 *forró* musicians, who went to the IPHAN bureau in downtown João Pessoa, accompanied by the sound of accordions playing *forró*, *xote*, and *baião* rhythms.

The move from a request for *forró* to a request for "the traditional origins of *forró*" thus took place in the first half of 2011, resulting from a dialogue between *forró* musicians and IPHAN professionals from Pernambuco and Paraíba, and perhaps also the Department of Intangible Heritage of IPHAN, in Brasília. In July 2011, IPHAN accepted the request, opening the application number 01450.008052/2011–50, which refers to the candidacy of the "traditional origins of *forró*" for heritage status.

The mobilization of Paraíba's *forró* musicians grew, empowered by IPHAN's decision to accept the application. A few weeks later, on August 24, 2011, the legal "foundation" of the Fórum Forró de Raiz took place. According to the meeting minutes, a group of *forró* musicians and supporters had already been talking since March earlier that year to deal with issues common to them all. In the minutes, moreover, the issue of heritage figures as one of the entity's main objectives; but, once again, its point of reference is "*forró*" rather than *forró's* "origins."

The Fórum, now officialized and going through a process of increased mobilization, organized an initial conference for October 11–12, 2011, in João Pessoa. The name – yet again without reference to "origins" – is *Forró: Patrimônio cultural. E aí?* (Forró: Cultural Heritage. What's up?). But in the text of the flyer that announces the event, we finally see the emergence of "traditional origins":

> Considering the current socioeconomic situation of some of these professionals – composers, performers, accordionists, tambourine players, triangle players, zabumba drummers –, given that the labor market is precarious, unbefitting the importance of their traditional knowledge and considering, furthermore, the growth of industrial manufacturing processes and the homogenization, in all aspects of music, of the traditional origins of *forró*, which put the musical quality and cultural diversity of our people at risk, the Fórum raises a fundamental issue for the contemporary reality of the artistic production in the State of Paraíba.

The origins of *forró* are thus cited as being under attack from "industrial manufacturing processes and the homogenization" of music. This attack is said to bring risks to the "musical quality" and the "cultural diversity," not just of *forró* or its origins, but of popular music as a whole ("of our people"). The "stylized *forró*" of Mastruz, Aviões, Safadão, and others is not explicitly mentioned, but the reference is clear to all of the people involved: "poor quality" and "homogenization" are accusations frequently leveled against pop music. *Forró* is not an exception.

On the other hand, the aforementioned text emphasizes that *forró* "professionals" find themselves in a "precarious" labor market. Among the mentioned "professionals" are those who play the instruments often used in Luiz Gonzaga's performances, what Santos (2013) calls a *trio gonzagueano* (or "Gonzagan" trio): accordion, *zabumba* (bass drum), and triangle.

In 2015, a national meeting finally took place concerning the heritagization of *forró*. It is the "Encontro Nacional para Salvaguarda das Matrizes do Forró" (National Meeting for the Safeguarding of the Origins of *Forró*), which is convened in João Pessoa on September 10 of that year, with participants from Pernambuco, Ceará, Alagoas, Maranhão, Piauí, Bahia, São Paulo, Rio de Janeiro, and Brasília, in addition to local participants from Paraíba. Resulting from the Encontro was the creation of a "Carta de Diretrizes para a Instrução Técnica do Registro das Matrizes do Forró como Patrimônio Cultural do Brasil" (Letter of Directives for the Technical Information of the Register of the Origins of *Forró* as Cultural Heritage of Brazil) (IPHAN, 2010–2015). The document proposes an elaboration of what "traditional origins" is designed to suggest:

> The origins concern the musical genres (*baião*, *xote*, *xaxado*, *arrasta-pé*, *rojão*, etc.) and also dances, festivities, instrument-making techniques, particular places in which these cultural references are very symbolic, etc. . . . [T]hey are inspired by, among other influences, African and native Brazilian artistic-cultural

> sources; . . . its traditional musical instruments (though not limited to these) are: the piano accordion, the diatonic button accordion, the zabumba and the triangle (in the 'Gonzagan trio' model); the fiddle; the tambourine; and the agogô [double bell].

The view presented here is much less clear than it was in the case of samba in Rio de Janeiro (which was, as we have seen, limited to three sub-genres). It includes musical genres, some of which are difficult to define ("rojão," e.g., although often mentioned in the recordings of Jackson do Pandeiro, still represents a true mystery for researchers); instruments, broadened now to include the diatonic button accordion, the fiddle, the *agogô*; dances, which, due to their aforementioned "suite"-like character, tend to be more diverse than we see in samba (there is a marked difference, for instance, between *quadrilha* and *xote*).

Whatever the case, the view proposed by the traditionalist *forró* musicians concerning its origins is clear enough to mark them as distinct from the "modernized" Mastruz com Leite-type groups. As much as some may insist that "stylized *forró*" is anything but *forró*, what we know for certain (and it is possible that not even the creators of Mastruz com Leite, Aviões do Forró, and other new *forró* bands would contest) is that "stylized forró" is not a part of *forró*'s "traditional origins." It is, therefore, outside of the scope of the heritage-making process.

11.5. Of bearers and researchers, from the coordinator's point of view

A word on my participation in the heritagization processes discussed in this article can be useful. From 2004 to 2005, I was the coordinator for the candidacy dossier submitted to IPHAN and UNESCO in order to recognize *samba de roda* as a part of Brazilian ICH (Sandroni, 2005, 2010). Between 2019 and 2021, I occupied the same role in presenting the origins of *forró* to IPHAN for heritage recognition (Sandroni and Santos, 2019, 2021). One of the main differences between these two processes, as far as my work as coordinator was concerned, was related to the topics discussed in this article.

In the case of *forró*, as we have seen, traditionalist musicians wanted heritagization to work as a defense "against" the post-1990s modernized versions of *forró*. For example, they generally expected the public institutions (mainly city governments) that hire the musical acts to play for the annual June Saint John's Day festivities would be prevented from hiring stylized *forró* groups. The argument was that the time-honored music suited for these celebrations was traditional *forró* and not any other.

The challenge for the researchers was to ensure that culture bearers understood that our job was not to censure "modernized *forró*" but rather to valorize traditional *forró*. Since musical taste is not a zero-sum game, accomplishing the latter did not necessarily mean we had to do the former. The tension regarding this issue, however, remained palpable throughout the entire process. Many culture bearers saw IPHAN as an institution with the power to regulate the musical market, the decisions of employers, and public taste in favor of the traditionalists. Of course, IPHAN did not have this power; nevertheless, as we insisted over the course of the research period, heritagization can arguably have long-term effects that end up benefiting traditional *forró* in the musical market.

In the case of *samba de roda* from the Bahian Recôncavo, this problem did not exist. After all, the commercial versions of samba that had developed in Rio de Janeiro starting in the first half of the twentieth century had already been widely legitimized for decades, even among the culture bearers of traditional *samba de roda*. The use of heritagization as a tool for giving *samba de roda* more visibility in the musical market was not accompanied by a critical discourse in relation to "other sambas." As a result, there was no tension, on this point, between the "discourse of the culture bearers" and the "discourse of the researchers."

For me as a coordinator, there was an additional problem in the case of *forró*, related not to the culture bearers but instead to the researchers. Some of them were accustomed, by way of academic habits, to problematize traditionalism; they believed they could perhaps convince traditionalist forró musicians that modernization was not necessarily bad and that it was moreover inevitable. From the point of view of the work of heritagization, however, this discussion ended up being counterproductive. After all, this was decidedly not designed as an effort to "convince" musicians/dancers of anything, but rather to find with them a common ground from which knowledge about *forró* could contribute to keeping the genre relevant according to a heritage perspective (i.e., a perspective sufficiently compatible, for them, with what they defined as "traditionalism"). I will leave it to other observers of the forró/ICH process to judge if this common ground was found.

11.6. Conclusion

"Música popular brasileira" or "MPB" is a term created in the late 1950s that became common over the course of the 1960s; it specifically demarcated a type of Brazilian music seen as "popular" and "national." The diverse genres of this "música popular brasileira" were produced and transmitted from "within" the recording industry and mass media outlets, by way of the accompanying technological advances. On the other hand, *samba de roda*, *jongo*, *tambor de crioula*, and other forms of dance/music already recognized as Brazilian ICH are all relatively absent from the pop music industry. These musical forms, performed primarily "outside" of the creative industrial media complex, were called *folclore* (folklore) until the 1970s, *cultura popular* (popular culture) in the 1980s, *música tradicional* (traditional music) in the 1990s; since the 2000s, they have been the focus of new ICH policies. Despite the (partial) transformation of *tambor de crioula* into a "spectacle" (Ferretti, 2002), and attempts by Mestre Darcy da Serrinha to fit *jongo* into "música popular brasileira" by adding guitars and other instruments, thus taking the genre to the "stages" (Gandra, 1995), the fact is that these musical expressions continue, in essence, to remain peripheral to the music industry and mass media outlets. That is why (among other reasons) they were ideal candidates for treatment by ICH policies.

For the opposite reason, samba and *forró* were much more complicated candidates – and maybe also more interesting from an ethnomusicological perspective. In both cases, the idea of "origins" was used as a means of maintaining the heritage dimensions as distinct from the commercial dimensions, given that these two dimensions are equally important in these music/dance genres. In the case of traditional music/dance genres in which the commercial and media dimensions have not become prominent, to speak of "origins" would be redundant. The case of *samba de roda* from Bahia illustrates this quite well. After all, it would be of little interest, in the context of heritage recognition, to emphasize *samba de roda's* particular "origins," as the genre itself is often viewed as the very "origin" of different styles of Brazilian samba.

From a distance, distinctions such as "*samba de roda*/samba from Rio de Janeiro," "traditional *forró*/stylized *forró*," "ritual/spectacle," "roots/stages" are of undeniable social efficacy. However, when examined more closely, we can temper such distinctions. In the case of the origins of Rio de Janeiro's samba, for example, the inclusion of *samba-enredo* in the ICH dossier is complex. If the composition and choice of a given *samba-enredo* song for the parade of a samba school is a process that takes place entirely within the cogs of the samba school itself – with all of its community but also hierarchical qualities, as we learn from Maria Laura Cavalcanti's classic study (1994, pp. 79–125) – it is no less true that, once composed, recorded, and mixed, the *samba-enredo* song is transformed into a highly lucrative product that works perfectly well within the larger cogs of the commercial and media production and diffusion machine. The separation between these two aspects, operating under the notion of "origins," is instrumental. But "embarrassment" is always ready to crop up in the debates and disputes (which are often heated and competitive), as soon as television networks, the music industry, bookies, drug dealers, more or less respectable money launderers, and other partners show up in the practices surrounding *samba-enredo*.

In the case of *forró*, the participation of many self-described "roots" musicians (accordionists, singers, etc.) in modern and mass media-friendly professional activities is an obvious issue that arises. The widespread mobilization that has taken place since the creation of the Fórum Forró de Raiz in João Pessoa in 2011, even the organization of "forums" in other states, and the creation of a permanent National Forum in 2018, was largely catalyzed by the *forró* musicians who, in the past 30 years, have watched with dismay as bands such as Mastruz com Leite and those that followed their lead have become a part of the *forró* industry. This group of *forró* musicians has seen heritagization, among other things, as a possible means of defending themselves against what they feel is an unfair usurpation of the name with which they affectively and culturally identify – and of the respective professional opportunities.

These analyses – as well as the reiteration of the theme itself, in the case of Rio de Janeiro's samba in 2006–2007, and of *forró* since 2011 – suggest that the idea of "origins" (*matrizes*) in Brazilian ICH policies might not only be an effective tool in dealing with the continual flows between the spheres of "pop music" and "traditional music" – and the respective "heritage embarrassments" – but it might also be a suggestive topic in thinking about how musical categories relate to each other in Brazil, and perhaps also in other parts of the world.

Notes

1 This chapter was written with the financial support of CAPES (Brazilian Coordination for the Improvement of Higher Education Personnel) during the Estágio Sênior (Senior Lectureship) that I held at the École de Hautes Études en Sciences Sociales (Paris) between August 2017 and July 2018. During this period, I participated in the research group "Unesco Frictions: Heritage Making Across Global Governance," led by Chiara Bortolotto, whom I thank for receiving me, for the discussions, and for the exchange of ideas. I also thank the participants of the group, Philipp Demgenski, Panas Karampampas, Simone Toji, and Marcelo de Paiva, for all of the exchanges. Finally, I thank CNPq (Brazilian National Council for Scientific and Technological Development) for the Productivity in Research stipend that, since August 2018, has also been crucial in helping me write this chapter.
2 "History" and "identity" do not always go together in the examples of popular music that I will present here, but it can be argued that the heritage perspective implies a specific articulation between these two aspects.
3 I borrow here from Howard Becker, who coined the term "moral entrepreneur" (Becker, 1997).
4 Tango had been proposed in the previous edition of the "Proclamation of Masterpieces of ICH" and subsequently rejected for failing to demonstrate that it was in need of "urgent safeguarding."
5 Among which was the author of the present essay, who was at the same time beginning his work on this topic.
6 Literally, "Northeastern Basket Association," but *balaio* refers to a special kind of traditional northeastern basket; it is further a type of basket that is supposed to be filled in with all kinds of traditional/local items.
7 In this section, I rely on documents housed at the Superintendency of IPHAN in Paraíba, made available by anthropologist Emanuel Oliveira Braga, a professional expert at the institution, whom I thank (IPHAN, 2010–2015).
8 Pinto do Acordeon passed away in 2020.

References

Albuquerque Jr., D. M. (2014 [1999]). *The invention of the Brazilian Northeast*. Durham (NC): Duke University Press.

Alencar, J. (1993). *O nosso cancioneiro*. 2nd edn. Campinas (SP): Pontes.

Andrade, M. (1972). *Ensaio sobre a música brasileira*. 3rd edn. São Paulo: Martins.

Asfora, A. C. (2004). "Fax from the Brazilian Ministry of Foreign Affairs to IPHAN's president, Antonio Augusto Arantes, about the visit of Brazilian Minister of Culture, Gilberto Gil, to UNESCO's Director-General, Koichiro Matsuura." IPHAN's document 01450.005987/2004–55, May 27th.

Associação Balaio Nordeste (no date). *Por amor ao forró*. Available at: www.youtube.com/watch?v=c14cbU53S8I. (Accessed 13 February 2023).

Augras, M. (1998). *O Brasil do samba-enredo*. Rio de Janeiro: Fundação Getúlio Vargas.
Bastide, R. (1945). *Imagens do Nordeste místico em branco e preto*. Rio de Janeiro: O Cruzeiro.
Becker, H. (1997). *Outsiders: Studies in the sociology of deviance*. 3rd edn. New York: The Free Press.
Bortolotto, C. (2017). "Como comerse un patrimonio: construir bienes inmateriales agroalimentarios entre directivas técnicas y empresariado patrimonial." *Revista Andaluza de Antropologia*, 12, pp. 144–166. Available at: https://idus.us.es/handle/11441/87315. (Accessed 1 September 2020).
Bortolotto, C. (2021). "Commercialization without over-commercialization: Normative conundrums across heritage rationalities." *International Journal of Heritage Studies*, 27, pp. 857–868.
Cavalcanti, M. L. V. C. (1994). *Carnaval carioca: dos bastidores ao desfile*. Rio de Janeiro: UFRJ/Funarte.
Cunha, F. L. (2004). *Da marginalidade ao estrelato: o samba na construção da nacionalidade (1917–1945)*. São Paulo: Annablume.
Ferretti, S. F. (2002). *Tambor de crioula: ritual e espetáculo*. 2nd edn. São Luís: Comissão Maranhense de Folclore.
Frota, W. N. (2003). *Auxílio luxuoso: samba símbolo nacional, geração Noel Rosa e indústria cultural*. São Paulo: Annablume.
Gandra, E. (1995). *Jongo da Serrinha: do terreiro aos palcos*. Rio de Janeiro: Giorgio Gráfica e Editora.
Hacking, I. (1999). *The social construction of what?* Cambridge (MA): Harvard University Press.
Herder, J. G. and P. Bohlman (2017). *Song loves the masses: Herder on music and nationalism*. Oakland (CA): University of California Press.
Hertzman, M. (2013). *Making samba: A new history of music and race in Brazil*. University of Illinois Press.
Herzfeld, M. (2014). "Intangible delicacies: Production and embarrassment in international settings." *Ethnologies*, 36 (1–2), pp. 47–62. Available at: www.erudit.org/en/journals/ethno/1900-v1-n1-ethno02680/1037599ar.pdf. (Accessed 4 January 2023).
IPHAN (2000). Decree-Law 3.551. Available at: www.planalto.gov.br/ccivil_03/decreto/d3551.htm. (Accessed 3 February 2023).
IPHAN (2010–2015). Documents related to the forró mobilization in Paraíba for the recognition of *forró* and of *forró* origins [*matrizes do forró*] as Brazilian cultural heritage. Iphan's local bureau in João Pessoa (PB).
Lima, I. M. F. (2018). "Batalhas para além de confetes e serpentinas: A espetacularização no carnaval pernambucano e nos maracatus nação." In I. C. M Guillén and A. N. Silva (eds.), *Tempos de folia: estudos sobre o carnaval no Recife*. Recife: Massangana, pp. 217–245.
Marcelo, C. and R. Rodrigues (2012). *O fole roncou! Uma história do forró*. Rio de Janeiro: Zahar.
Nogueira, N. (ed.) (2014). *Matrizes do samba no Rio de Janeiro (Dossiê IPHAN, 10)*. Brasília: IPHAN.
Robinson, M. and H. Silverman (eds.) (2015). *Encounters with popular pasts: Cultural heritage and popular culture*. Nova York: Springer.
Romero, S. (1954). *Cantos populares do Brasil*. 2nd edn. Rio de Janeiro: José Olympio.
Sandroni, C. (2005). "Questões em torno do dossiê do samba de roda." In *Registro e políticas de salvaguarda para as culturas populares*. Série Encontros e Estudos, 6. Rio de Janeiro: CNFCP/IPHAN/MinC, pp. 45–53.

Sandroni, C. (2010). "Samba de roda, supernal heritage of humanity." *Estudos avançados*, 24 (69). Available at: https://doi.org/10.1590/S0103-40142010000200023. Accessed 8 February 2023.

Sandroni, C. (2021). *A respectable spell: Transformations of samba in Rio de Janeiro*. Urbana (Ill.): University of Illinois Press.

Sandroni, C. and Santos, C. O. (2019). "Música local, políticas culturais e gêneros musicais: notas iniciais sobre forró como patrimônio cultural." In *Anais do IX Encontro Nacional da ABET/XII Encontro de Educação Musical da Unicamp*. Campinas (SP): Associação Brasileira de Etnomusicologia/Unicamp, pp. 174–180.

Sandroni, C. and Santos, C. O. (2021). "Festival São João na Rede: celebração do forró em meio à pandemia." In M. L. Cavalcanti and R. de S. Gonçalves (eds.), *A falta que a festa faz: celebrações populares e antropologia na pandemia*. Rio de Janeiro: Museu Nacional, pp. 76–90.

Santos, C. O. (2013). *Forró: a codificação de Luiz Gonzaga*. "Batuque Book" Series. Recife: CEPE.

Silvers, M. B. (2018). *Voices of drought: The politics of music and environment in northeastern Brazil*. Urbana, Chicago: University of Illinois Press.

Trotta, F. (2010). "A reinvenção musical do Nordeste." In F. Trotta, A. C. Bezerra and M. A. Gonçalves (eds.), *Operação forrock*. Recife: Massangana, pp. 9–64.

UNESCO (2001). "Proclamation of masterpieces of the oral and intangible heritage of humanity: Guide for the presentation of candidature files." Paris: UNESCO. Available at: http://unesdoc.unesco.org/images/0012/001246/124628eo.pdf. (Accessed 1 September 2020).

Vianna, H. (1999). *The mystery of samba: Popular music and national identity in Brazil*. Chapel Hill (NC): University of North Carolina Press.

INDEX

For Product Safety Concerns and Information please contact our EU representative GPSR@taylorandfrancis.com
Taylor & Francis Verlag GmbH, Kaufingerstraße 24, 80331 München, Germany

www.ingramcontent.com/pod-product-compliance
Ingram Content Group UK Ltd.
Pitfield, Milton Keynes, MK11 3LW, UK
UKHW020007200926
475702UK00015B/2515

* 9 7 8 1 0 3 2 1 5 4 3 3 6 *